"THIS IS THE WAY IT WAS IN THE SOUTH PACIFIC . . .

"Foster knew the ordinary men, too, whose names do not appear in the record books as Marine Corps aces, the tireless crewmen who kept the rugged bent-wing Corsairs flying. It is their unsung story that is the heart of his account.

"The book is authentic war literature, more than thrilling reading. It is a fitting tribute to men, alive and dead, who deserve remembrance.

"Foster's eye saw everything. He felt, he heard and remembered. The reader hides under a flimsy table when the air raid siren sounds, breakfast is canned grapefruit juice and coffee, the tent leaks above the cot, but Foster does not become engrossed with detail for the sake of detail.

"His men live."

—*Air Progress*

Author's Note

Everything I have written (except for the scuttlebutt) is as historically true as I have been able to describe it, with the help of interviews with various people and reading official and other reports.

In cases where the true names would reveal the gruesome manner of death to their families, I have labeled the men just X and Y.

Many of the songs in this book are being published for the first time probably, and I cannot give acknowledgment to the composers, for nobody overseas knew who originated them. They were usually learned by ear and added to as they passed around.

CAPT. JOHN M. FOSTER, USMCR

HELL IN THE HEAVENS

CHARTER
NEW YORK

A DIVISION OF CHARTER COMMUNICATIONS INC.
A GROSSET & DUNLAP COMPANY

HELL IN THE HEAVENS

Copyright © 1961 by John M. Foster

Published by arrangement with G. P. Putnam's Sons.

Charter Books
A Division of Charter Communications, Inc.
A Grosset & Dunlap Company
360 Park Avenue South
New York, New York 10010

To:
Major Pierre Carnagey, Captain "Willie" Moore,
Lieutenants "Joey" Craig, "Huck" Lassiter, Jesse Leach,
Lieutenants X, and Y, and Sergeant Axel Larson, all of
VMF 222
and to Lieutenant junior grade Samuel "Goldie" Goldberg
of the Navy

IN MEMORY
this book is dedicated.

Manufactured in the United States.

CONTENTS

FOREWORD

LIKE SO MANY boys of my generation, I eagerly read all the war books I could lay my hands on, particularly about the flying aces of the First World War. After progressively wanting to be a cowboy, locomotive engineer and President of the United States, I reached the stage where I wanted to be an aviator. How many Richthofens I shot down in imaginary dogfights in my Spad I will never know. Despite the accepted attitude of my time that war was something to be hated, I secretly hoped another one would come along when I grew up so I could get up in the air as a fighter pilot.

I did grow up and World War II came along and I became a fighter pilot—not in the Army but in the United States Marines. Instead of fighting Germans, I was sent against the Japs. Instead of shooting them down—they nearly got me. There were to be no Parisian mademoiselles for me, but we did manage to get down to Sydney, Australia. I came back covered with tropical ulcers instead of glory and much less interested in heroics than fresh eggs and cold milk.

It seems to me that I have hardly begun to live yet, but here is my son, John III, growing well past the five-foot mark already. He wasn't born with a silver spoon in his mouth—but with an aluminum dog tag.

He belongs to the new atomic age. Possibly when he reads these pages he will ask, "Why did you waste all that time island-hopping? You could have destroyed the whole of Japan with a few atomic bombs." Or will he ask, "Why did you want to fight an ole war anyway?"

In these pages I have tried to answer the question, "What was it like over there?" I have tried to tell faithfully and honestly what a man overseas does, hears, sees and feels, and I have tried to write the story of one squadron of combat pilots in World War II.

What happened to me and to others in this story was not far different from the experiences of every fighting man. Some had more arduous experiences, others less, but we all had the same feeling when we heard the whistle of a bomb on its way down. We all felt the same way about dehydrated potatoes. We were all just as anxious to get back home. And for most of the men who went over and did their job well it was return without glory.

"The Flying Deuces" was a fighter squadron made up of a group of average Americans, from little and big towns all over the country. There were twenty-eight pilots in the original outfit that arrived in the Solomons, along with five ground officers and approximately 250 enlisted men. Four of the pilots and one enlisted man were destined never to leave. In the course of combat the squadron received seventeen additional pilots of whom three never came back.

Captain "Willie" Moore of Los Angeles, California, was considered one of the hottest pilots in the squadron, but he never returned from his first aerial combat. "Joey" Craig and his friend "Benjoe" Williams both landed in the water in one engagement when Benjoe protected Craig's disabled plane from the Japanese pilots until his own fuel supply gave out, but Joey (who sometimes composed music) never returned from his last crash. Then too, there was big, burly "Huckleberry" Lassiter, always good-natured, and drawling Jesse Leach, who thought he was going crazy when he heard a piano playing practically on the "front lines" and couldn't believe his ears, and Lieutenants X and Y, all of whom were lost.

Johnny Morris, of the dental-cream grin, saved himself by unsnapping his safety belt and catapulting into the water as his plane somersaulted into the ocean. He had just recovered from this crash and a hole in his arm when he had to bail out again near Munda. Again he was saved. Captain Pierre Carnagey, a former New York adman, bailed out after being badly shot up and was rescued. After he was transferred to another squadron he failed to return from a heavy aerial combat. John Fitting had a close call, parachuting into the ocean in a semiconscious condition. He was grabbed by "Doc" Brittingham on the rescue boat just as he was about to go under for the last time. "Doc" had a wife in Perryville, Maryland, who provided him with more mail than anyone else in the squadron, and he collected firearms at any price from $300 up or down (but mostly down). R. A. Schaeffer was shot down into the ocean close to the Jap positions, but was rescued in time to recuperate from major burns on his body and return to the States with his buddies.

"Steve" Yeager had been racing motorcycles and midget automobiles before the war and owned a shoe store in Kansas City. He gave an impromptu war dance every time he doctored his tropical fungus infection. John "The Face" Nugent often wore protective cream on his face, because if there were ever any poison ivy or insects around they always got to him first. Bill Carrell had sold automobiles in Dallas and owned a drugstore, which was operated by his parents when he went away to war. Charles D. Jones was nicknamed "Mother" because he once whipped up a batch of fudge while the squadron was at Midway Island. The top sergeant, John Saint, was a former bank teller. James Walley had been an antique dealer in New Orleans. Henry Turner's folks owned a big dude ranch in Montana and he brought his guitar along to sing cowboy songs to us. I bought an accordion to accompany him, but had a hard time getting it away from some of the fellows so I could practice. Fred Hughes, who survived a downward spin of over two miles with smoke pouring from his plane, bought a cornet to join in the concerts and evoked more frowns than cheers. Intelligence Officer George Schaefer, once a photographer for Warner Brothers, was the most popular man in the squadron even though it was his job to wake the pilots up for the day's work at any hour from 0230 to 0530. He rarely got more than four hours' sleep each night himself. Major Max Volcansek Jr. of Santa Barbara, California, was the first C.O., followed by the popular Major Al Gordon, an Annapolis graduate with a Kansas drawl.

VMF 215, "The Fighting Corsairs," was the sister squadron to my VMF 222, "The Flying Deuces," and preceded us all the way through combat by three weeks—a time interval that caused 215 to see action when fighting was toughest over Rabaul, New Britain. It broke the record by shooting down 135½ Japanese planes in eighteen weeks (85½ in one month), and had ten aces among its forty flyers.

Thirteen of its men were lost. However, VF 17, a Navy squadron, soon surpassed this record with 154 planes—losing twelve pilots and twenty planes itself. In the South Pacific too was VMF 214, "The Black Sheep," the famous squadron of Gregory Boyington who got his 28th plane and failed to return from the battle until after eighteen months in Japanese prison camps.

These, then, were the Marine pilots of World War II in the South Pacific. Their lives were a mixture of great excitement and great boredom, of narrow escapes and, in certain cases, tragedy. I was proud to be one of them, and it is their story I have sought to tell.

1.
GUADALCANAL TO MUNDA

THE RISING SUN touched the mountains of the Solomon Islands passing below our starboard wing and melted their foundations into a mass of hills and ravines.

Six weeks of combat were ahead of us and, unless my squadron upset the tables of calculation, four out of our twenty-eight pilots would have seen the Island of Guadalcanal for the last time. Yet I was in high spirits and eager to share in the new adventure.

The airplane crossed over the mountains and skirted the shoreline on the opposite side. The terrain became grassy flatlands with hundreds of acres of coconut-palm trees interspersing areas of brown.

Halfway up the Island of Guadalcanal we came to Henderson Field, with several other landing strips nearby. As we circled the field and came in for a landing a happy exclamation came from up front: "Gabriel—we is heah!"

We were taken to the Hotel De Gink—nothing more than a Nissen hut—a concoction of metal, wood and mosquito netting shaped like a hot dog that has been split lengthwise, with only the upper half being used.

Our back yard consisted of a plantation of coconut trees replete with an occasional nut. But mostly the tops of the trees were frayed from the battle that had raged a year before. Three battle-worn light tanks sat under the trees. They still showed the holes that had disabled them. I wondered if any of the American crew had escaped. In front of my tent on the way to the messhall the lower part of an old Jap tank helped to protect a nearby foxhole.

We were only given time to unload our baggage when an enlisted man rode up in a truck. "Operations wants all of you down at Fighter number two right now. Take your flying gear with you."

In the intelligence shack near Operations we sat on benches while an Army lieutenant colonel named Tyler gave us a talk on what we might expect from the Japanese and what our chances of getting rescued were if we should go down. He told about one pilot who came back weighing more than he had when he had been shot down. After floating in his one-man life raft without any water for several days, he thought, If the birds can drink sea water without any harmful effects, why can't I? He caught a bird that lit on his boat and proceeded to investigate its digestive system. He found a fatty material and decided that it was the secret of the bird's success. From then on he drank sea water, chewing some of the fatty tissue whenever he did. He was rescued after nine days on the raft and was an astonishingly healthy example of sea-survival.

Tyler wasn't halfway through with his lecture when the telephone rang. His voice was casual when he came back and announced, "We will have to call the rest of the lecture off. There has been a large flock of Jap planes reported by our coast-watcher on Choiseul; they seem to be rendezvousing for a strike on Guadalcanal. We'll need some of you pilots to fly twelve Grumman Wildcats we've got here. Most of our fighter planes are farther north on a strike so we'll have to use every plane we've got available. I suppose you have all flown a Wildcat, haven't you?''

Major Max J. Volcansek, our skipper, immediately asked all the most experienced pilots to handle the twelve Grummans. Yes, we had all flown Wildcats before, but we newer pilots in the squadron only had five hours in them and the older pilots up to fifty before advancing to the 2,000-horsepower Corsair. It had been so long ago that we had forgotten how much fuel the planes held, and most of the pilots had forgotten how to start the engine.

The twelve Grummans trundled past the truck where those of us who didn't get assigned were waiting to be taken to a foxhole, if a bombing attack developed. Some of the Wildcats had droppable wing tanks slung on one or both sides. Two of them taxied by with their wings tilted at a steep angle; one side of their landing gear happened to be low on hydraulic pressure. It was indeed a motley array of planes and pilots, waiting at the end of the runway for the signal to take off. The signal never came, for the reported Jap formation had disappeared. Perhaps it was for the best that no plane even had to take off, because some of the pilots confessed later that they had forgotten how to charge the guns, and some were not at all sure they knew how to retract the landing gear properly.

That night I visited a hut where most of VF 33 was staying. They were a Navy fighter squadron flying the new F6F, the Grumman Hellcat. Shortly before my arrival at Guadalcanal they had given their new airplane its first real combat test. Two pilots I had known when we were cadets learning to fly at Corpus

Christi, Texas, belonged to the fighter squadron. I hadn't seen Stacey or Stolfa for many months, but I found them that night.

Their squadron had returned from a big strike on the formidable Japanese air base of Kahili. The skipper, "Jumping Joe" Clifton—a colorful husky-voiced character who had received his nickname because of his habit of hopping up and down when angry—was discussing the events of the day. "Did you notice how wide apart those Corsairs were flying?" he said. "There must have been close to a half a mile between sections. Now, I don't want you men to fly like that. Get right in there and stay close together, so you can help each other out when a Zero jumps you. I know we had quite a rough time today, but when we have been up here as long as the Marines, we'll be able to give a good account of ourselves. We are lucky as hell to have escaped as well as we did. One more day like today and we're bound to take some heavy losses. I want each man here to think over what mistakes he made and see that it doesn't happen again, because the second time—you may not get back to think anything over. That's all for now."

After a few days of combat VF 33 was flying with just as much distance between each two plane section as the Marines in their Corsairs. They had learned there was a reason for such a distance: to allow plenty of room for the pilots to turn to shoot Zeros off the tails of friendly planes.

Stacey told me about Ernie Jackson. Ernie had been a cadet with me all the way through training. He was always the clown of the class. "Ernie was following his division leader down a canyon over Attu when they ran into a williwaw and crashed into the ground. Only the last man in the division escaped. He saw what happened to the others and managed to get out of the way."

"What's a williwaw?" I asked.

"It's a wind that springs out of nowhere up in the Aleutians. One minute everything might be perfectly calm and the next, you might get struck with a 150-mile-an-hour wind that blows straight up, straight down or in any direction of the compass!"

I felt deeply shocked at Ernie's death, but the pain was taken partly away by the return of another good friend the following day, who had been shot down on a strafing hop on Santa Isabel. After two weeks in which no word had been heard from him, we had practically given him up.

I now greeted my good friend and ex-roommate, George P. Sanders from Pawhuska, Oklahoma. He had arrived that day after nearly three weeks in the jungle, loaded down like a Santa Claus with Japanese gear and native souvenirs. He brought with him a Jap radio set, diary, documents, pistol, letters and native-carved wooden figures inlaid with mother-of-pearl.

Glancing in the diary I saw a map of the Pacific area and several Japanese bases with lines denoting the various routes of supply. Whether or not our intelligence people already knew that information, I didn't know, but it looked like valuable data for our submarines and bombers.

"Let's hear what happened to you, George," I asked. Four others were gathered around him looking at his mementos. Only a few months before he had belonged to our squadron before he got transferred to VMF 215—"The Fighting Corsairs."

"Okay, it will help me to refresh my memory on it

for the report I've got to write for intelligence tomorrow. First of all though, you fellows don't appreciate how happy I am to be back. You couldn't—not unless you've been through the same thing yourselves. Anyway, on August the 19th, Harold Spears and I were strafing at Rekata Bay. I was flying wing on him and we made several passes at some float planes. That was our mistake. If we had only made one or two and gotten out of there everything would have been all right, but we kept going back. That gave the Japs plenty of time to man their guns and draw a bead on me. Spears waited until one float plane just got off the water before he shot it down. There were three of them altogether.

"The AA hit my engine and it began to smoke badly. The oil pressure dropped to zero. I also think my radio was hit. About that time I became pretty worried. I knew I had to make a water landing because I was losing altitude fast. There are two islands opposite the Jap positions at Rekata. I decided to land outside them and try to keep my landing place behind the islands, so the Japs couldn't see.

"I tried to jettison my hood, but I couldn't. While I was fooling around with the hood I almost let the air speed get to the stalling point. When I found that the hood wouldn't release, I latched it back and held my arm over the side so it wouldn't slam shut and lock me in.

"Just before hitting the water I pulled her back and skimmed over the surface until she stalled in on a good water landing. I crawled over the side of the plane and inflated my life jacket. The plane sank in about 15 seconds. The chute gave me some trouble when I tried to get out of it, but I inflated my boat and crawled in without any difficulty. I shouldn't have inflated the boat just then though, because it made it easier for the Japs to see me. I was more afraid of sharks at the moment, although I didn't see any. The current kept drifting me northwest up the coast of the island, so I threw out my sea anchor.

"When it became dark I started paddling down the island and toward the shore, landing on the small easterly island off Rekata at about 0330. After scouting for Japs a short distance in all directions, I hid for the rest of the night.

"That morning I saw a float plane Zero and in the afternoon eight F4U's came over searching for me, but they were way too high to see anything. I spent the rest of the day and night about a half mile east of where I originally landed. All this time I thought I had arrived on the mainland and I was waiting for some natives to come along that might be friendly. I saw what I thought was a native fishing in a canoe just offshore that afternoon and yelled at him. Luckily, he didn't hear me, because I suddenly realized it was a Jap. That night I chose a nice sandy spot to sleep in. Earlier in the afternoon I had chased a crocodile out of the spot. After I had been lying there for quite a while and was sound asleep, I woke up and thought I heard a noise close to me. I kept very quiet, thinking it might be a Jap coastal patrol. Then I heard a kind of a crunching sound. I turned my head and there was the biggest mouth I had ever seen—wide open. It was that same crocodile and it had come back to reclaim its bed. Boy! Was I scared! I ran for the nearest tree. I heard something beside me and looked down. There was the croc. We were running almost side by side, me for a tree and him for the water. We were both scared as hell. It seems funny now, but it was anything but—while it was happening.

"The third day I went westward to examine what I thought was a native village. When I came across some foxholes and some Japanese printed paper I got away as fast as I could. I worked my way down the coast in the opposite direction and in the middle of the afternoon I started to paddle my boat the 2½ or 3 miles to the mainland of Santa Isabel. That was sure tiring. I was damn lucky the Japs didn't see me. I landed at about 1800 and found an abandoned native hut. During all this time, since my crash, I had used my deflated lifeboat for a cover at night. I had lost my pistol and jungle pack when I left the plane and opened my life raft. All I had to eat were coconuts and small green crabs.

"The following morning I made up my boat into a back pack and started to work my way down the coast. The ground was so rough and the jungle so dense I was only able to make about a mile and a half by 1400. I found myself a big oyster bed and ate a few—raw of course.

"It was in the morning of August 24th that I came upon my first native. I had traveled about a mile and was resting up, when I heard somebody coming and saw the native. I stepped out and said, 'Me friend, me American.' I smiled as big a smile as I could. He answered me in good English, 'Yes, I know!'

"This native took me to his village located only six miles from Rekata Bay. The natives fed me native potatoes, nuts and pineapple; we had boiled pig to eat at night. They sent a messenger to the coastwatcher and he radioed a few days later and told the base at Guadalcanal that I had been found."

George then told us how the natives paddled a thirty-foot war canoe a distance of nearly forty-five miles to take him to Captain Michael Forster, the

British District Officer. Forster turned out to be a rather dark-complexioned, pleasant chap about the same age as George. His cook, Orlando, provided a dinner of roast pig. After a bath and fresh clothes George felt like another man. They tried to call Guadalcanal on a captured Jap transmitter, but did not receive any answer.

By 0400 the next morning they had started their journey back to the captain's home at Totamba, stopping at native villages for their meals. That night the children of the village approached and gave George shells, beads, bracelets, and each of them shook hands with him. After supper Captain Forster asked a native if they would sing for them, so about 1930 they gathered about the porch of the hut and sang songs of many kinds. There were old native canoe songs and battle chants. Some of the more recent belittled the Japanese and praised the Americans. The natives asked George what his name was and then sang a song about him. George thought it only fair after that to teach them "The Eyes of Texas," after which they finished up the recital with "God Save the King."

On August 28th they continued on their way, traveling in a forty-foot canoe paddled by twelve men and accompanied by two thirty-foot canoes which were paddled by eleven men each. Then they arrived at Totamba where George was surprised to find Captain Forster's house beautifully situated on a 200-foot hill with landscaped grounds and a view of the sea and mountains. They immediately sent Guadalcanal a message of safe arrival.

The captain gave George an American 38-caliber pistol which had been taken from a Jap pilot at Kahili by some natives who had killed him. He also gave him a native walking stick, and his top sergeant brought a present in the shape of a native canoe paddle.

On August 30th the two were doing some target shooting with a rifle when they heard what they thought were bombs exploding to the east. A plane came from that direction and flew directly overhead at 12,000 feet. When he got four miles west of them he went into some loose spirals, righted himself momentarily, then dove straight in. A couple of days later a native brought word that the plane had been Japanese. He brought the Jap pilot's pistol and told them that about half of the pilot's body was all that was left. The next few days were wonderful for George. He was served breakfast in bed if he wanted it that way. The meals were all very good. He spent most of his time walking in the jungle with the native sergeant and three other natives, learning jungle lore, and taking sunbaths and hot water baths in a tub.

That morning about 1000 the Dumbo (Consolidated "Catalina" PBY flying boat) landed and took George aboard to fly him to Tulagi. After a three-hour delay, he got a boat to Guadalcanal and then finagled a truck to take him to Fighter One landing strip.

"Those coastwatchers sure have what it takes," George told us. "They live right up there within a few miles of the Japs, sending reports on all the Jap movements to Guadalcanal. They've got scouts out everywhere looking for our lost pilots or watching the Japs. It gets pretty hot for them too, sometimes. The Japs know they are there, but just can't find them as a rule."

"George, just who are the coastwatchers anyway?" I asked. "How come they are so familiar with the natives and the territory?"

"Well, most of them owned or worked on plantations around here before the war, so they know the country and the natives very well. You just can't imagine what a valuable service they perform."*

"I'm almost afraid to face the rest of the guys in my squadron when they come back from Munda," George told us. "They've been up there since August 12th going through hell. Even when we weren't fighting we had terrible living conditions. They've been doing their duty and I haven't."

"Good gosh, George—what can they expect of a pilot who's been shot down?"

"Did they lose many men, George?"

"Yes, we had a pretty rough time of it. On our very first mission we lost two men. We were operating from Guadalcanal, waiting for our ground troops to capture Munda. We were escorting some G-25's to Munda when Pickeral crashed into the sea. All that we could figure out was that he fainted from oxygen failure. Our skipper, Major Neefus, came back from the same flight and told us D. B. Moore had been shot down while he was following his leader in an attack.

"We thought we had lost Stidger after he bailed out near some enemy installations, but he got help from natives and made his way back. Nichols was shot down on the 30th of July near Gizo Island.

"That's all that happened before I got lost, but intelligence told me today that Major Tomes was shot down just a couple of days ago. He led a strafing hop up to Kahili, but instead of staying clear of Ballale

*From the Solomons to the Phillipines the coastwatchers killed nearly 4,000 Nipponese, took 74 prisoners and rescued more than 5,000 Allied airmen during the war.

Island, he was turning in on the north end of the runway at fifty feet, when small-caliber and 20-mm AA fire opened up on him. Cantrell and Rathburn reported that his plane exploded and crashed in flames on the island. I sure hated to hear about that; if he had only lasted two or three more days he would have been relieved. He had four Zeros to his credit.

"Don Aldrich has been doing all right, too; he's bagged five Zeros and Spears has got four. Several of the boys have one or two."

At last we said good-by to George and returned to our own hut. We hadn't been there long enough to take our shoes off when the air raid siren wailed mournfuly three times.

Outside we sat around the edge of the foxhole and dangled our feet, waiting for action to begin. The tent lights went out one by one, but the moon still provided enough light for me to distinguish the outline of the abandoned Jap tank in front of our foxhole.

"So you've finally got here," I told myself. I remembered all I had gone through to get this far, how I had spent nearly a year and a half trying to pass the physical examination to join the Army or the Navy as a flying cadet. I had accumulated sixty hours of flying, struggling to live on what was left of my wages after paying for the rental of an airplane. Then had come the letter from the Eagle Squadron officially telling me they would accept me when I got a total of eighty hours. I tried hard, but my money wouldn't permit enough flying, so I had tried to get into the R.C.A.F. I was all ready to take my savings of $29 and hitchhike from Utah to Canada on December 8th.

Then the Japs struck on the 7th and that changed everything in a flash. I didn't want to fight with England or Canada any more. On December 9th I passed both the Army and Navy preliminary physical exams. Which service should I join? Finally, I arrived in San Francisco on the last day of 1941 and started through the three-day Navy physical.

I passed and was sworn into the Navy. When I walked outside, I heard the newsboys shouting that Bataan had fallen. Nothing had been heard from our Marines on Wake Island for ten days. A month and a half later came the fall of Singapore. Finally on February 19, 1942 I was called to active duty and began my aviation training as a seaman, 2nd class, at Oakland, California.

Halfway through our cadet training, after we'd moved on to Texas, volunteers had been asked for the Marine Corps. "Goldie" (my good friend S. E. Goldberg) wanted to be a Marine badly and his enthusiasm communicated itself to me. One hundred and fifty out of our group at Corpus Christi applied, and eighteen of us were given the nod. Bob Wright, D. C. Gill, and myself were the only three out of the twenty-five in our original Oakland class to become Marines. Bob was subsequently killed on the East Coast (he had been a boyhood friend of mine), Gill was at Midway in the squadron that relieved mine—and I went on to the Solomons.

After getting my commission I learned how to fly the old Brewster Buffalo (F2-A), then went to North Island, California, across the bay from San Diego, and learned how to land on an aircraft carrier. Then I was sent the fifteen miles to Miramar to await overseas orders. It was at Miramar that I had met some of the men I was to fly and fight with.

We shipped overseas and joined Marine Fighting Squadron 222, called "The Flying Deuces" because of the winged playing cards in its insignia. After a few hours in the North American Texan (SN-J), we learned to fly the Grumman Wildcat and then advanced to the powerful Corsair (F4U-1), the most powerful and fastest Navy fighter plane in the world, equal to if not surpassing any of the Army planes.

The Fighting Corsairs and the Flying Deuces were sister squadrons. They were formed at the time and shipped over together on the U.S.S. *Pocomoke* to be stationed at Barber's Point, twelve miles from Honolulu. Then suddenly The Fighting Corsairs (VMF 215) had been sent to Midway. Three weeks later my squadron followed.

And now we had followed VMF 215 to the Solomons. Tomorrow, we were to fly up to Munda and relieve them. And the boys of 215 had been having one tough time. Would we too have nearly one man shot down out of every four pilots? Only the next few weeks would tell.

The wings of our transport tipped precariously, then leveled out. The water that had been passing beneath us ever since we left Guadalcanal was displaced by solid ground. A couple of seconds later the end of the landing strip approached, rising fast to receive us. The plane settled down in a three-point landing in the center of the dirt and coral runway. On each side the wing tips extended beyond the width of the strip and were nearly clipped off by the hazards lining the edges.

We passengers craned our necks to peer out of the windows and watch the logs, boulders, dirt embankments and crashed remains of Japanese and American airplanes flash by. Brakes groaned as the transport neared the end of the landing field. The left engine speeded up and the plane swung around to the right and taxied off the runway.

We had scarcely taken a dozen steps from the plane when we were deluged by a happy group of pilots. They rushed at us, pumped our hands up and down and shouted with joy. These were the men of our sister squadron, whom I had last seen at Midway. I looked around curiously to see what change three weeks of intense combat had wrought on their youthful appearance.

What I saw surprised me deeply. A rough growth of whiskers made them look like the sourdoughs of Alaska. Their eyes were red-rimmed and bloodshot, with a blank, haunted look. Creases lined their drawn faces, their thin cheeks. The expressions were those of men who had seen death too often, who had worked too hard and too long without enough food and sleep. They greeted us with the joy of men who were to be granted a few more days of life.

We had little time to exchange salutations, because the transport plane presented an inviting target to the Japs and had to leave as soon as possible. There was work to be done. We formed a line similar to the old-fashioned bucket brigade and unloaded our parachutes and baggage from the plane.

Even before we had finished the job of unloading, the boys of 215 brought their gear close to the plane, all ready to "get the hell out of this godforsaken hole." Many of them carried souvenirs: officers' swords and pistols, snipers' rifles, Jap flags, gas masks, cannon shells and belts of a thousand stitches.

The walking ghosts of VMF 215 piled into the plane. Just before the door closed on of them yelled to us, "Don't ever let 'em talk you into strafing

Kahili.'' The starter whined and the engines coughed and started one at a time. The plane taxied out quickly and took off.

It is hard to forget that first day at Munda. It was past the middle of the day when we arrived. An overcast sky, gray and dull, hung over the island. The deep brown of the earth seemed even darker and capable of engulfing us all as it had swallowed several thousand Japs a scant three weeks before.

As far as the eye could see—seaward toward the island of Rendova and along the water's edge north-ward across the narrow landing strip which was not yet sixty feet in width and on to the ridges and hills rising inland—nowhere was there a tree untouched by bombs, shellfire, grenades, rifle or machine-gun fire. A plantation of stumps, fallen trees and naked trees still standing marked the place where many thousands of coconut trees once stood in a steady array. Large craters broke the crust of the earth, most of them now filled with water from the many tropical cloudbursts.

And there was mud. A vast sea of it. Seemingly solid earth would dissipate when you stepped on it and you would sink to your knees. It was easier to walk in the mud puddles and let the dirty water swish on your shoes—it kept your feet comparatively clean.

There were roads at Munda. They turned into a morass of mud every time it rained, smelling like a hog-wallow from the rotted jungle vegetation. The continued presence of death hung heavy in the air.

Such was the road leading from the landing strip, winding through the tents of the Seabees and Army soldiers, up ravines and over hills to the pilots' area. When that road became muddy and the wheels sank down as far as nature would permit, they discovered a surface lying beneath the mud—a surface that pitched and rolled the transportation truck like a light craft in a heavy sea, providing unexpected bumps and jolts.

During the daylight hours, flies swarmed over everyone trying to catch up on sleep. The flies in the Solomons are either braver or lazier than those in other localities. It took more than a mere wave of the hand to frighten them away. We became adept at catching them in our hands, making allowance for the fact they take off backwards, and giving them sufficient lead. And before the sun went down, mosquitoes buzzed out to relieve the flies and gnats patrolling over us. Their size made our wisecracks about their carrying away dead Japs seem logical. They, too, were very brave and would not frighten easily. Like the Japs they clung to their positions until annihilated.

Our attitude toward the flies and mosquitoes was not just one of annoyance. We feared the disease they carried. Malaria, dengue and dysentery were not uncommon. To combat disease, a special detail had been named "malaria control" and assigned the task of spraying stagnant pools of water and enforcing such measures as the use of a mosquito net at night. No bare legs or arms were permitted after sundown. As to dysentery we soon learned why the messhall along the landing strip was named "Dysentery Chowhall."

The pilots' ready room consisted of a tent only fifty yards from the shoreline. A rough lumber table was piled high with two-month-old newspapers and magazines. There was usually a can of lemon drops available as well as some packages of D rations. Sometimes there was a two-quart can of grapefruit or pineapple juice to refresh those who had just come from a hop. Twelve folding canvas cots took up all the available space on the dirt floor. At one end of this tent was a field desk with two roughly made chairs, where the intelligence officers interviewed pilots and wrote up their reports.

In an adjoining tent, flight operations kept the record up to the minute on the planes in commission and the pilots available to fly them. Here, too, were several large scale maps of the area and the latest vital information regarding Japanese movements and locations.

Usually each of the four-man divisions took turns at assignments. When headquarters or the operations officer decided on a mission—such as a barge swept or a patrol over a friendly task force or a dawn or dusk patrol—the pilots who had been sitting around the ready tent longest were generally assigned.

No sooner had we landed at Munda than some of us were immediately put on scramble alert, while the rest took the gear up the hill to the tents. We returned to the strip as soon as we could to listen to Captain Wiley Terry, one of the intelligence officers. Terry was a large, ruddy-complexioned man, with a hail-fellow-well-met personality. In civilian life at San Francisco he had been one of America's top insurance salesmen. He called us together to tell us where the Japs were located, where we might expect to find friendly natives or coastwatchers if we were forced down, where the greatest concentrations of antiaircraft fire were and the latest Jap tricks.

The picture was not very bright for us. New Georgia had been captured from the Japs after a bloody struggle that had taken much longer than originally expected. Facing us now was all enemy territory, except for our small beachhead on Vella Lavella. The island of Kolumbangara was easily visible thirteen miles to the northwest. It looked as if a great peak had once risen from the sea and the entire top had been blown off. On this circular island Vila airfield had been built, but was rarely used. An estimated 20,000 Japs occupied the island.

Over forty-five miles on the other side of Kolumbangara lay Vella Lavella, upon which the Marines together with some Army and New Zealand troops had just established a toehold. Farther to the northwest across a long unbroken stretch of water the Shortland Islands were located, not far from the largest island in the Solomons—Bougainville.

It was in the 1700's that the first white explorers found these islands. Lieutenant Shortland, an Englishman, had been on his way to Botany Bay, Australia, with a shipload of convicts when he happened to be blown off course and land among the islands that now bear his name. Then there was the Frenchman, Bougainville, who gave the largest island his name. Santa Isabel had been named after the Queen of Portugal. New Guinea also had its share of explorers: the German Finschafen, the Englishman Owen Stanley, and others. How disappointed those first sailors must have been when they learned that those glittering war clubs were not made of gold from the mines of King Solomon as they supposed, but instead were shaped from fool's gold (iron pyrites). They had named them "The Islands of Solomon."

Now Lieutenant Shortland's islands provided a well-protected seaplane base for the Japanese invaders. Bougainville's jungle-clad namesake had four Jap airbases on it; one of them, the most formidable in that part of the Solomons, was named Kahili and stretched inland from the southeastern shore. This landing strip pointed like a dart to Ballale, thirteen miles across the water and just large enough to contain another airbase and one of the greatest concentrations of antiaircraft fire in the South Pacific.

Strange names these, but names that were to become familiar to thousands of Americans and their Allies as the first great game of leapfrog began in the Pacific area—a strategy that was to save thousands of American lives and lead to the end of a long struggle.

That evening we drove along the muddy, bumpy road up the hill to the pilots' camp area and ate our chow in a long, low building with a slanting dirt floor. A sign over the entrance pictured three nude girls and beside them was printed MAUDIE'S MANSION, A HOME FOR WAYWARD PILOTS.

The chow consisted of meatloaf, canned peas, canned carrots and dehydrated boiled potatoes that had become waterlogged in their reunion with water. A tepid cup of lemonade made from a powder extract, and a small square piece of pie finished off the meal.

"If all the meals are as good as this one, we'll get along pretty well," Yeager remarked.

Our morale was dampened by an officer sitting across the table. "Wait until you've eaten at Dysentery Chowhall, before getting your hopes too high," he told us.

We stumbled and slid in the muddy path leading to our new homes. A jeep was mired up to the floorboards in the mud and a truck had become stranded in the ooze trying to pull out the jeep. We successfully evaded similar pitfalls and arrived at our new home.

All the tents were the same, except that some were more crowded. They all had the luxury of a wooden floor, however, with built-in foxholes. At the foot of my canvas sleeping cot a trap door covered the entrance to one foxhole; the other was located beside Nugent's cot. Five bunks lined one side of the tent and four were on the opposite side. There was just enough room between cots to permit you to take off your shoes without dangling the laces in the next man's face. Four round sticks arose from each corner of every cot to support a generous amount of netting. The sticks generally tilted and the netting had the habit of sagging in the middle so that it lay atop one's bed like an extra sheet. Any mosquito well schooled in the art of dive-bombing would be afforded the opportunity of sticking his nose into personal matters. I solved the problem by tying a cord dangling from the canvas roof to the netting, thus eliminating the sag. There was one tall pole in the center of the tent, which not only supported the weight of the canvas but three nails as well, providing a place for nine of us to hang our clothes.

As soon as it became dark—which was as soon as the sun went down because there is practically no twilight in the tropics—we went to bed. There were no lights except for our flashlights.

Nugent's flashlight flicked on and I saw it move over the inside surface of his net canopy. The light went out, then it came on again. Suddenly he let out a yell, threw away the side of the netting he had been so carefully tucking in and roared, "Jumping Jehosharphat, let me outa here. I've got an animal in bed with me!" By that time he was ten feet away and still going.

He had noticed a pair of eyes glistening directly

above as he lay in bed and shined the flashlight on them, but the glare hadn't permitted him to see what it was at first. The second time though, he found a good-sized spider dangling on the inside of his netting, giving him the eye.

Every night after that, Nugent examined the interior of his sleeping enclosure as well as the outside and upon several different occasions found the same spider or its relatives, trying to play a return engagement.

Talk among us as we lay on our cots that night—our first in the real front lines, so to speak—revealed that we all were thinking of what the next few hours, days and weeks would bring. We evaluated our chances of coming through the next six weeks of combat alive. The odds were a little better than four to one in our favor. If we followed in the footsteps of VMF 215's pilots, an average of every other man would shoot down a Jap plane. Gradually, the conversation died out as one by one we fell asleep.

It was 2330 when suddenly a great moan rent the air. It scared us half out of bed as it started, because the siren was located in a tree only fifty feet away.

"This is a helluva time to be starting this sort of thing—our very first night here," remarked our pilot from Crystal Springs, Mississippi, Jesse Leach.

"It's just a friendly greeting the Japs are giving to welcome 222 to the beautiful South Pacific," came back Frederick Hughes, the tall, curly-headed pilot from St. Paul, Minnesota, who looked like Bob Hope. "Listen—you can hear Washing Machine Charlie!"

The buzz of an airplane's engine became louder. Long fingers of light probed the sky, moving slowly to and fro, criss-crossing each other in a supposedly scientific pattern most likely to pick up the marauding airplane. They failed, but the plane went farther away; then came the sound of two distant explosions reminiscent of the beat of an Indian tom-tom. A few distant shots were heard from the antiaircraft guns along the shore facing Kolumbangara.

"Does this happen often?" I asked a figure whom I recognized in the moonlight as the major from the tent next to ours.

"They're after those new 90-mm AA guns we've got tonight," he replied as his dog rubbed against his bare legs and whined. "He'll be coming back later on to keep us from getting too much sleep."

The searchlights flicked off one by one and we hit the sack.

Just as we were on the brink of sleep the siren wailed again—the long steady *brrr* of the all-clear. I turned over on my other side and started to go to sleep again. This process was interrupted by the siren ringing its warning of another air raid. I decided to wait until the guns started to fire before getting up. The noise of the Jap's engine came, but again the searchlights couldn't find him. He stayed a good distance away and then left. Once more the all-clear came to disturb anybody the other warning had failed to awaken.

We began to doze when a Navy enlisted man came into the tent. "It's time to get up."

He was answered by a chorus of groans and moans. "What time is it?"

"It's 0430 and you'll have to hurry or you're gonna be late," he answered. "You men stayed in the sack an extra hour this morning. We got some of the more experienced divisions up for the alert and dawn patrol."

Somebody yawned and commented sleepily: "I don't mind giving my life for my country, but why oh why do we have to get up so early to do it!"

2.
FIRST MISSION

I LIFTED UP one edge of my mosquito netting. Swinging my feet I located my heavy field shoes with my toes; then I lifted the wall of net over my head and picked up my socks. I shined my flashlight on and off to conserve the battery as I walked past the open foxhole to the center pole and began the search for my flying suit. There was only one nail on my side of the pole and it had about five different articles on it—mine at the bottom. My flying suit still felt damp from the perspiration it had absorbed the previous day as well as from the high humidity of the atmosphere.

Outside, I poured some cold water from a bucket into a steel helmet and washed my face. Politely leaving the water in the helmet for the next man, I tripped over tent ropes and returned once more to the tent.

I slung the leather shoulder holster containing my 45-caliber automatic over my neck and buckled the belt, strung with my hunting knife, first-aid kit, extra cartridges and canteen, around my waist. After I had put my baseball cap on and grabbed my flying helmet, goggles and gloves, I stumbled and slid my way fifty yards to Maudie's Mansion for breakfast.

Two kerosene lamps glowed from the two vertical wooden poles supporting the roof, while pilots on both sides of the aisle gulped down the last of their coffee and ushered forkfuls of fried Spam to their mouths, interspersing these with occasional bits of imitation scrambled powdered eggs.

After breakfast, we climbed aboard one of the trucks provided to haul pilots down to the landing strip. We waited until there was a load—which meant stacking us in two layers—then jolted our way down the winding road in the murky light of the coming dawn.

Far away an air raid siren reached its triple crescendo monotonously. Another began its warning cry closer to us, followed immediately by others until the din swept past us to the area we had just left. The driver of our truck turned out the lights and we jumped out to find cover.

The high-pitched whine of an airplane became audible, increasingly so until it sounded as if it was heading directly for us. We crouched as low as we could in a drainage ditch. In a few seconds the plane was directly overhead. Now was the time that we should be hearing a bomb if any had been aimed at us. Nothing happened and we heaved a sigh of relief.

Five small red flashes appeared in the sky as our ack-ack went into action and seconds later we heard the *plop, plop* of the exploding shells.

The plane turned around and headed back for the landing strip. Then we heard the bomb. It was like a fluttering whistle as it fell, the sound increasing rapidly in its intensity and punctuated at the climax by a sharp, groundshaking CRR-ACK.

The engine droned softly now and soon disappeared. The last red blossoms in the heavens died out.

We loaded ourselves into the truck again—glad to be alive—and wheeled down the road until we were out of the small hills and rolling across the slanting ground near the airfield.

On the road ahead of us we saw a parked jeep. A few yards away a few men were gathered together. "It looks like the bomb hit right over there," Witt remarked, pointing to a small crater not far from the men.

We were already late so we didn't stop to investigate. It was not until the afternoon that we learned what the little group of men had been clustered about. The driver of the jeep had stopped when the air raid alert sounded and had taken cover behind a tree stump. Unfortunately, he chose the wrong side of the tree. The bomb had burst close to him, spraying him fatally with shrapnel.

As soon as we arrived at the ready tent we were assigned to duty. A couple of the divisions took off on the moonbeam patrol (the code name for the dawn and dusk patrol). The rest of us got into a truck marked PILOT TRANSPORTATION ONLY and drove along the circular road through the airplane dispersal area. On each side we saw F4U's parked in sturdy stone revetments built by the Japanese. As we came to each airplane an enlisted man called out the name of the pilot who was to fly it and the truck stopped while he disembarked, loaded down by a parachute with a seat-type rubber lifeboat attached and a jungle pack, all weighing sixty-five pounds.

The first two planes I was assigned to each had something wrong with it. On the first one the left magneto was bad; the other had a broken generator. The third plane was satisfactory. After testing, I taxied the ship from its revetment to the end of the take-off string where the rest of the planes that were to be on scramble alert had been parked. I shut off the engine, prepared for a hasty take-off, then joined the other pilots who were gathered under the wing of a Corsair.

Every half hour we started the engines up to warm them so we could take off immediately in case we were scrambled. After a couple of hours the transportation truck came by and eight pilots got out.

"Where do you think you're going?" I asked one, who was heading for my plane.

"They want us to go out on a barge hunt over near Choiseul."

"That's a hell of a note—here we sit on our duffs for hours and then when there's a chance for a little fun, they give it to you boys."

"Sorry, old man, but orders are orders and besides, you'll have plenty of time to catch up before we finish this tour."

As I helped the pilot into the cockpit and assisted him in fastening the shoulder straps I gave him a word of advice. "You want to watch these mechanics around here, Reid. The one on this plane didn't even know where to put the gas. Everything is all right now, though. I checked the gas and oil and the ammo. Some of these 'mechs' haven't touched a plane before. They have been pulled off their regular jobs to help out until we can get some trained men here. I notice the generator charges quite high; you'll have to keep an eye on it."

We got into the vacant truck and drove around the end of the landing strip to the ready tent, with little more than the width of the road between the strip and the ocean. We passed a shell hole containing hundreds of rounds of Jap 20-mm cannon shells, then a

Jap three-pounder coastal defense gun.

A couple of hours later the pilots returned from their barge hunt. All of them tried to talk at once as they gathered around Gunner George Schaefer, our squadron intelligence officer, who had a wife and two children waiting for him in Los Angeles.

"Now, now, boys—take it easy," George said soothingly. "I can only handle one of you at a time. Now then, Gher, what do you have to say—did you see anything?"

"Sure did, George. Up along in here," the pilot said, pointing to a map of Choiseul, "we were fired on by some AA guns. Just around this bend, Moore noticed a barge hidden under some bushes along the shore. All the rest of us had passed by without even seeing it. He called us over the radio and we all went back and strafed. There was one measly ack-ack gun popping away at us, but we soon quieted him down. The barge was just a mass of smoke and flame when we left. It must have been loaded with barrels of oil."

After interviewing each pilot and finding the exact spot at which the barge had been found, as well as its length and appearance, who flew top cover to watch for Zeros and who did the strafing, George and Captain Terry telephoned headquarters and reported all the facts. They had a time limit of a half hour to report back to headquarters after each mission.

By this time it was nearly noon and the sun was beating down unmercifully. The canvas tents protected us from the direct rays, but even so, the humidity in the air prevented the escape of the heat to the outside. Consequently the tent became the lid to our oven.

"Okie's division—go over to chow now and come back as soon as you can, you've got to relieve the fellows out on scramble alert."

"Don't worry," Carl McLean replied in his best Ardmore, Oklahoma drawl. "I won't be staying over there even long enough to eat if the food is anywhere near as bad as they say it is."

Four of us donned our shirts, which instantly clung to our wet, perspiring backs. We were joined by Ace Newland's division in the truck which drove us around the strip, along the taxi-way, past some wrecked Jap airplanes and up to Dysentery Chowhall.

Outside the low wooden frame building, the lower halves of three fifty-gallon barrels formed the dish-washing unit.

We opened the screen door and entered. The first sight to greet us was the seating arrangement. There wasn't any. Six rows of men stood side by side along both sides of waisthigh tables which extended the length of the room.

We picked up metal trays which had been divided into compartments to prevent the peaches from mixing with the potatoes. Here we flyers were favored, because most of the enlisted men were eating from mess kits. There were no spoons or knives at the moment, so we got along as best we could with a fork. In a few minutes the supply of spoons and knives was replenished.

In the wall separating us from the kitchen were three large openings. From the first, a large spoonful of gritty spinach was dumped into my tray, followed by a heaping spoonful of dehydrated potatoes. I moved on to the next window for a slice of Spam. After a couple of stewed apricots had been splashed into the niche adjoining the meat, I moved on to the next window. Here my canteen cup was filled with what I called chocolate milk.

To all appearances the food was good, but the telling was in the tasting. The potatoes were so water-soaked that I had to force myself to eat them. The Spam was like all Spam. The spinach was so gritty that even the men who liked it ordinarily, rebelled at this gastronomical insult. The chocolate milk would be more aptly described by the name of watered cocoa. It tasted much the same. With the use of sugar it became drinkable, however. Its temperature was about the same as a human body, but fifteen minutes after drinking it, sweat came more profusely. There was only one enjoyable part of the food—the apricots.

In the days to come, many of us fasted at noontime, or else just ate the fruit the messhall had to offer—invariably apricots or peaches.

When we had finished eating we carried all our utensils out the back door. First we stopped at a barrel and emptied all the uneaten food into the garbage can. Then we slid our cup, knife, fork and spoon onto a wire which projected from one corner of the dirty eating tray. Holding the end of this wire, we dunked the whole shebang into the first tub of hot water. Next we dunked the utensils into the middle tub, which washed off the particles remaining from the previous rinse.

Fires built under the tubs of water kept them hot, although not always boiling as they should have been. It was an ingenious system the Seabees had rigged up to feed the fires with liquid fuel. Leaning over the hot, steaming tubs with the heat of the fire blasting from below and the sun blazing from above was almost suffocating.

After a third and final rinse in comparatively clean

water we took our ware back into the messhall and
left it on a table for the next shift.

Once again we carried our parachutes to the truck
and were driven to the planes. Again we checked and
made preparations for a hurried take-off. We sat in
the cockpits this time, hoping for an order to scramble. Operations had given us special instructions to
remain in the plane ready for an immediate take-off,
evidently expecting some Jap activity. The sun was
very hot and I remembered the old saying: "Mad
dogs and Englishmen go out in the midday sun." The
words "United States Marines" should be inserted
next to "mad dogs."

Finally, after one more midafternoon trip to the
ready tent, the operations officer came in and asked,
"Who wants to fly?"

My division leader, Okie, was the first to volunteer. We were to cover the withdrawal of some supply ships and their escorts, which had completed
unloading at Vella Lavella and were anxious to get
out of range of Jap dive bombers before darkness
came with its "bomber's moon."

We took off and turned to our compass heading. As
we left the vicinity of our base we each moved away
from the leader to assume our battle formation on a
line abreast, so that each pilot could watch the tails of
the others and have space enough to turn into any
enemy plane that might attack.

We were at ten thousand feet now, and climbing
steadily. I picked up my oxygen mask and curled my
legs around the control stick to keep the plane flying
as smoothly as possible, while I struggled with the
face mask. The elasticity of the rubber bands was
nearly gone and a tiny clamp continuously came un-

fastened as I twisted my head from side to side, keeping an alert lookout for the Japs. The little clamp permitted the lower part of my mask to rest loosely against my face instead of snugly.

Ahead of us lay a small island about fifteen miles distant. I took my map out of the knee pocket of my flying suit. Gizo Island, I thought to myself; and off to the left, that island rising like a hog's back from the sea for nearly fifteen miles must be Ganongga. . . . Only a few miles of water separated Ganongga from the comparatively large island of Vella Lavella, which tucked tiny Baga in its side, much like a white corpuscle about to envelope a germ.

"Fox base from Red one leader. Over," crackled Okie's voice over the radio.

"Red one leader from Fox base, go ahead. Over." One of the destroyers, which we could see far below leaving a long white trail of foam behind, was replying to our call.

"Fox base from Red leader. Have arrived on station with three other chickens. Over." Okie was telling the destroyer that four fighter planes were now overhead and ready to relieve other planes in protecting it from Japanese aerial attack.

"Red one leader from Fox base. Fly at angels ten. Over."

"This is Red one leader. Fly at angels ten. Wilco. Out." We began to climb up to angels ten, which happened to be 20,000 feet for that particular day. Several flights of fighter planes were covering the withdrawal of the supply force and were stacked up at altitudes assigned them by the fighter director officer on the destroyer, so that he had planes at all levels to intercept raiding Japs.

At 20,000 feet it is possible to see a lot of country.

The land and the water spreads out beneath you as if you were perched high above a gigantic, varicolored map. I could make out the shore of Bougainville with the Shortlands this side of it. Farther toward the south I could see the long island of Choiseul and Santa Isabel.

Yes, this part of the world all looked so close from my flying foxhole, but I knew it might take many months and many American lives to bridge the gaps. It had taken one solid year to capture Guadalcanal and build up sufficient strength to take Munda. That conquest had ended one great chapter in Marine Aviation, in which men like John Smith, Marion Carl, Joe Foss, Zeke Swett, Kenneth Walsh and other pilots became aces many times over.

Marine Aviation had since changed to the offensive, but at the same time had to defend our hard-won positions. No longer were the pilots able to rise daily and try to knock down as many attacking Jap bombers and fighters as they could before supper. The Jap planes were no longer as plentiful, although they were still very much a real menace. The Marines had to range far afield to utilize their effectiveness to the maximum. They began to strafe Jap barges and installations and to escort Allied bombers far from their home base.

It had not been easy—those first days in the Solomons—but now our pilots had proved at Munda and again at Vella Lavella that they could take and hold an aerial beachhead anywhere within fighter plane range. They could provide an aerial umbrella for the bombers and for the Marines who landed on enemy-infested shores.

It had taken a year to wrest 190 nautical miles of water and jungle from the Japanese—as far as

Munda. Then we had hopped over the thousands of Japs on Kolumbangara, Ganongga, Arundel, Gizo and other small islands to Vella Lavella, forty miles away.

Where would we strike next? The Shortlands, Choiseul, the Treasuries—or Bougainville?

Judging from the past record, it would take six months for us to move up as far as I was able to see from my altitude. The time might be shortened, because we now had large quantities of supplies at Guadalcanal and our other bases. Even so, it looked like a long long way to Tokyo.

Undoubtedly our progress in the Solomons campaign had been made easier by the death of one Japanese, one of the smartest, most experienced and most arrogant of them all, one who predicted early in the war that he would dictate peace terms in the White House at Washington, D. C. Those American commanders who had known him in prewar days when he was a military attaché in Washington, and others who met him in Japan, thought so highly of his military capabilities that when the chance came to destroy Admiral Isoroku Yamamoto on Sunday, April 18, 1943, the project took precedence over all others of the moment.

In one of the most efficient and amazing examples of Allied Intelligence work during the war we had at last broken the Japanese code—and at a very opportune moment. One of the first messages decoded revealed that Yamamoto and his staff were to fly on an inspection trip from Rabaul to Kahili, his main base beyond Rabaul. They were to fly in two Bettys (twin-engine bombers) and would arrive over Kahili about 1135. Headquarters at Pearl Harbor sent orders to ComAirSols to get Yamamoto. With Admirals

Halsey and Mitscher closely involved, the detailed planning was assigned to the exec of Mitscher's ComAirSols Fighter Command, Lieutenant Colonel L. S. Moore. Some officers wanted to attack when the Japanese would be motoring in his launch from Kahili to Ballale, but others decided an aerial kill would be more certain. The longest-ranged fighters were assigned the job. Eighteen Army P-38's were to leave Guadalcanal. Six of the best shots were assigned to do the shooting and the other twelve planes were to protect them from Zeros. Major John W. Mitchell commanded the P-38's. Major John P. Condon, the operations office, plotted a course to take them outside The Slot. Lieutenant Colonel Moore gave instructions to fly at an altitude of fifty feet off New Georgia to try to avoid detection by radar. They were to get Yamamoto at all costs—even to the extent of ramming his plane if necessary.

Two of the six sharpshooting pilots failed to get off the ground because of belly-tank fueling failure and a tire that blew out.

The Japanese were punctual, arriving at the expected time. The Zero fighter cover assumed their job was completed when the transports began to circle in preparation to land. Before the Japs knew what had happened, the Army fighters had dived from the clouds and Captain Thomas G. Lanphier shot down the plane carrying Yamamoto. It crashed into the jungle. Lieutenant Rex T. Barber shot the other aircraft down. It crashed into the sea, carrying Yamamoto's Chief of Staff, Vice-Admiral Ugaki. The nine Zeros which had been covering the two planes were frantically fighting the twelve P-38's acting as cover for the triggermen. Three Jap fighters were shot down. One American was lost—Lieutenant

Raymond K. Hine. Miraculously, it was learned later, Ugaki survived the crash.

On the anniversary of the Doolittle raid on Tokyo which had flown from Mitscher's carrier, *Hornet,* Admiral Halsey sent a message to Mitscher regarding Yamamoto's death that day: *Sounds as though one of the ducks in their bag was a peacock. April 18th is your luck day.*

My mind stopped concentrating on the past. For over two hours we had been on patrol. For two hours I had just been sitting in the cockpit, moving my hands and feet occasionally and twisting my neck constantly from side to side, like the rotor of a washing machine. We had strained our eyes for the sight of an unfamiliar speck that might materialize into a Jap plane. We had listened carefully to the radio to be sure we wouldn't miss any bogey reports. The radio popped and crackled and finally came to life and a voice told the destroyer that Red flight two had arrived on station. Fox base called our division, thanked us for our efforts and told us to return to base. We felt disappointed at leaving, because the Japs' favorite time of day for attacking was fast approaching.

We pointed the long smooth snouts of our Corsairs homeward and with a sun low in the sky at our backs we dived at a shallow angle, chopping the miles off the distance at the rate of one every twelve seconds.

We raced over the Munda airstrip, then one by one peeled away from the formation in three-count intervals with steep chandelles to the right. When we had lost sufficient speed we let our wheels down.

Never had I attempted to land a plane on a field as narrow and short as the Munda strip. It was about fifty feet wide. And of all fighter planes, the Corsair is perhaps the worst with which to attempt such a landing. The nose projects so far ahead of the pilot, without narrowing to a point as some fighter plane noses do, that when the plane is on the ground in a three-point attitude, forward visibility is nil.

I hoped for the best and swung in for my landing. The plane touched the ground gently and swished down the runway. Everything ahead was blotted from sight, except for a little triangular patch of the runway between the lead edge of the wing and the nose on each side. Unless I kept each of those patches the same width, I would run off the runway into deadly obstacles.

There was very little wind and my Corsair seemed unwilling to slow down as it should. A coral road went by on the left. I knew the end of the surfaced runway was fast approaching, so I applied the brakes, meanwhile keeping the plane rolling straight ahead. It soon slowed enough so that I was looking for the wide taxi road leading from the far end of the strip. In a few seconds I saw it, but I saw something else too—*mud!* Before I could unlock my tailwheel and turn off the runway, I felt the plane hit something and mush down, simultaneously coming almost to a stop. I felt like a fly stuck in molasses. I knew in a flash if the plane ever stopped rolling, a truck would be needed to pull it from the goo. I had to keep it rolling and try to plow through the mud. I shoved the throttle forward for more power and a fraction of a second later pulled the flap lever up so the mud wouldn't damage the flaps as the plane mired deep. I pulled back on the stick to lessen the tendency for the front wheels to dig in and flip me over on my back.

The plane slowed almost to a standstill, but I gave it more throttle and eased the stick forward to make the tail lighter, yet not so far as to endanger going over on my nose. The engine roared loudly and the plane shuddered with its mighty effort, but the wheels kept rolling as I gave it left rudder to get to the nearest solid ground and the taxi road.

Just as we reached the edge of the mud the plane slowed almost to its final stop. I quickly added more throttle and must have had nearly 2,000 horsepower to pull me up and onto the hard ground.

It had all happened in a period of fifteen seconds or less. I grinned and waved to a mechanic who was standing nearby, waiting for me to get stuck. He waved back and grasped both of his hands together in a handclasp and shook them over his head—just like a victorious prize fighter.

That night as we lay in bed, we heard piano music floating up to us from some place down the hill. Whoever was playing was an accomplished pianist with a strong resonant bass.

"Do you boys hear what I hear?" Leach asked us in that peculiar Mississippi drawl of his.

As if by one accord we all decided to play a little joke on him.

"Why no, Leach—I don't hear nothin'."

"What are you talking about, Leach?"

"I don't hear a sound, Jesse."

One after another we denied hearing anything. The music stopped as if the player was in on our little game.

"Why, I could sworn that I heard somebody playing a piano just a few minutes ago. It's stopped now though," Leach said.

"Ace, you better go get Doc Brittingham over here. Poor ol' Jesse has been out in the sun too long today," I suggested.

When he heard that remark, Leach proclaimed adamantly, "I don't need no doctor—I'm as well as any man in here." He paused for a moment and added, "At least I think I am."

"That patrol was just too much for Jesse," piped up Hughes.

"Fools," drawled Leach, using his favorite invective, "there was somebody playing a piano, I am as sure of that as I am that I'm lying here next to Hughes."

"Oh, but you're not lying next to Hughes, old man, you happen to be lying next to me." Ace Newlands of Pasadena, California, interspersed that statement with one of his mock accents—this time an English twang. We all believed Ace was an escaped vaudeville comic, although he claimed to be a graduate of UCLA. He was as thin as a bean pole.

Leach was by now getting excited, judging from the rising inflection of his voice as it tried to surround the darkness shrouding our conversation. "Good Gawwd—what is this? Are you all ganging up against me or am I really going crazy?"

The music started again. Leach tried to call our attention to it and once more we denied hearing anything.

"Jesse, come to your senses and let us go to sleep. How in God's world would a piano ever get away up here at Munda, where they just cleaned the Japs out only a few days ago, let alone anybody around here that could play the damned thing like you claim he can?"

"That's what's worrying me. I just can't believe it could be true."

And so, with the mystery of the piano still unsolved, we dropped off to sleep.

A great noise spurred the air at 2330. My heart momentarily stopped beating. Without delay, I swung my feet over the cot and into my "air raid" shoes, which I had placed in such a position that my feet would fall into them every time I got up.

One chorus of antiaircraft guns was augmented by a second, very close to our tent. The bang of that gun caused me to drop my efforts at reaching for my steel helmet—and run. I took two steps and practically fell down the incline leading to our foxhole. I hit my head on the top of the foxhole doorway and was just ducking it lower for another try, when I felt somebody's feet land on my back. This bit of impetus sent me the remaining five feet into the dugout and I crashed into the opposite wall of our shelter. Dirt crumbled and slid down my back as I slumped to a crouching position.

"What's the idea of blocking the entrance, Zed?" asked Nugent right behind me.

"I couldn't help it, I hit my head. What's the idea of jumping on me anyhow?"

"Good hell, I didn't want to waste any time getting in here with old Washing Machine Charlie headed right this way and those guns shooting so fast."

There were three Johns in that one foxhole. John Witt of Wauwatosa, Wisconsin, was a dark-haired, rather stocky lad who was buddy-buddy with John Nugent, who hailed from Chicago. We called Nugent "The Face" because if there were any insects around, poison ivy or other skin maladies, they always got to him first. He was the same height as Witt, but not quite as heavy. I was the third foxhole John. With my shoes on I was almost six feet tall. My 10,000 odd brown hairs were cut short in the GI manner. I was nicknamed "Zed" because I was one of the three pilots in the squadron who had acted as Fighter Director Officer at Midway and in that capacity used Zed as my code name. I was soon to pick up another nickname, "Belts Foster," because of the jingling buckles of the three belts I wore every day—one to hold my trousers up, one to carry my knife, canteen, first-aid kit and extra cartridges, and the third to be accessible for a tourniquet in case I should get wounded badly in the air.

In front of our tent I found Ace Newlands, Leach and Hughes. They burst out laughing as I approached, thinking I looked funny in just a pair of shorts with my clodhoppers and steel helmet on. And we all laughed when we saw Jules Koetsch from Brooklyn. He was standing out there in the bright moonlight enjoying the air raid—stark-naked with the exception of his meerschaum pipe. The moon made his balding head glisten.

Two of our veteran "sack" men—Texan Paul Pankhurst and Okie—hadn't stirred from their bunks during the entire aerial barrage.

We had just returned to our sacks for a few minutes when we heard the distinctive moan of a Jap airplane. Their engines had a high-pitched anemic roar compared to the deep, throaty resonance of American planes. Jap night raiders are called Washing Machine Charlie after the original pest that harrassed our boys on Guadalcanal. At various times he had been called

Louie the Louse, Maytag Charlie, and other names less printable.

Despite their impotent sound at night, the Jap bombers sometimes performed accurate bombings, but what was more remarkable was the small amount of damage they did compared to what they could have done.

This particular Louie the Louse was coming back for another try. The searchlights came on and caught a reflection.

"They've got him—they've got him in the lights," Nugent and I yelled. The rest of the men trouped out of the tent to see the sight.

Red polka-dots appeared on the black velvet of the sky. The orange flashes missed him by hundreds of feet. A fellow from the next tent shot his 45-caliber pistol into the sky at the Jap as a gesture of contempt for our AA.

We hit our foxhole just before the ground shook and dirt tumbled down from a near hit. Shrapnel chopped holes in our tent and rattled around in the trees. Then we returned to our still-warm sacks.

Time to get up. After a breakfast of hotcakes we arrived at the strip in time to see Willie Moore make two forced landings. The second plane he took up that day left a trail of black smoke and the propeller stopped turning when the engine froze up, just as he landed.

After the day's flying was over the sixth and the seventh divisions were assigned the dawn patrol and the scramble alert for the next day, which meant we were to sleep in the ready tent alongside the runway, a most undesirable place to spend the night.

3.
EAGLES IN THE AIR—
VULTURES ON THE GROUND

THE SUN WENT down and the world became lovely again for a few minutes. All the flying and the bombing, the mud, sweat and heat, seemed to have been somebody else's lot. I felt a momentary deep contentment.

At 1915 we saw two red flares shoot up from the tower across the strip and the siren began its wail. Soon we heard the pulsating unsynchronized engines of a Jap bomber.

Searchlight beams were cut short by a layer of clouds.

The bomber circled around for a few minutes, while we impatiently waited for him to drop his bombs and depart. But he was in no hurry, safely protected by the clouds, and he was enjoying harassing us. Soon he went away without dropping anything.

The *clop* of a green flare and a blast on the siren notified us all was clear.

A freshening wind brought the smell of rain. I chose a cot near the center of the tent for my bed in anticipation of the squall. The wind grew stronger. Dust swirled and eddied about our cots.

"Here she comes," Newlands exclaimed at the patter of raindrops on our tent. Within thirty seconds of the first warning drop we were deluged by what would be called a cloudburst in the States, with little cloud and lots of burst.

As if each raindrop stirred its own particle of air in passing and each of these had formed together, a small gale sprang up with the storm and blew the mist from the splattering drops inside our unwalled tent. A cold chill spread through our shelter and drove out the humid heat of the day. The wind blew the rain in from the open sides. A roof, its loose canvas corners flapping is, of itself, small protection against the storms at Munda.

Witt, immediately realizing the hopelessness of his position, salvaged what he could of his half-soaked clothing and bedding and ingeniously converted a wooden shelf under the table into a bunk. Leach's bed was wet completely through. He left it and went to the leeward side of the tent to an extra bunk. Nugent, Okie and Pankhurst all pulled their cots as close to the center of the tent as possible, so close that they began to get rained on from the hole in the center, where the supporting tent pole passed through.

Newlands and myself were the only ones who had no serious troubles so we just lay there and laughed at the discomfort of the others. I happened to look down at the ground between laughs just in time to rescue my shoes from a young river that was starting to flow through our tent. Then the tent roof started to leak over my cot. I tried to move out of the way, but I was blocked on all sides by the others. There was nothing to do but take it, along with the wet flurries of wind. I thought of my mosquito netting and set it on the poles over me. It worked. The coarse netting caught the droplets and prevented them from coming through and calmed the wind in my cubicle.

Then, as suddenly as it had violently arisen, the rain stopped, except for a very fine drizzle.

The air raid alarm sounded and the blurry form of a rising red flare lit the sky.

"I don't care if that son-of-a-bitch has got me in his sights, I'm not going to move out of this sack." Witt's voice floated up indignantly from underneath the table.

Entirely unexpected, because we had heard the Jap plane buzzing what seemed a long distance away, we heard the rising snarl of a diving engine. We didn't know whether it was to be followed by a falling bomb or not and didn't wait to see. We ran for the foxhole, ten feet outside the tent.

Witt went past Newlands so fast that Ace only felt a gust of wind in the dark and although Witt had nearly a five-foot head start on me I was right behind him and ready to pass as we jumped into the foxhole and scrambled for the far wall to avoid the thundering herd behind us.

At that moment we heard the deep *ka*BALOOMPH of a large bomb as it exploded far away. It had landed near a point where some 90-mm AA guns had recently been placed and also near our artillery which lobbed shells toward Kolumbangara. There was ack-ack fire—too little and too late. Finally, near midnight, we got to sleep.

Breakfast consisted of canned grapefruit juice and coffee—and some other things, too, which were left untouched. Newlands division took off on the dawn patrol; the rest of us went on scramble alert.

Thus began what was to be a hectic day for the Flying Deuces.

The skipper of our squadron, short and lively Max

J. Volcansek, was a great believer in competition, always challenging someone to a game of acey-deucy, knife throwing or just plain coin tossing. He had the idea that his squadron should have one or two divisions containing all the best pilots, according to his judgment. The rest of the men in the squadron were supposed to vie with each other to see who would get "promoted" to fly in the chosen divisions. He thought that these few of the best should go out on every mission when enemy contact was expected. (At that time he didn't realize how busy flying we would be because of the few pilots and fewer planes at our disposal, and of course he had to change the policy later on.)

A big strike was ordered on Kahili and every flyable plane on the field was to get into the air as cover for the bombers, along with some of the fighters from the Russell Islands. This was the big chance for contact with the enemy our squadron had been waiting for. The Flying Deuces sent all the pilots whose turn it was to fly, plus the chosen few, into the sky. We watched them circle the field and then head for the rendezvous with the bombers.

Doc Brittingham, Leach and I stood on top of a coral mound alongside the taxi strip. This vantage point was known as "Vultures' Hill" because it permitted a person to watch the planes take off, land and sometimes crash. We used powerful binoculars to scan the horizon for low-flying planes, which might be Japs coming in for a strafing attack.

A report came in that there were some unidentified planes approaching Rendova. A few minutes later through our glasses we saw twelve Army B-25's followed by the same number of B-24's.

All of the planes disappeared toward the northwest

into a solid line of darkening clouds, an ominous portent of approaching bad weather. Those of us who hadn't gone on the strike walked back to the ready tent and played cards, while we inwardly sweated out the return.

1000 came and still none of the planes had come back. An extended line of rain crept toward us from Kolumbangara and enveloped the tiny islets ahead one by one. You could see the calm surface of the water before the storm and then look past the streaming curtain to the water behind, which appeared to be foaming in torment from the beat of the rain. The fresh invigorating smell of the storm wafted to those of us at the brown airfield at Munda.

Out of the mist a gray figure materialized, then another. They possessed the distinctive inverted gull wings of a Corsair. The planes zoomed over the strip and peeled up and off, then came in over the water and landed from west to east, downwind.

The fighter planes straggled back by ones, twos and threes. We counted every plane to find out if our boys had all returned.

"It looks like they've had a fight from the way they are straggling in."

"Yeah, either that or else the weather broke them up."

We had returned to the top of Vulture's Hill to watch. Two Corsairs approached at 1,000 feet. Suddenly the wingman broke away from his leader and lowered his landing gear.

"That boy is in trouble—he's coming straight in!"

The pilot in the Corsair maintained plenty of altitude so he would be able to glide to the field if his engine conked out. We had all been in a similar posi-

tion and knew he was straining every fiber to antici-
pate any trouble and to get down safely. If he made
one mistake it would very likely be his last, for
airplanes don't usually give a man a second chance.
When he saw he could reach the runway even if his
engine failed—he popped his landing flaps to slow
him down.

"*Good Gawd!* Look what's coming in at the other
end of the strip!" Another pilot dropped his landing
flaps at the other end of the field. The two pilots were
landing head on! Neither of them seemed to see the
other, because of the long nose of their planes.

"*Watch out!*"

"*Take a wave-off, somebody!*"

"*Don't land!*"

We stood on the sidelines and yelled hoarsely and
with futility, our bodies tense with excitement, a
helpless feeling filling our insides.

Both planes were now skimming along just above
the deck in the final stage of landing and both were
landing long. At the last desperate moment the 2,000
horses of the first plane's engine roared into life, its
nose rose in the sky, the left wing dipped violently,
missing the ground by only three feet or so as the pilot
made an emergency left turn to evade the oncoming
plane.

He gained a few feet of altitude and swung in a
steep right turn to head toward the water as quickly
as possible.

I turned my eyes to watch the other Corsair land.
He had no sooner rolled the length of the runway and
turned toward the taxi strip when his engine stopped.

I looked again for the plane that had taken the
wave-off. It was not to be seen.

A B-25 came in for an emergency landing, shot through with large holes and a wounded crew member aboard.

Quiet settled down upon the flying field. It began to rain.

The pilots back from the raid had been given a small two-ounce bottle of Lejon whiskey. Some of them refused it, some sipped it and others downed it in one gulp as they were being questioned by the intelligence officers. Even with that nerve-calmer, I noticed how their hands shook as they held a cigarette.

"Four men are missing," I heard Schaefer say. This shocking news made me feel strange, much the same feeling I had received when I was a little boy and my pet dog had been run over by a car. "It must have been Pappy Reid who took the wave-off. We just got a report that two F4U's crashed into the water and Pappy must have been in one. Who the other one was, we won't know for a while, although we think it was Morris. Now then, does anybody here know anything about Craig and Williams other than the fact they were last seen heading for home?"

Shortly afterward, I was carrying my parachute out to the truck to go on scramble alert when I saw the brown skin of a black-haired pilot clad only in shorts. It was Johnny Morris. His white-toothed, dental-cream grin was as broad as ever, though he was wet all over and covered with many scratches and bruises. Doc Brittingham was patching him up.

In due time, I learned what had occurred: Morris had made a landing approach, but when he saw he was not in the correct position he decided to take a voluntary wave-off and go around again. He had reached the edge of the water when without warning one flap collapsed, while the other remained at the full fifty degrees. The airplane went into a dive from his height of 200 feet and started to roll over on its back. Just before it hit the water, Morris succeeded in getting the wings leveled to make a good water landing—except for one serious defect. His wheels were down—there hadn't been time to pull them up. As soon as the water struck the wheels it flipped the Corsair over on its back at nearly 100 miles per hour.

When Morris felt the plane going over, he unsnapped the safety belt and was catapulted completely out of the cockpit with his parachute. He hit the water and a couple of seconds later the tail of his plane smacked beside him with a great splash— missing his head by inches.

The mechanic of plane #4, who was one of the men to rescue Morris, told me he saw the plane go over and land on its back amid a tremendous splash. He didn't see anyone get out. The rescuers swam and waded out to the sinking plane, thinking the pilot hadn't possibly escaped. But then they arrived near the plane, they saw Morris' head bobbing on the waves.

After returning from an uneventful scramble alert, I found another very damp and bedraggled pilot, clutching a tangled mess of soaking-wet flight gear. He was streaked with the green and yellow of his emergency dye marker. It was Lieutenant Winfred Reid, the high-stepping ex-drum major from Delight, Arkansas, and the Casanova of Waikiki.

Pappy Reid had had a lively day. He was the skipper's wingman and had followed him as Volcansek attacked a Zero from behind, poured in a burst of 50 calibers until he was as close as fifty feet from the

Jap, then pulled away. The Zero turned on its back and went down in a split-S. Reid was to the side of and behind the skipper and was able to put in a good slug from his own .50's. The Jap plane headed straight down from 25,000 feet, trailing smoke until it disappeared from view.

Craig and Williams had left the division 20 miles southeast of Ballale. Craig was trailing black smoke, which changed to white and looked like the emission of a cropduster. The skipper and Reid had stayed to protect the bombers and watched the other two men of their division head for home.

There had been a mix-up in the rendezvous and the fighter planes had thirty minutes' less gasoline than they had anticipated. When their fuel got down to sixty gallons each, Reid and his leader started back for Munda. They were cruising along comfortably when Reid looked behind and saw several Zeros sneaking up.

"Volcansek from Reid. There's six Zeros on your tail!"

Both of the Corsair pilots then "bent their throttles over the throttle-quadrant," using 2,700 RPM (used only for extreme emergency and take-offs). After going into a shallow dive they gradually pulled away from the Japs. Two more seconds and the Japs would have been within firing range. As it was, the skipper found some holes in his elevators.

As they neared the Munda fighter strip, both pilots realized they only had about three to five gallons of fuel. Reid decided to break off and make a straight-in approach, but Volcansek heard the tower call and say that the landing course had been reversed. The skipper continued on and made his approach according to the new course. Reid made his an emergency approach. Both were justified in their actions.

When the skipper saw the other airplane approaching head on, he knew he never had the gas to take a wave-off and go around the field again; so he decided to wait until the other plane had landed before setting his own down.

Reid saw that he was safely over the runway, when he observed the other Corsair coming head on. He continued in his approach hoping the other pilot would apply throttle and take a wave-off, because he thought his own gas supply would fail if he tried it. The other plane kept on coming so Reid decided that he "would have to get the hell out of there" to avoid a collision. He poured the coal to his plane and banked to avoid passing too close, then banked again to the right to get over the water as quickly as possible, for if he should run out of gas over the rough, crater-strewn shore at Munda it would spell finish. Most pilots had been able to survive crash landings in the water, unharmed.

When he reached the water his engine suddenly stopped for a second, then started again. After this warning it ran a few more seconds then conked out for good. Reid had already retracted his landing gear. He stuck the nose of his plane down to keep from stalling, then leveled off just above the water and settled down in a neat water landing. He had time to get out of the cockpit and save his parachute before a rescue boat came by and picked him up.

It had been a black day for the Flying Deuces. We had lost four airplanes and two pilots, although we hoped to see these pilots come back alive in the near future.

Every day a Marine, soldier or Seabee wandered

up to the pilots with something to sell for cash or whiskey. Jap rifles cost from $25 to $100, or one to three quarts of whiskey. Japanese invasion currency or their national currency sold for three pieces per $1 for the bills with the larger dimensions and $1 for four pieces of the smaller-sized dimensions. The monetary value of the bill apparently was not as important as the physical size. The 10,000 yen notes brought no more money than a mere 100 yen.

The price of a Japanese flag consisting of a square piece of white silk with a large red round sun in the center, with various Japanese hieroglyphics (and perhaps a bloodstain or two), was from $50 up to $300, or three to six quarts of whiskey.

One of the officers went whole hog one day and bought a Nambu light machine gun complete with ammunition. Doc Brittingham immediately tested it. He had a hobby of collecting firearms and during the entire time at Munda was constantly on the lookout for a certain type of pistol he needed for his collection.

The enlisted men seemed to think that we pilots were made of money and had hundreds of dollars as well as several cases of whiskey each. They found it difficult to understand that most of us had brought only about $10 with us into the combat area. Some of the gamblers were better supplied with money, although much of their gambling was conducted on a credit basis.

As for whiskey, the majority of pilots had brought along one or more bottles for trading or drinking purposes—not nearly enough.

I had wanted a small cannon mounted on wheels with wooden spokes to take back home with me as a souvenir. It was the "Pistol Pete" that had pestered the men at Munda Point after all organized resistance had been wiped out. Every little while the Japs would drop some shells into the captured area. This constituted a very unhappy situation for the pilots and enlisted men, who never knew when they might get hit. Patrols were sent out after the gun, but it was so light the Japs moved it continuously from position to position. Finally, our men had succeeded in its capture. My plans for the cannon were never realized due to transportation difficulties.

"Don't let 'em talk you into strafing Kahili."

That had been the last word of farewell we heard when VMF 215 left us. Now, the time had come. One hop from another squadron had gone out early in the morning to strafe the airfield, but had missed finding the spot by three or four miles. Consequently, Major Sapp volunteered his division for a strafing attack to arrive at Kahili just at dusk, when the Japs would find it hardest to see them.

Nothing worked out right. After they had taken off, Sapp had to land and get another plane. He took off again, but he was already 20 minutes behind his time schedule. He increased his speed to arrive at the turning point at his estimated time, but this increased his carefully planned fuel consumption. To top it off, the division ran into bad weather!

They were flying low over the water so the Japanese radar system couldn't pick them up. Their low altitude and the storm prevented them from seeing any landmarks, so it was a remarkable job of navigation—as well as a lot of luck—that when Sapp started his turn to the right he was only a few hundred feet off target. They stayed just above the tops of the jungle as they approached the enemy airfield—the largest south of Rabaul. They then zoomed up and over the hill that hid them from the Japanese.

To their dismay they were just a little too far north of the strip and they couldn't sweep across the width of the field in a line abreast. Sapp did a wingover to the right and went down the lower length of the runway on the right-hand side. Plane after plane flashed beneath him. They were parked in revetments, but his 50-caliber slugs found them. He arrived at the water's edge and turned to the left to rendezvous.

Meanwhile "Montana" Turner and "Mother" Jones were finding some juicy strafing targets as they went down the other side of the runway. They caught what they thought was a messhall, as well as several Jap planes. "Kitty" Hobbs hadn't been able to turn as sharply as the others, so he drew a pipper on some buildings and spat his .50's out in the personnel area, where many of the Japs were quartered. Near the shore he cut down the Japs manning a gun position, then found himself heading directly into the corruscating display of interlacing tracers coming from the defense of a destroyer. He bore down upon it firing as he went, with deft handling kicking his rudder from side to side to rake the entire ship with his spraying bullets.

The fireworks display from the intense AA defenses of Kahili had lifted the hackles on the hair of all our pilots, but they were able to look back on a field blazing with numerous fires. The Japs at Kahili had had the macabre honor of feeling the first newly born wrath of the Flying Deuces in retaliation for the loss of our two pilots.

Our pilots hightailed it for home. Everyone landed except Jones. Nearly a half hour went by and still he didn't come in, and we were almost ready to give him up for lost when we happily heard the whistle of the wind rushing through the intercoolers of his plane as it went overhead. No wonder the Japs called the Corsair the "Whistling Death"!

Jones had started back flying the YG radio beam. He hit a false fade and thought his compass was out and he must be going in the wrong direction, so he turned around and headed back—toward Kahili. The radio signals really began to fade then and he realized his mistake.

We added up the score and decided twelve Jap Zeros had been destroyed, as well as a number of Japs killed and untold damage to matériel. Kitty hadn't stayed around long enough to see what happened to his destroyer, and all the Texan could say was, "This is the toughest way to make a living I know of."

The time came when it was my turn to sleep in the ready tent again. This was unpleasant duty, because the strip was easily visible to Jap bomber pilots and therefore the installations along each side received most of their attention.

After the flying for the day had ended and the sun was sinking low, we were seated in front of the tent engaged in our evening bull session when an Army enlisted man came strolling up. He had been through the battle for Munda. The Marines and some Army units had landed and captured beachheads from the Japanese in several places. Upon being relieved by the Army some of the Marines had returned to Guadalcanal. After several days of hard fighting it had been necessary to send for the Marines again for reinforcements.

The soldier talked constantly without pause, and his story was very interesting to us. From the way he looked and acted we judged that he had been affected by his experiences and this incessant talk was a form of shell shock or war neurosis.

"You can't ever tell what's gonner happen aroun' this place," the soldier remarked. "When we got the Japs all kilt we thought it'd be safe aroun' h'yar. The other day just before you fellers came we had a plane blow up and got thirteen men killed."

"That's right," corroborated George Schaefer, "a TBF (torpedo bomber) couldn't get its bomb bay doors open while it taxied back after a hop and some gas fumes must have accumulated. The pilot was seated on the wing in the parking area waiting for a mechanic to come when something caused the TBF to explode, probably a spark. That caused the bomb it was carrying to go off too. It got two gas trucks and obliterated two more planes. I was sitting all the way over here and the blast and shock nearly blew me off my seat. Flames went up over a thousand feet into the air. Nobody will ever know what really happened."

Darkness came and I began to feel slightly woozy. The voices seemed to come from far off. I felt as if I were someplace far away. Then things came back to me clearly and I realized where I was. A few minutes later the voices again sounded faint and a long distance away. I couldn't hear anything but the distant voices and the rush of blood in my ears. Again my mind cleared. I stood up and everything went dark for a moment. Then I walked over to Doc Brittingham, the squadron physician.

"Doc—something's wrong with me. I just came close to blacking out two or three times."

The doctor asked for more symptoms, then he felt my forehead. "You have some fever, Zed. Come on over here by the lister bag and I'll give you something to drink."

"That's what I was afraid of, Doc."

He mixed some white powder with the lukewarm water, stirred the mixture and handed it to me. "Here, drink this."

I took the small glass and downed the awful stuff in two gulps.

I remembered how Frederick Hughes had looked the previous afternoon as he lay under the hot canvas of his tent. He had come down with gastroenteritis. He lay there panting for breath, his face redder than I had ever seen it. He had opened his eyes when three of us visited him, but didn't say anything—just lay there breathing hard and so weak he could hardly move without help. I wondered if I had the same thing.

Shortly after drinking the medicine, I began to feel cold. I knew the air hadn't cooled off from the heat of the day, yet I felt as chilly as on a cool, crisp morning in the mountains. I touched my forehead and my hand came away damp with moisture. As if commanded by an inner self I automatically weaved and swayed my way to the bed for the night, which I had chosen closest to the foxhole.

It was eight o'clock according to the luminous figures of my wrist watch. The chilliness had faded away under the weight of my sheet and two blankets plus a spare mosquito netting that I was using for a quilt. In its stead I began to feel as if I were being roasted in an oven. The perspiration stood out all over my body, and even though I threw off all the blankets I was panting for breath. My head throbbed and I heard a sound like the ringing of a distant doorbell.

I shut my eyes, trying to lapse into sleep, but I felt that I was riding a small rowboat in a maelstrom. Although my eyes were closed I could still see my surroundings in a twilight, but they were all rocking back and forth, faster and faster until they were going at a furious pace. They could stand it no longer and began to spin around like a top, slowly at first and then ever faster. I had to open my eyes to stop the mad sensation of dizziness. The whirling would slow down and finally stop after a few seconds. After I had steadied my world and the buzzing and the chimes had become slightly softer and my mind clearer, I became conscious of a tug deep inside my stomach. A cord inside was growing increasingly tighter.

I desperately tried to think of other things: of when the next bombing would come, of the predawn take-off in the morning, of what had happened to Craig and Williams. I wondered if I would ever see the States again. How far away that life I used to lead seemed now, and how immaterial. Here, we were stripped to the fundamentals of life itself and the survival of each day without death or injury was one of the uppermost desires in all our minds.

Finally, I fought my way into a feverish slumber. Someone yelled. I awoke sweating profusely. Red flares struck the ground across the strip and continued to burn, giving a violet tinge to the blackness outside. The field telephone rang. Somebody answered it. "The air raid siren is broken and the field is on condition red." I put on my shoes and lay down in bed again with my feet poking out near the foot.

A few minutes later the AA guns began to fire and we all went to the foxhole. No sooner had I arrived there than I had to leave. I walked twenty feet away to an old bomb crater and threw up, while the Jap plane devoted its attention to the bivouac area. I arrived back at the foxhole at the same time the Jap headed our way. Bursts of ack-ack appeared close to the plane, which by now was clearly visible in the rays of our searchlights. The Jap became discouraged by the intense, accurate fire and desisted from his approach to turn off toward Kahili. We left the foxhole and returned to our sacks.

When the AA guns fired again, all of us headed for the foxhole. Before I reached it, however, I had to make another run for the bomb crater. Again the enemy plane tried to make a run on the airstrip. Again the antiaircraft guns changed his mind.

Time after time throughout the long night we had air raid alerts. Each consisted of one or more raids by enemy planes. I counted seven alerts. Each time that I changed from my horizontal position my stomach emptied itself. I arose only when the Jap planes got too close.

Shrtly after midnight the telephone rang and gave us some good news. Craig and Williams had been rescued and were safe on Vella Lavella!

At 0400, Major Al Gordon from Desoto, Kansas, the executive officer of the squadron upon whose wing I was supposed to fly that morning, woke me up and said, "Zed—you're too sick to fly with us this morning."

I was too tired and sick to say anything, but mentally I thought, As if I didn't know! I was worried for fear I was coming down with malaria. If so, I would probably be sent back to Guadalcanal for rest, then be sent back into combat with another squadron. Even if it took several months between malarial spells, I would be kept away from home until I had put in three combat tours of six weeks each.

The doctor woke me up about eight o'clock and gave me two capsules of white powder. A couple of hours later he procured a command car and took me to my tent on the hill. There he gave me eight chalky white tablets and a small glass of spirits of opium. I was put to bed and left with more tablets to take at two- and four-hour intervals.

The skipper had also come down that morning with the same thing I had—gastroenteritis. The previous night scuttlebutt had spread saying that Italy had surrendered. During one of our frequent meetings the next day the skipper told me that a Seabee had told him Germany had also surrendered. I only hoped so—then we could get back home that much quicker—but knowing how the Seabees liked to spread "news," I was afraid it was only a false rumor.

By the third day I felt considerably better, but weak. The enlisted messmen at Maudie's Mansion knew me and kept my canteen filled with some lemonade made from a powder extract and containing the luxury of genuine ice.

Hughes was recovering from gastroenteritis and Morris was recovering from his crash landing and a deep hole in the arm. We three strolled down the hill to a tent where an enlisted man made bracelets from the aluminum of wrecked Japanese planes, which he sold for $5 to $10 each. Back at Guadalcanal he used to make $100 per week with 12 to 15 bracelets or watchbands. Hughes placed an order for one.

We then walked around the hill and passed a tent where church services were being held—our only reminder that it was Sunday. Around the rim of the hill from the church tent we followed a ridge down-ward into the jungle. We found several cans of food scattered all over the ground. The printing on the cans was mostly gone so that you could only guess at the contents. This old Army food dump was ran-sacked from time to time by soldiers and Marines who desired canned vegetables and fruit. Most of the choice items had been taken and the bulk remaining was of the Spam variety. Army gas masks were scat-tered all over the hill.

Jap sniper's shoes with the customary split toes, hand grenades, bullets, GI ration tins, Jap Helmets and gas masks were scattered about on the trail. Wet, moldy, green Jap blankets, woven mats, baskets and woven sacks floated on the water of a series of Jap foxholes. These were built with connecting tunnels and on two levels—one foxhole near the brow of the ridge and the other down the side a short distance. One of the foxholes contained thousands of rounds of belted ammunition for Jap machine guns. Another contained a Jap mask in excellent condition, and a Jap machine gun barrel which showed evidence of superior bluing qualities by its lack of rust. These two articles I kept for souvenirs. Near the bottom of the ridge, bulldozers had dug a deep trench and hundreds of Jap bodies had been thrown in and covered with dirt.

The fourth day I had been grounded I was still weak and tired easily, but felt much better except for an ache at the back of my eyeballs. Rather than be faced with a monotonous day around the camp area with nothing to do, I decided to go down to the landing strip. In the ready tent a surprise awaited me: Lieutenant Glasscock, whom I had last seen as an Aviation Cadet in Texas. I had flown with him on a crosscountry training flight to Austin, Texas. He had graduated the next week. Now after a lapse of eight months I found him with six bombers and Zeros to his credit.

It was almost old home week in the ready tent for I spotted another pilot I knew, Lieutenant Milton Vedder. At Oakland, California, he had been in one of the newest classes of cadets and had made himself remembered for just one innocent remark. It was after taps and lights were off. All talking, according to the rules should have stopped. Instead, there was a loud rumble of voices. Cadet Vedder had come walking down the aisle fresh from a shower and said, "All right, you high school prima-donnas, knock it off." Everybody had burst out in laughter at this remark and used it over and over for months. He had shot down three Zeros.

These fellows were in the other half of VMF 213 and had arrived to relieve the part of their squadron that had been spending the past few days at Munda.

A big Kahili strike was scheduled the day they were supposed to arrive. If they didn't get to Munda on time for the hop, some of the divisions from my squadron were going to have to fly. Because Kahili was a very unhealthy place, our pilots were anxious not to have to take the hop for somebody else. Twenty minutes before take-off time the C-47 (DC-3) landed with the relief for half of VMF 213. Our pilots were holding their parachutes all ready for the new arrivals to get into as soon as they stepped foot into the ready tent. Within half an hour they were on their way to cover the bombers!

Army P-39's, P-38's and P-40's were using the base at Munda as well as New Zealand P-40's and sometimes the Navy F6F squadron. Once in a while SBD's and TBF's would have to land to refuel after a strike or because they couldn't get back to their own base. Mostly, all these transient planes and pilots only stopped at Munda long enough to refuel and head for home—they didn't like to remain overnight if they could help it.

While reading an old newspaper that afternoon, I heard a dull distant noise that sounded like a muffled explosion, but I didn't pay any attention to it.

"A plane went in—a plane went in," someone yelled.

I ran outside and jumped on the running board of a command car. We drove down the taxi-strip toward the east.

A tall column of black smoke funneled into the sky from fifty feet offshore. We stopped and I stood on a coral boulder that provided a good view.

"My hell!" I exclaimed at the full scene. Only fifty feet away a piece of metal showed above the water, burning with the flame of a gasoline and oil fire and sending the cloud of smoke skyward. A propeller poked one of its blades above the surface of the burning water. Farther out in the water and a few feet away, another part of an airplane was partly above the water. There were five men pulling something out of the metal.

They waded through chest-deep water with a body and carried it toward me. It was the limp, still form of the pilot. They carried him to within five feet of me. I could see the face burned black, with its scorched remnants of a beard. The white bones of the knuckles protruded from a blackened hand from which a glove had been partly burned off. A steamy smell of char- red hair and flesh came to me as they passed.

The pilot was not dead when he was carried past

me, amazing though it was that he could still be alive. The doctors did all they could to maintain that spark of life and fan it into flame. They injected adrenalin, administered oxygen and plasma. Fifteen minutes later he died.

The casualty list would rise by one tiny digit in the KILLED IN ACTION column. In a few days his next of kin would receive a telegram informing them of that fact. They would cry and feel very bad. The neighbors would try to console them. A funeral would be held with praying and singing and sentiments expressed—perhaps by someone who had never known him.

A few lives would feel empty, as they had while he was away at college and out in the Pacific, fighting. The father and mother and the sisters and the brothers would always remember him and regret that he had to die so young. The sweetheart would be brokenhearted and hysterical.

Time would pass and the family again would laugh at jokes and enjoy the dancing, the threatres and their fellow men; the sweetheart would find that someone else could matter. She would marry, have children, and soon but faint remembrances of the pilot who died so young, so long ago, would remain.

Very quickly in the lives of mankind all is forgotten. All that remains is the record—DIED IN ACTION.

In the flying game one little thing forgotten often spells disaster. Everything is important. Onlookers said the Army P-39 took off and tried a sharp climbing turn to the right, nearly stalled out, then leveled out for a short distance and tried again—this time going into a stall and falling off on one wing into the water. The droppable belly tank caught fire. Other observers thought that the engine had missed at the crucial moment. Nobody would ever know.

We welcomed two lost sheep back into the fold that evening: Joe Craig of Savannah, Georgia, a small taffy-haired practical jokester, and Benjoe Williams, mostly dark haired, but with several prematurely white ones already visible.

Some Zeros had peppered Joey, who was flying tail-end Charlie (last man of the division). "After a few seconds of that stuff it got kinda old, dontcha know. Those old 7.7's sounded like hail on a tin roof. I began to smoke a little so I decided I better get my little tail for home and broke out of the formation. Benjoe stuck right with me in a battle formation and boy was I glad to see him. He drove I don't know how many Japs off my tail. My oil pressure dropped to zero and I knew that I couldn't stay up much longer. The Zeros followed us for quite a ways but they must have got tired or ran out of ammunition. About twenty miles the other side of Vella Lavella I had lost so much altitude I decided to bail out."

Williams had circled him and saw that he was all right. Then he located a rescue boat and flew low over it blimping his engine, and flew off in Craig's direction.

Williams knew he didn't have enough gasoline to get back to base, so before he ran out of fuel he made a water landing within a short distance from Craig. Both of them were picked up by the crash boat soon after and taken to Vella Lavella, where some of the enlisted men of the Navy gave them some of their own dry clothes. They were treated royally by the men at Vella.

"Munda is like home compared to conditions up on Vella," they told us. "Mud and rain and hardly anything you could call a road. The chow was terrible. Spam would be considered splurging up there. At night the Japs don't seem to have anything else to do than send their bombers over Vella."

Radio Tokyo had finally admitted the loss of Munda. They had also threatened that by the next full moon all the Americans on Munda would be driven into the sea. We all laughed at this threat, because we felt the Japs couldn't prevent the arrival of reinforcements if they did try to reinvade our island.

Our smiles very nearly turned upside down that night. The moon was full and beginning to set when the air raid siren sounded four times in the distance.

"Four times—that means invasion!"

"What do we do now?"

"Grab your guns, boys."

There was no commotion and excitement in the other tents so we all went back to bed and decided somebody hadn't learned to count very well. All the same, I located my 45-caliber pistol and placed it and my hunting knife within easy reach—just in case.

The dog next door howled mournfully—his master had not returned from the day's attack on Kahili.

4.
TALLYHO!

THE MOST NOTABLE day of every month was the thirteenth. On this day the Japs always engaged in more vigorous activity. Scuttlebutt had it that Tojo's son had been shot down by Americans on the thirteenth and the Japanese were trying their best to make us feel remorseful over that regrettable occurrence.

Whatever the real reason, we were glad when September 13, 1943 arrived. We had all been griping over the lack of real aerial combat. Now the one day above all others had come when we should see some action. With the optimistic fatalism that is characteristic of most fighting men—without which few could mentally survive combat—we all thought that none of us would get killed. Each man thought if anybody got it, it would be somebody other than himself.

Captains Willie Moore and Pierre Carnagey had their divisions on the morning scramble alert standby, when an order came to "get 'em in the air."

The Corsairs took off down the runway one after another, without waiting to make sure the others ahead had gotten off safely. Another group of pilots was immediately placed on the scramble alert stand-by in the event a call came for reinforcements.

In the ready tent we had a radio set that could

receive on the airplanes' frequency. We gathered around to listen.

"Tallyho!"

One of the pilots had sighted the enemy, but static and buzzing blotted out the rest of his transmission.

Half an hour later the planes came back. One was missing.

We watched one pilot fly his plane a safe distance from Munda so that it wouldn't crash among us, then saw the white umbrella of his parachute open and swing the dark speck it supported in great arcs, like the arm of a pendulum, until it hit the sea. A crash boat raced for the spot.

The intelligence officers were nearly swamped at first until they were able to get the fellows calmed down enough to tell their stories singly.

"Willie Moore never came back. The last I saw him was right after we peeled off in a dive to go after some Jap bombers. Maybe he didn't see the Zeros covering them. The rest of us were kept busy with the Zeros. Each of us knocked down a Zeke on our first pass. Hazlett got a Tony."

The newest Jap fighter plane, the Tony, looked a lot like a German Focke-Wulf 190, had an inline engine and was reported to be very strong and fast enough in a dive to keep up with American fighter planes. The Japs were beginning to make up formations of both Zekes and Tonys. If you outdove the Zeke, the Tony could stay with you. If you tried to outmaneuver or outclimb the Japs, both of them could surpass you except in a long, gentle climb at full speed ahead.

No, it was not quite the same news the people in the States were hearing about their planes. We too had been told about the superiority of American planes—even in intelligence reports—and had to learn the hard way those areas in which we were actually superior.

Carnagey, leading his division, failed to see the Japs, and made a turn which placed them in an ideal position to come down on his tail. His wingman, Wayne C. Gher of Urbana, Illinois, kept several Japs off the tail of his division leader. Meanwhile five Zeros made runs on Gher and shot up his plane so badly he had to dive away and into a cloud to escape. Carnagey was shot up himself, but made it home. He didn't consider his plane safe to land, so he bailed out.

I. E. Moore's plane had been hit by 20-mm cannon shells and 7.7-mm bullets. The Zeros usually opened up with machine guns until they were on the target. Then they fired their cannons.

We wondered what had happened to Willie Moore. Some of the pilots thought he had been so intent on shooting the bombers that some of the Zeros were able to pick him off. Others thought he had tried to dogfight with a Zero. Back at Midway he used to tell us he could out-dogfight any Jap. We used to reply that he wouldn't live to tell about it if he tried.

He was considered a hot pilot, and we knew that if he never came back some day, he had taken some Japs with him. Most of us felt that he was probably forced down and would turn up in a few days or weeks.

Those pilots just back from their first aerial combat were changed men. Less than an hour before, they were all anxious and willing to fight the Jap Zeros. Now they no longer ached for a tangle.

"I don't want to ever see another Zero as long as I live—not unless I'm right behind with my pipper on it!"

"I don't want to see another Zero—period."

"It gives you quite a thrill when you see those balls of fire from the 20 mm's shooting past your cockpit. You feel like reaching out and grabbing one. When one hits your armor plating behind, it sounds like somebody is pounding on the back of your seat with a baseball bat."

"Those 7.7's sound like hail when they hit your plane."

"All my guns jammed except one, just when I had a chance for a good shot."

"Boy! Didja see the one I hit blow up into a big round ball of flames!"

"The pilot of the one I hit jumped out of his plane without a parachute, it got so hot."

"Didja ever see such a screwy formation as them guys was flying—looping and slow-rolling all over the place trying to keep their speed low enough so they could stay with the bombers!"

That afternoon we had been waiting half an hour in the hot sun in the cockpits of the planes because we thought we might get scrambled. On the other hand, the Japs had already tried one raid and they might decide it was enough for the day. I watched a truck tearing across the strip and heading for us with a big cloud of dust pursuing it. The truck came to an abrupt stop and an enlisted man yelled, *"Scramble! Get 'em in the air!"*

My mechanic gave me the thumbs-up signal. I gave the engine a three-second prime and pushed the starter lever. The engine caught. I moved the mixture control into Automatic Rich and watched the oil and cylinder-head temperatures and pressure go to normal.

I looked around and saw the other planes with their propellers turning over. Major Gordon taxied to the center of the runway and took off. Johnny Morris, who like myself, was also on his first flight since being grounded—took off right behind Al Gordon. After Bob Wilson started his take-off I taxied into position and waited a few seconds. Then I pushed the throttle forward, streaked down the runway and became airborne.

The division leader had turned to the right as soon as he got into the air instead of continuing straight ahead for forty-five seconds as he usually did. His idea was to get to the Japs while they were as far from the field as possible and for us to make a running rendezvous with him.

We were all strung out in a column. Every few miles I watched the men ahead catch up to the major, until they were all in battle formation except me. I was getting the utmost out of my plane within the safe operating limits and soon had caught the formation. I had neglected to gain altitude with the formation, however, so that I was able to gain that much more forward speed to catch them. I now moved ahead of the battle line before I began to ease my Corsair skyward. I gained altitude and dropped back even with the other planes, but I was still five hundred feet below them.

Over the earphones crackled the latest instructions from the Fighter Director on the ground: "Vector three four zero distance twenty. Over."

I unhooked the oxygen mask from where I had it clamped handily near the check-off list and curled one leg around the control stick while I struggled to get the straps over my head. My plane began to nose down. I couldn't afford to lose the precious altitude, so I reached down and grabbed the stick with one hand.

After I had everything adjusted and had fired my guns and checked my gun sight and switch, I saw that Wilson had moved outward to the right-hand side of the formation, which was the position I was going to assume. He evidently realized it would put me behind to make the long cross-under and had moved out to leave room for me to slide up into the formation. I felt like giving the Minnesota boy a prayer of thanks.

Now I had time to draw a deep breath of oxygen and take a close look around. We were flying through a tunnel lying in a huge mass of clouds which towered up on both sides of us and closed over at the top. Occasionally we passed small chambers on either side. It almost seemed as if we were going down a corridor in a boardinghouse.

I began to get worried about Wilson. "What in the hell is he doing way out there?" He had strayed a little too far from me and the other pilots for his own safety and for mine, I thought. It was my job to stay the correct distance from the major, and his to remain in the proper position to me. I remembered that Yeager had told me Wilson liked to get off by himself where he could keep a constant lookout without devoting very much time to flying formation.

The rest of us were revolving our heads 'round and 'round like a beacon on a hilltop, because seeing the enemy before he sees you is not only good life insurance, but often the only key to shooting him down. My own head felt as if it was mounted on a ball-and-socket joint. I scanned the sky directly overhead and sometimes threw my plane into a slight skid so I could look behind better. I would tip the plane up on one wing and look below, then roll it over and stand it on the other wing to look down. My main business was to watch the sky behind the other planes and the skies directly ahead.

I felt excited and was very anxious to remain in good battle formation, but back of it all I retained a certain cynicism which said, "It'll probably be another false alarm. By the time we get to where the bogey is supposed to be, he'll have disappeared."

Then, in the course of their wanderings, my eyes suddenly became transfixed—they bulged. I couldn't believe it, but the sky ahead seemed alive with airplanes! My impression was of a swarm of bees flying en masse with some buzzing above and below and around the inner group—looping and slow-rolling. I gasped when it came to me a fraction of a second later that those airplanes were Jap Zeros and each one of them was out to kill me and the three boys with me, because we were American.

Grasping the microphone, I lifted my gas mask from the lower part of my face long enough to report, "Zeros at three o'clock!"

Then, in one of those cockeyed moments of imminent action, I remembered I hadn't followed the correct radio procedure, so I pressed the mike again. "*Tallyho*—from Foster, sixteen Zeros at three o'clock—up!"

A lightning tug of emotion squeezed my heart. Where was Wilson? We had started a turn as soon as I saw the Zeros. It would place Wilson close to where the Zeros were. Then I saw the blue form of a Corsair come shooting across the skies hell-bent-for-election and slide up on the inside of the turn, skidding to kill some of his excess speed. I heaved a sigh of relief.

The Zeros got closer, and their aerobatics gave them the damnedest appearance—like a bunch of playful puppies wriggling around in all directions. It was a miracle to me that they didn't collide in mid-air. The planes more or less in the center seemed to be flying more sanely. I counted up to ten and still had several planes to count, so I guessed at sixteen.

The major hadn't heard my radio report and had not seen the Japs when he went into a left turn. This was the worst maneuver that could have been made, because it presented our tails to the enemy—which is not only impolite but unsafe when all the guns fire forward. They were in a position three thousand feet above us and behind—a position that might have meant a massacre.

I crossed under to the left to the inside of the turn so I could keep up with the others. Wilson swung to the outside and the position I had just left, so he wouldn't overrun us. The turn continued in my direction. I knew we were all bunched together in the turn like a group of frightened rabbits and any moment I half expected to see the Jap tracers shooting past.

Wilson began to fall behind on the outside of the turn and I forged ahead. The other two planes scissored. Wilson started toward me. I thought that he too wanted to scissor and headed toward him. Then I whipped over into a steep left bank so the others wouldn't get too far away. Unfortunately the others had steepened their turn even more and had left me behind, because I had the greatest distance to cover.

My heart jumped into my throat. We had completed the turn and were headed in the opposite direction and I was trailing the others. Off to the left the mass of Japs had melted into several streams of Zeros, some of them diving for the planes ahead and five or more heading for me. I was really in a pickle. I knew I couldn't possibly catch up with the other F4U's before the Japs struck us.

The next few seconds would be a matter of life and death for me. Yes, I was scared—but not frightened to the point of helplessness.

I realized that I would have to do my fighting alone and that there was only one thing to do that might give me a fighting chance, unless I wanted to peel off and dive for home. I poured all the throttle to the Corsair and shoved the RPM into full low pitch and pointed its nose into the sky and climbed.

Twisting my neck from side to side was not enough to watch behind. I had to twist my shoulders too. The heavy jungle pack on my back and the safety belt, shoulder straps and parachute all fought my efforts to see better. I felt that I was clamped in a vise at a moment when my life depended on an unrestrained field of vision. My oxygen mask would rub against my shoulders and move awry. Pulling out of a dive, the mask would sag away from my face from the force of gravity.

Below and off to the left I could see the snouts of the Zeros pointing up at me with the great speed accumulated from their dive. Our positions were now reversed. I was above them but had lost most of my own speed in the rapid climb. They were trying to sneak up on me from below where I would be less likely to spot them. Ahead of me and below I saw the rest of the Zeros converging upon the other three Corsairs.

I thought out my situation calmly and in the tenth part of a second. It would be best to sneak off to the side unnoticed and then pick out some unsuspecting Jap at my leisure and shoot him down before he knew anyone was around. My problem was slightly complicated, however, by five Zeros, who were eager to bestow all of their attentions upon me.

In three or four more seconds the Japs would be within range of me. I couldn't sit there any longer and the only way out was to dive.

Below me three thousand feet was a Zero poised in a beautiful position to make a run from the rear upon two Corsairs that were flying close together. The third Corsair had disappeared. I pulled the stick to the left and went over on my back, then back on the stick and into a steep inverted dive.

My gun switches and electric sight had been on ever since the Japs started for me. I was breathing fast and my heart pounded like the keys of a concert piano. My speed increased rapidly. I hoped the approaching Zeros weren't close enough yet to fire at me. Now I rolled out of my steep dive, framing the Zero in my sight. I was performing some rapid mental arithmetic to estimate the amount of lead to give him. I pulled the throttle back to give me more time to get on the target. The red blobs of paint on his wings loomed large against the dirty brown wing.

I was nearly within range now. The Zero began to dive toward the Corsairs ahead. I followed and pressed my trigger. My tracers converged like a stream of fire just short of the Zero, but moved inward to cut it in two. My guns began to jam one by one until only two were shooting. Suddenly the Jap went into a snap roll and performed a split-S— impossible for me to follow. I rolled my plane with the Zero and tried to pull through with him, but my tremendous speed made it impossible and I began to black out from the tremendous centrifugal force.

Pushing the stick forward again I continued in a

steep dive with plenty of air speed. I leaned down and pushed the recharge button to try to clear my guns. Ahead of me and to the left I saw a jumble of airplanes. I kicked left rudder and gave it some aileron and headed for the center, hoping for a shot at a Jap. One swept by in front, but so fast I couldn't depress my nose to get on it. My speed was so great I couldn't turn upon the tails of two or three that were offered to me. I zoomed on through the dogfight and up on the other side in a high-speed climb.

To my right I saw three Zeros all coming for me. I still had plenty of time to look around before they got close enough to worry about. Even so, I couldn't help but marvel at the steep angle the Japs were climbing.

As my own air speed began to fall I looked downward. Three spots in the ocean attracted my attention. I wondered if bombs had been dropped. Then I realized it was an airplane that was causing the huge geyser that was just rising from the water. Another had just receded beside it and farther away great concentric circles were radiating outward just as they do when a pebble is dropped in a pool of still water, where a third had probably gone in. Were they Japs or my three buddies?

I tipped my wings vertically to look below me. I saw a Zero with its tail toward me. "This is going to be cold meat," I breathed into my oxygen mask as I ruddered into a left *chandelle* and dived for the unsuspecting Jap.

The Jap was not as unsuspecting as I thought. When I drew closer to him the pilot turned the Zero around in an incredible short space and I found myself facing him head on. I had heard they could do this almost unbelievable feat, but I hadn't been gullible enough to believe it, until then.

We hurtled toward each other, my six .50 calibers (if all were working) against his two 20-mm cannon and two 30-caliber machine guns. It is only good fighter doctrine never to look at anything more than three seconds continuously without looking around. I glanced to my left and saw the same three Zeros as before—very close to me. Smoke sprang from the leading Zero and streaks of light seemed to whizz beneath my cockpit.

"Shall I fight and run away and live to fight another day?" I asked myself the old fighter pilot's quotation. The appearance of the extra Japs had changed the color of the situation. It seemed to me four against one with everybody firing would be just too big a gamble for that particular shot, so I turned to the right and dived. With my rear-vision mirror I could see the three Zeros still following upon my very heels, so I turned on my artificial horizon and flew into a towering wall of clouds.

As soon as the white mass enfolded me into its protective bosom, I read my compass. Then I counted to sixty and turned to the left to the reciprocal heading. When I burst out into the clear air after four minutes in the clouds, I half expected to find the three Zeros waiting to jump me—but none were to be seen.

The huge amphitheatre in the clouds where the fight had taken place was now apparently empty of airplanes. Far away in a trench leading from the theatre toward what must have been Kahili, I saw three tiny specks which disappeared from view even as I watched. How I wished I was sailing around the clouds that formed the walls to that trench! I could ambush the Japs and knock down a Zero or two before they knew what hit them, but they were too far away now.

I climbed to 24,000 feet where there wouldn't be as much danger of getting jumped from above, in case there were still some Zeros around, and cruised back and forth to look for planes. That was not the only reason, however. I was lost. There was nothing below or around me except clouds. Since I was comparatively new to the country, it was doubtful if I could recognize landmarks even if I saw them. I remembered the compass heading on which we had left the base, but the fight had taken place over an area of many miles.

With that single particle of knowledge, I started for the base. There were clouds all the way, and it was necessary to search for openings through them because mountains might be hidden in their midst, and at the very least they might contain strong winds capable of tearing any airplane apart.

After ten minutes of snaking my way through the channels in the sky I came to an impenetrable barrier of clouds. I circled high and dropped lower. I caught a brief glimpse of land through a small loophole in the clouds as I swept past. On the next round I twisted the plane to the left and flew through the hole. Dead ahead lay the airstrip at Munda, looking like a white pencil mark on a dirt clod. It seemed like heaven to me.

When I walked into the ready tent glad to have come back from that hop in one piece, I was greeted more enthusiastically than I had expected.

"Glad to see you back."

"We thought they had got you for sure."

"Didja see anything of Wilson?"

After giving my report to the intelligence officers,

Wilson had not yet returned and we were on the verge of giving up hope for him when a lone Corsair came nosing over the field and, after one circle, landed. It was Wilson.

Morris came walking into the tent. He was in his shorts again. He was dripping wet with sea water—again. He had bailed out near Munda when his plane got shot up by the Zeros.

The Doc patched Morris up where he had been scratched and bruised when leaving the cockpit. He was a comical sight, covered by small bandages or strips of adhesive tape over his entire body—all spaced very regularly. Although this had been his first hop since his crash a few days before, he still kept that wide-lipped, white-toothed grin like a cat eating catnip.

Major Gordon had perched on the tail of one Zero and shot it down, then moved up on another Zero ahead and filled it full of holes. While he was shooting at them, however, a Zero had been putting a few slugs into his plane.

Morris had been able to get on the tail of one Zero, but when he pressed the trigger to blast it, only one measly gun popped away and the Zero escaped.

Wilson had succeeded in doing what I had wanted to do. He got off to the side undetected and saw a lone Zero, who didn't see him, and shot it down.

We all felt that we had seen enough of the Japs to last us for quite some time, and were all happy to have escaped alive. Morris and I were disappointed at not getting any Zeros, but this feeling was outweighed by the escape and safe return of every man in the division. I felt considerably relieved to know what it was like to meet the Japs and knew my chances for survival would be greater because of it.

* * *

The night of the thirteenth was also made exciting by our little yellow friends to the northwest. Thirty minutes after midnight we all went out in front of the tent to watch the beautiful sight of a Jap plane caught in the beams of our searchlights. A few shots of the hundred directed at the plane came close enough to scare the Jap and he dived toward Rendova, zigzagging as he went.

I wasn't able to get to sleep again, because of a slight headache and the compulsion to relive the events of the day. I couldn't get the vivid feeling of despair at being left alone with the approaching Zeros off my mind. I wondered what had happened to Willie Moore.

At 0330 I heard the faint sounds of an airplane engine and the whistle of a falling bomb as it fluttered downward and exploded with a very loud CRACK! Shrapnel from the burst rattled through the trees.

I had the head start, because I had been awake to begin with as we all hit the foxholes. The others arrived in a remarkably short time considering that they had been sound asleep. Four more whistles and explosions came with a few seconds—and then the air raid alarm sounded!

The next morning as we made the right-hand turn that led to the landing strip we saw the first signs of the bombings of the night. At this corner four Negro Seabees had built their home—a tent. They had dug their foxhole in the floor. Now there was no tent there at all—nothing but a gaping bomb crater, the remains of a shoe, a broken toothbrush and bits of powder. The four Seabees had met their end, far away from home.

5.
MUNDA—THE BITTER PILL

WE KNEW THERE would be a fight—there always was—when the bombers struck at the Jap base of Kahili.

Over the shortwave radio in the ready tent a clatter of voices came to us as the strike approached their target.

Army bomber pilots called to each other:

"Get up here into position—which flight do ya' think you're in?"

The bomber crewmen talked with each other over the intercom:

"My gun is jammed."

"It's sure cold up here."

"Wish we were headin' for the States right now."

As the formation drew closer to the enemy base the frivolous conversation stopped and reports began to come in:

"Bogey at three o'clock up."

"Watch him—he's coming in."

"Where's Jamison?"

"He's smoking."

"Got that Zero."

"Get the hell up where you belong—high cover."

"*Get off the air!*"

"Right in the middle of the runway."

"In the water!"

"Am returning to base."

"My engine is smoking. My oil pressure is dropping."

"We hit a gun emplacement."

"Where's number three?"

"I'm going in! I'm going in! My position is—"

"Get off the air, you Gawd-damned fools—somebody's trying to give his position."

Later the messages began to come in again:

"We'll beat you home, Bert."

"Diamond tower from Oboe eight one, we are coming in for a landing. We have a wounded man on board, over."

The Corsairs began to land. We stood on Vulture's Hill to watch and then went to the intelligence office to listen as they told their stories.

"I'm afraid we lost Hughes," Okie (McLean) was telling George Schaefer. "I swung over and shot the Tony down in flames. Then a Zero perched right on Hughes' tail, just blazing away. The last I saw of Hughes his plane was in a spin and trailing a big cloud of black smoke. I watched him go down for several thousand feet without pulling out and then I had all I could do to keep some Zeros from getting me."

"You're sure it was Hughes, Okie?"

"I'm as sure of it as I am of standing here—It couldn't have been anyone else."

Immediately, I thought of how Hughes' devoted wife would take the sad news—and his parents. I couldn't believe that Hughes had gone on his last mission and we would never see him again. Yet it sounded nearly impossible for him to still be alive. Even if he managed to pull out of the spin, the Zeros would probably have pounced on his smoking plane like a gang of vultures. With his disabled plane he would be cold meat for them.

Major Sapp had shot two Zeros off the tail of his wingman, New Yorker Charles D. ("Mother") Jones. They followed Jones in a dive and Sapp tailed in on the Zeros. He was able to pick one off and then move right up closer to Jones and get the other, who was too intent on following Jones.

Major Volcansek and Lt. Steve Yeager had each shot down one Zero.

Somebody outside the tent yelled, "There's a U coming straight in!"

We ran outside and watched an F4U approach the field, maintaining a high altitude so he could still make it to the field if his engine conked out. He ducked his nose and the landing gear went down. Smoke was trailing in a cloud behind him. No flaps came down as he arrived at the runway. He made a wheel landing—hotter than hell. A plane ahead of him was just turning off the runway. It appeared that he would run smack into it, but he passed on by. We saw smoke come from his brakes as he slowed down before reaching the end of the runway. He turned off the strip and taxied the plane into a revetment near the ready tent.

A black-faced pilot walked over to us. Two white circles showed where his goggles had been over his eyes. We gathered around him, slapped him on the back and congratulated on his getting back. Hughes.

"We heard you had gone in."

Hughes' jauntiness, quipping remarks and Bob Hope humor were gone. In their stead was a very subdued quiet manner.

"I sure came close to getting it."

"What happened?"

"I guess a Zero must have sneaked up on me. I was going along flying in battle formation when all of a sudden I saw tracers going by on each side of the cockpit and a rattle that sounded like someone throwing pebbles at my plane. Then I heard a thumping sound. I guess that must have been the 20-mm cannon. I looked out on the left wing and Jeez, there was a big ol' hole gaping at me.

"I was trying to skid to make him miss me until Okie shot him off. No sooner had that happened than another got on my tail and I felt him hitting my plane all over with 7.7's and 20 mm's. I tried to pull up and skid to make him miss, but my plane went into a spin.

"A lot of smoke and dirt came up and choked me. I thought I was on fire. I guess I must have nearly passed out for a few seconds, 'cause when I came to I thought I was dead. It seemed like it was all a part of a bad nightmare. The force of the spin kept me thrown over on one side.

"Finally I realized that I wasn't dead and that I still had a chance. I tried to bring it out of the spin and couldn't. Then I thought of my wife and something made me keep trying to get out of the spin after I had practically given myself up for lost.

"At about 3,000 feet above the water she came out and left me so dizzy I didn't know where I was. I had been at 16,000 feet when I went into the spin. My compass was all shot to hell; my air speed and every other instrument but my gas gauge and oil pressure was shot up. I headed in the direction I thought home was and opened my hood to let the fumes get sucked out of the cockpit. I nearly went unconscious from the fumes and my engine was smoking like a bonfire with my indicator showing zero oil pressure.

"I thought This is it, and expected some Japs to

start pounding away at me any moment, but I was lucky—I guess they didn't see me or else they were too low on gas.

"When I got near Munda I discovered my wheels wouldn't go down—I had lost all my hydraulic fluid—so I used the emergency CO_2 bottle to force them down. I sure prayed that they would 'cause I didn't want to make a belly landing with all the fluid floating on the floor of the cockpit. My windshield was coated with oil and I had to stick my head out to see. My throttle was stuck quite a ways open so I couldn't cut it down enough to land very slow, and on top of that my flaps wouldn't work and with the holes in my wing and my air speed indicator gone, I was afraid of stalling out too high. I'll bet I burned those brakes out trying to stop before I got to the end of the runway and I nearly ran into a plane that was just turning off."

"That was me," said Koetsch.

"I'll bet my wing didn't miss your tail over six inches when I went by."

Hughes was still shaking from his narrow escape, but he was eager to take some of us across the road to the plane he had brought back. On the back of the armor plating which protects the pilot from the rear, we counted over eleven 7.7 mm's plus a hit by some 20-mm cannon shells, which had exploded. The left wing and the engine each had a 20-mm hole.

We walked to the plane Koetsch had flown. His high gear supercharger had burned out and he hadn't been able to get the speed he should have had. Some Zeros had chased him, but his wingman Willie Hazlett had scared them away. Koetsch didn't know that he had been shot at until he landed and had seen some small holes from 7.7's near the tail.

As we looked the plane over we not only found the holes Koetsch had seen, but in addition there was a large hole in his main gas tank about five feet in front of the pilot where a 20-mm shell had gone in. It was only luck that the shell hadn't hit five feet farther to the rear and it was also luck and scientific engineering the gas tank hadn't exploded or caught fire.

That afternoon we watched another strike return from Kahili and Ballale. A Navy F6F made a beautiful water landing along the shore. The pilot landed with the use of only the left arm. His right arm had received a compound fracture when hit by shrapnel from AA. Another F6F pilot landed and his wheels caved in. He had been wounded in an arm and a leg. Within the space of a few minutes an F4U landed and went up on its nose.

The Army bombers came all the way from Guadalcanal and picked up their fighter escort near Munda. The fighters came mostly from the Russells and from Munda. The SBD's and TBF's came from the Russells.

I saw an F4U pilot by the name of Boyington report to intelligence that he had shot down four Jap planes plus one more probable. The fellows told me he was a major in the Marines and used to be in the Flying Tigers where he had shot down six Jap planes. He was commanding officer of a new squadron that had just started combat, VMF 214, known later as "The Black Sheep Squadron."

Fifty Zeros had attacked the TBF's and SBD's and the fighter escort he was leading had roared in to protect them. During the carnage that followed, a Zero flew up close to Boyington and waggled his wings, evidently mistaking him for another Jap.

Boyington let him get directly in front of his guns and then gave him an answer from his .50's. The Zero crashed into the sea in flames.

The next Zero exploded as Boyington came in on a stern run. He had to fly through pieces of debris that put dents into his wings.

He got his third Zero after it had been shooting at two Corsairs and was going into a loop. It too fell in flames.

On the fourth, Gregory Boyington nearly got sucked into a trap. The fight was nearly over and most of the Zeros were heading back for Kahili. As a lone Zero passed below him heading for its home base, Boyington was about to dive on it when he remembered his fighter's doctrine and looked above to make sure all was clear. He pretended to dive for the lower Zero, then pointed his nose up and went into a sharp turn head on at the other Jap. Pieces of metal flew from the Jap plane and it left a trail of smoke as it dove toward the sea.

As Boyington headed for home he saw a lone American plane being chased by two Zeros. He was too far away to get within his usual firing range so he let loose a few tracers in their direction to scare them. One Zero went up and over on its back, followed by Boyington who opened fire and shot the Jap plane while upside down.

One of the minor tragedies of war had happened that day. An F4U pilot mistook an F6F for a Zero and shot it down near the Shortlands. Luckily, the pilot was picked up later by the PBY rescue plane, "Dumbo." On top of that a trigger-happy F6F pilot shot at an Army P-40, but missed. The poor Army never got to shoot any Allied planes; they confined themselves to Japs. The new Jap Tony looked a lot like the P-40, however. The P-40's had all been painted with white stripes on the wings and fuselage to help identification.

The Navy F6F squadron remained at Munda overnight, doubling the number of planes on the field. There were also some SBD's and TBF's that stayed over. A full moon gave a brilliant light for the bombers we knew the Japs would send over.

We had seventeen raids that night. They drove a Navy chief past his last ounce of self-control and he put a 45-caliber pistol to his head and fired. Thirteen men had been wounded and a total of five had died. The F6F pilots wouldn't permit anyone to taxi their planes and they hadn't been dispersed properly. One direct hit burned up one F6F except for the tail. The heat from the fire caused its machine guns to go off and damage another F6F parked directly in front. Altogether eight F6F's were put out of commission—not a bad night's work for the Japs.

Munda was getting to be a busy airfield and capable of handling larger planes as the Seabees widened and lengthened the strip every day. It was still short and narrow enough to give a pilot fresh from the States the shakes, however.

One night a bomb landed so close to us I thought the end of the world was at hand. A terrific explosion shook the ground, dirt fell down upon our heads and the sudden concussion felt like someone had put my head in a paper sack and tied the entrance, then clapped his hands with the sack between them.

We were almost out of the foxhole when an explosion occurred and we heard metal swushing through the air above us.

"What in the hell was that?"

Another report, then another. Something hit the trees over our tent and a branch fell down and struck the ground with a rustle of leaves.

"Those must be delayed action bombs going off."

We saw flames rising above the rim of the hill beyond Maudie's Mansion, but we decided to get to bed.

We were in the sacks trying to get some sleep, when a voice came that sounded deep and gruff and familiar.

"Get into the foxholes, men. They hit a 155-mm ammo dump and the shells are exploding."

I looked through the doorway and saw a dim figure standing in the moonlight and the reflection from the fire.

"Who says to get out of bed?" asked Okie, one of our most ardent sack-time men who usually stayed in bed during all but the most vicious air raids.

"This is General Mulcahy," the dim figure answered. "Now get out of those sacks and into the foxhole—we've already had one man killed."

"Yes sir," Okie replied.

"Yes sir," Leach said.

"Yes sir," I added—as I hit the foxhole.

After the general had gone, Nugent commented on him. "I never knew that generals took such a personal interest in our safety but then I haven't known many generals."

"Yes," I answered, "what is he doing out in the open warning everyone else to stay under cover?"

"He's liable to get hit and spoil those hands of his so he can't play the piano any more," Hughes said.

Leach spoke up with renewed interest. "So that's where that piano music was coming from—I thought I was hearing right all the time."

"Yeah—they say the general used to be a musical prodigy when he was a child."

Our ten days at Munda were about up when the official word came that we were going to be relieved.

"This squadron has got by with murder," Hazlett told me. "We've lost six planes and through the grace of God only one man and we've accounted for thirteen Japs sure."

"Well—I'll bet the Japs have racked up one F4U as a sure kill—eh Hughes?" I remarked. "Besides we might get Willie Moore back one of these days. He's probably feasting on coconuts right this minute."

Our first week at Munda had been a period when the Japs had not ventured a single daylight attack on our positions. After this comparatively quiet week one of the officers reported officially that the enemy air force had been "reduced to virtual impotency." We flyers, however, took a different viewpoint. One trip over Kahili or Ballale was enough to convince us that the Japs still swung a wicked left hook. True, the Japs were facing problems in other areas and were probably siphoning some of their forces off to New Guinea. True, also, was the fact they had lost a reported total of 781 planes during the months of June, July and August for an average of 260 per month in the Solomons alone. Yes, and the Jap seemed unable to provide air protection for his barge and supply lines. The "Tokyo Express"—the destroyers and cruisers that used to cruise up and down The Slot— ventured out only infrequently. But it was plenty dangerous to fly all by yourself any farther northwest than Kolumbangara. You never knew when you might get jumped by a swarm of Zeros.

In one day's strafing missions one division of our squadron had destroyed five barges in Warambari Bay and nearby coves on the northern tip of Vella Lavella, within eighty miles of Kahili. Other squadron planes had destroyed four more barges the same day. No effort had been made to protect the barges (though some types of barges were outfitted with guns).

Every night a prowling "Black Cat"—a PBY painted black, or an Army Liberator (B-24)—flew all the way up The Slot looking for enemy submarines, shipping or air activity. They liked to circle near Kahili and keep the Japs awake, much as the Japs were keeping us awake at Munda and Vella. When they ran out of bombs they would drop empty bottles.

On the night of September 2nd one Liberator sank at least two barges off the coast of Choiseul. Five days later two Corsairs damaged three and the next day Corsairs destroyed two more barges around Kolumbangara. Army Mitchells and Marine SBD's often found several barges to work over on their way back to base after a bombing mission to Kahili. Almost every day a bombing attack was made on Jap supply dumps on Kolumbangara, from Surumuni Cove on the east around the southern end to Ringi Cove on the west. The airstrip at Vila was bombed so that it was kept almost out of action throughout most of September. Typical of the activity from Munda field during the first half of September would be a noon attack by 16 B-25's on the barge and bivouac area west of Dulo Cove, exploding one of the Japanese ammunition dumps, followed a half hour later by 20 SBD's and 15 TBF's who bombed and strafed enemy positions at Bambari, Parapatu and

Suramuni. This attack was followed fifteen minutes later by a strike at gun positions northeast of Vila by eighteen B-25's.

From the 14th to the 30th of September the air attacks were directed more to the Bougainville area, particularly Kahili and Ballale. Fifteen air attacks were made on these two bases alone during that time, mostly by Army Liberators. Between 75 and 100 enemy planes were thought to have been destroyed in the air and on the ground in these raids.

I had been successful in finding and attacking some Jap barges and had become enthusiastic over the opportunities to find and strafe them. One evening after my duties of the day had ended I went to the main intelligence center and copied a large scale map of Kolumbangara, which named every little cover and showed the positions of all the main barge hide-outs. I had hopes of getting permission to search these barges out when there was no other mission assigned to me.

My optimistic hopes were blasted the next morning by the operations officer. "We don't have the planes to spare to go out on an extra mission like that. We've got all we can do to keep enough in commission to furnish patrols and cover for shipping and strikes."

"But sir, it would only take one plane and quite often there is an odd plane left over."

"I couldn't let you go out by yourself—that's against orders. We not only don't have the planes for that idea, but you would have to go on up to see the colonel or the general to get permission and I personally don't think it would do you any good."

When I learned about all the red tape involved I threw up my hands in despair.

The Army fighter pilots were flying P-38's, P-39's, and P-40's. The P-38's because of their high ceiling were usually given the job of high cover of the bombers. The P-39's and P-40's were not much good except at the lower altitudes and shorter distances. New Zealanders were also flying the P-40's. Those P-39 and P-40 pilots held the admiration of us Marines because much of the time any Japanese planes they met would hold the altitude advantage over them. They had perfected their tactics, however, taking into account the disadvantages of their planes, and were able to put up a stiff defense. The New Zealanders in particular were noted because of their flying skill and guts.

Everyone except we Marines was based far to the rear, at the Russells and at Guadalcanal. Except for part of another squadron, we of VMF 222 were the only pilots living at Munda early in September. By the time we were about to leave Munda a Navy squadron flying F4U's arrived at Munda. Their planes were not quite like the ordinary fighter. On the right wing a large round red bulb projected, like a carbuncle, from the leading edge. Inside the cockpit they had some special gadgets including a screen. These planes were fitted with expensive and heavy radar equipment. Their sole job was to act as night fighters. On nearly our last night at Munda we had our first night without an air raid. The Japs soon got wise that we had some night fighters using radar and they began to fool our ground and airborne radar by dropping "window"—metal foil cut into lengths to match the radar wave lengths. This foil gave electrical echoes similar to that of a real plane. Our fighters would be directed to intercept these pieces of metal foil, while the bomber made his bomb run or made good his escape.

The Allied policy of strangulation and blockade began to get real results. One enemy position after another was either abandoned or mopped up. About the time I had arrived at Munda, patrols reported that no Japs appeared to be left on Santa Isabel Island and a large quantity of foodstuff and ammunition had been left behind. Indications were that the Japs were also preparing to evacuate Rekata Bay, once an advance seaplane base for attacks on Guadalcanal.

On the same day as my first aerial combat, patrols on Ganongga, the island south of Vella Lavella, had reported the destruction of a large enemy bivouac area. Living quarters plus a quantity of food, clothing, weapons and other stores had been abandoned. In four more days our troops on Arundel Island expected to complete their conquest after having killed over 500 Japs.

Of all our battles on land against the Japanese we had swallowed the most concentrated pill of bitterness in our battle for Munda. From talking to many soldiers and from intelligence officers I got an inkling of what that fight had been like. As our SCAT plane lifted us off the ground after what had seemed an eternity at Munda and pointed its shadow toward the peaceful Russell Islands I looked out the window at what I was leaving. From our installations around the airfield I could see a barren sweep of ground cut into the jungle for miles where some of our forces had landed and fought their way with shot and shell to the landing strip. War must have been hell in the jungle. New chapters in methods of warfare had been written on that scarred earth 200 feet below. The contest had been a bitter one indeed. Only a handful of men were intended to be used in the battle for the airfield, yet the successful taking of the landing strip and the driving of the Japs from the island of New Georgia wrote an entirely new chapter in the Pacific war. It marked the turning point for the Japs and the spot where our own forces had completed their first real offensive—a drive that was to be sustained with the capture of the Philippines as its immediate and the streets of Tokyo as the ultimate objective.

All of our other victories—Guadalcanal and the Aleutians—were desperate thrusts to stave off the wave of Japanese conquest. New Georgia was the first visible sign that we had started rolling the Japs back in the direction from whence they came.

The New Georgia group lying 200 miles northwest of Guadalcanal are mountainous islands of volcanic origin. Off their coasts barrier islands and reefs had formed lagoons which in times past were the habitat of a people known throughout the Melanesian world for their maritime aggressiveness.

After their failure to gain command of the air over Guadalcanal in November, 1942, the Japanese began to construct an airdrome near Munda Point on the southwest coast of New Georgia Island. The location of Munda Point was such as to render it almost immune to invasion from the sea. There were only two approaches: one from the north through Diamond Narrows, a deep but very narrow channel; the other from the west across Munda Bar, which had only two fathoms of water and was therefore dangerous during a heavy sea or swell.

So cleverly did the Japs conceal the construction of their strip that our reconnaissance planes failed to detect any signs of activity until the project was well under way. The Japs strung heavy wire cables between the tops of the palm trees in such a way as to form a net. The trunks were then cut out from under the branches, which remained in place supported by the cables. After the runway was completed, this camouflage was rolled back and further attempts at concealment were abandoned. The first reports of these concealed clearings were provided by the scouts of Australian coastwatchers, D. C. Kennedy and Harry Wickham. Meanwhile the Japs began to build a second airbase near the mouth of the Vila River on the southern tip of Kolumbangara Island.

The threat offered by these bases to our position on Guadalcanal was obvious. Beginning December 3, 1942, the day the Munda field was discovered, aircraft from Guadalcanal made repeated attacks, bombing and strafing gun emplacements, buildings and runways. During the ensuing three months, our flyers conducted more than 80 raids. Some of these promised spectacular success, yet none interrupted Japanese use of the installations for more than a day or two. On the night of January 4, 1943, a task group of cruisers and destroyers opened the first of a series of naval bombardments of Munda. After thinking they had done a great job of destruction, the Navy learned to its chagrin that eighteen hours afterward hostile aircraft were again operating from the field!

The only answer to the situation was invasion.

We began to build additional landing fields on Guadalcanal to improve the dispersion of the airplanes and relieve the congestion of Henderson Field. Fighter #1 and #2 were built for our fighter planes. Carney Field was built principally for heavy and medium bombers and long-range search planes. We also had completed two fields in the Russells after invading them without opposition. Great stores of supplies and equipment were accumulated for the coming offensive and were located largely at the Russells.

Several landings were to be made on the 30th of June, 1943. Our plan was to bottle the Nips up and drive them into the sea and avoid the long costly chase that we had been led over the length and breadth of Guadalcanal. The reef at Munda and the possibility of flank attacks made for a complicated landing operation. Our advance intelligence operations in collaboration with the coastwatchers were becoming so noticeable that there was danger of the Japs moving into the area near Segi Point at the opposite end of New Georgia Island from Munda Point. This upset our timetable and our landing there had to be made on June 21 in advance of the main New Georgia operation by 400 Marine Raiders of the 4th Battalion. The landing at Viru had to be delayed one day beyond the time originally planned, because of the late arrival of the advance unit which was supposed to silence the land batteries.

The second and main landing in the New Georgia area took place at Rendova against 150 Japanese. Our boats went ashore in the face of machine-gun fire from the beach on the 30th of June. At a few minutes after 1700 the Japanese batteries on Munda Point opened up. The first salvo registered a hit in the engine room of the *Gwin*—the only destroyer surviving the battleship night action of November 14 and 15, 1942. Other batteries opened up from Baanga Island and Lokuloku. Our destroyers returned the fire and put seven of the enemy positions out of action. Intermittent exchanges of gunfire between the ships and shore batteries occurred the rest of the day.

Throughout the landing operations a 32-plane combat air patrol was maintained by fighters based at Guadalcanal and the Russells. June 30th was destined to be a heyday for VF 21, VMF 213, VMF 221, VMF 121, and VMF 122, with a total of 101 Jap planes claimed shot down in aerial combat. Fourteen American planes failed to return to base, but seven pilots were rescued within 24 hours. (Radio Tokyo reported the fight as 32 American planes shot down with no Japanese losses.) In spite of the fierce resistance put up by the fighters and the AA fire of the ships, which shot down all but two bombers of the first attack made by 24 torpedo bombers escorted by an unknown number of Zeros, the transport *McCawley,* which had been serving as the flagship of Rear Admiral Turner, was left dead in the water, the victim of a single plane. It was apparent that it could no longer be kept afloat so the destroyer *McCalla* eased alongside and all hands were ordered to abandon ship. At 2002 the destroyer was ordered to prepare torpedoes for sinking the transpot if the settling of the vessel should warrant it. The transport's end came more quickly than expected—much to everyone's surprise. At 2023 the doomed ship was struck by three torpedoes; thirty seconds later she sank stern first in 340 fathoms of water. It was at first believed that she had fallen prey to an enemy submarine, but it was later learned that she was sunk by friendly PT boats which mistook her for an enemy! They hadn't expected any but enemy vessels in Blanche Channel.

Even before the first echelon has arrived at Rendova, steps had been taken to secure one of the entrances to Roviana Lagoon in order to make landings east of Munda possible and to prevent reinforcements from other parts of New Georgia or from the island of Kolumbangara where over 9,000 Japs were located, among them many veterans of Guadalcanal. At 0230 on June 30th units of the 169th Infantry of the 43rd Army Division were debarked.

Two days later a good beach was located at Zanana on the south coast of New Georgia, six miles east of Munda. A company of SoPacFor Scouts was landed there. Landing craft began to ferry 43rd Division troops to Zanana Point when a flight of eighteen to twenty-five Bettys attacked under cover of thirteen Zekes. Approximately fifty bombs were dropped in the Rendova area, killing 59 and wounding 77. Most of the casualties were among headquarters personnel of the 43rd Division; about a fourth consisted of sailors and Marines. This constituted the greatest number of American casualties of any single raid in the South Pacific.

The strange thing about this raid was that it occurred at probably the one time during daylight hours when our forces were most defenseless. At 1201 the fighter patrol was ordered by Admiral Mitscher to return to Guadalcanal because of a storm that was brewing. Between 1325 and 1335 the only radar on Rendova was out of service while it had its oil changed. The raid came at 1330 as a complete surprise. A large number of our men thought the Japanese had intercepted the radio reports telling our air patrols to reutrn to base, but General Mulcahy was of the opinion the attack was entirely coincidental. Surely the Japanese would not know the time the radar would be out of commission, whether or not they had heard the orders concerning the fighter cover.

That night reinforcements by units of the 169th and

172nd Infantry was completed by the assault boats at Zanana. Combat patrols moved ashore and took up their positions along the Barike River, the Army's line of departure. By July 8th all artillery and troops were in position for the jump-off against Munda.

The first landing in the Wickham Anchorage Area was made at Oloana Bay at 0630 on the morning of June 30th with companies of the 4th Marine Raider Battalion of the 1st Regiment participating. At 0335 the task unit hove to off the west side of Oloana Bay. Ten minutes later embarkation of the first wave commenced under extremely hazardous conditions as a result of heavy seas, low clouds, and high wind. The outline of the beach was not readily discernible at any point. After one or two boats had been loaded it was learned by the commanders of the ships that they were lying off the wrong side of Oloana Bay. They immediately moved 1,000 yards to the east and resumed the embarkation.

The first wave of boats was thrown into confusion as a result of LCI's, carrying Army personnel, breaking into their formation. All attempts to regain contact were unsuccessful, so the coxswains were forced to guide their craft to the beach individually. No course had been given them and they became widely separated, landing the troops along a stretch of seven miles of terrain to the west of the designated landing beach. Six boats were lost in the heavy surf.

By 1000 all landings there had been completed without opposition.

Vura Village, several miles inland, had been designated as the objective in the original operations order, but after landing it was discovered that the main body of the enemy was situated at Kaeruka. In the fighting which followed, a force of 300 Japs was wiped out. By July 3rd our objectives in this area had been realized.

On the morning of July 5th, after a 24-hour postponement, landings were made at Rice Anchorage on the north coast of New Georgia by two battalions of the 37th Infantry Division and the 1st Raider Battalion in order to make possible an advance on the Bairoko-Enogai area and thereby prevent the Jap garrison at Munda from receiving reinforcements from Kolumbangara. By this time our beachheads east of Munda were firmly established and preparations were being made to advance on the airfields.

While the drive against Munda was getting underway, the northern force was slowly moving south from Rice Anchorage. Maintaining an overland supply line after the departure from the initial landing beach proved well nigh impossible. Our troops carried with them sufficient food rations to last three days. It was hoped that Enogai Inlet would be occupied in two days, whereupon all supplies could be brought by boat to that location. The seizure, however, required seven days. As a result of the delay the troops were without food for a period of 48 hours and were finally supplied by airdrops on the sixth and seventh days. Colonel Liversedge's Marines blocked the Munda-Bairoko trail and turned back two enemy attempts to reinforce Munda from Bairoko. On July 11th the Jap garrison at Enogai was wiped out and preparations made for a drive on Bairoko, which turned out to be the last scene of enemy resistance.

A highly kept secret was the fact that one day before D-Day one of our Navy units laid a submarine cable from Rendova to within 100 feet of the New Georgia shore. By merely completing the gap, the forces we landed near that point were able to telephone instructions to the artillery at Rendova and tell them where to place their shells.

The big guns proved to be a life saver for a two-star Army general. This high-ranking officer had the habit of not only getting up to the front lines with his men, but sometimes advancing ahead of them! On one of the latter occasions when he should have been comparatively safe in spite of his advanced position, the Japs cut in behind him with native canoes. The general discovered his difficult position and immediately ordered an artillery barrage from the guns on Rendova. On the first salvo a direct hit was scored on the Nips within 300 yards of him. He it was who was largely responsible for the success of the Munda operations.

Our forces that had landed below the airstrip came in at the spot the Japanese had anticipated. They encountered strong fortifications. A huge ring of pillboxes numbering over eighty-seven, barred the way. These pillboxes were well dug in and equipped with ample food and ammunition for a long fight. Each was about two stories deep and interconnected with the others by underground tunnels. They were built with interlacing fields of fire for mutual protection. That was the first extensive Japanese use of pillboxes our troops had found in the Pacific war.

Volunteers were asked to assault the pillboxes. Because of the suicidal nature of the mission no married men were accepted. With flamethrowers spurting a tongue of flame well over a hundred feet, the men drove the Japs from their machine guns down to the bottom room of the dugouts. A concussion grenade dropped through the machine-gun slit created a terrific explosion and a quick end for the

Japs. Sometimes another new ordnance weapon—the incendiary grenades—was used. Thousands of white-hot particles of burning metal showered on the skin and the clothing of the Nips. This, too, made many of the Japanese very, very homesick.

Seven hills like the one fringing part of the Munda airfield had to be conquered. Each hill had its own Jap pillboxes and foxholes. In the wake of our advancing troops a wide swath was cut by bombs, artillary, grenades and mortars in the extremely dense jungle growth. We blasted the jungle apart as we went, leaving the Japs no place to hide. Only a few stumps, tattered foliage and battle-scarred earth remained of nature's scenery, which was further despoiled by the bodies of dead Americans and Japanese lying in the grotesque postures of their dying, discarded ration tins and boxes, gas masks, cartridges, *shambos* (the shoe of the Jap sniper) and other remnants of battle.

I talked to many of the men who took Munda and learned much of their ordeal. One Army soldier described some of the terrors of the long nights in the foxholes. Nearly every night some Japs, who had been trained especially for night tactics, slipped through our outposts and into our lines.

''One night my buddy and I were in a foxhole together. It was his turn to hold the knife and my turn to be the grabber. Pretty soon we heard a voice say 'Hey—Joe!' in a whisper. Neither of us made a sound. We just crouched there with our hearts pounding like hammers. Scared? Boy, I've never been so scared before in all my life. After a long pause the whisper came again. My buddy answered this time with a quavering 'What?' 'Do you want a grenade?' the whisper asked. '*No!*' my buddy replied.

"In a few minutes we saw an arm upraised, silhouetted dimly against the sky, then it disappeared. We didn't know whether it had thrown a grenade into our foxhole or not. A few moments later there was a loud explosion in the foxhole next to ours and screams of pain from some men that had been in it. That foxhole was large enough for twelve men, but only three were using it that night. The Jap had felt out the dimensions of their foxhole with his hands, then while measuring ours he had tried to cover up with his conversation. After he found theirs was the largest he threw his grenade at them, thinking he could get more men.

"There is one other night that I'll never forget," the soldier continued. "This time I held the knife— you have to hold it like this." He placed the butt of the handle against the palm of his hand, which he had against his chest. He took the other hand and curled it around the grip with the blade of the knife sticking straight out from in front of his chest, something like a unicorn. "You have to use your palm at the back of the grip to provide enough support. Anyway, this particular night my buddy and I were in the foxhole was a cold night, and we were huddled close together for warmth with our arms around each other so we would know where each other's arms were located. Suddenly my pal whispered quietly. 'Somebody's got hold of my ankle, is it you?' 'No,' I answered. We remained motionless and silent.

"Pretty soon a voice said, 'Is there any BAR (Browning Automatic Rifle) men in there with you?' 'No,' we replied. Then we were hit by three or four objects thrown into the foxhole with us. We scrambled madly to seize them and throw them out. We thought they were grenades."

"The Jap gave a hideous laugh and crept silently away. He had found out all he could and not having any grenades evidently he tossed some pieces of coral at us.

"Another Jap trick was to jump into foxholes with our men and then jump right out again, while our men stabbed each other in the darkness.

"It was a serious offense to shoot during the night as that would reveal our positions, so all our night work was done with bayonets used as daggers. One of us would sleep while the other would watch. Much of the time, neither of us got a chance to sleep."

The battle for Munda was considered bloodier and more terrible than even monumental Guadalcanal by many men who fought at both places. They ascribed this to the improved technique of the enemy. The wily Jap had learned his lessons well from Guadalcanal. He had developed new tricks and knew the answer to most of ours.

At Guadalcanal, the snipers proved to be more of a nuisance than a real threat, due to the poor marksmanship of the Japs. At Munda, the snipers seemed to be superior marksmen and became a definite threat to our forces, causing a great number of casualties. One of their favorite tricks was to kill a man who had already been wounded, just as he was being carried to safety. They also delighted in purposely wounding an American instead of killing him. Then when stretcher bearers or other help had arrived, he would try to kill them all.

At daylight on July 20th the northern force opened its drive on Bairoko against from 500 to 600 Japs armed with automatic weapons and heavy mortars and supported by one battery of heavy artillery on the west bank of Bairoko Harbor. The Japs were inclined to view the intrusion of our force from Rice Anchorage as a primary danger and therefore concentrated reinforcements from Vila at that point. After advancing to within 300 yards of the east bank of the harbor our forces encountered heavy enemy artillery fire, suffered heavy casualties and were forced back to Enogai, where the Japs surrounded and practically cut them off from all supply for a time. To keep our force contained, however, required almost the entire attention of the Japs at Bairoko, and their communications with Munda were impaired, so that from a strategical viewpoint the diversion was highly successful.

Following the second ship bombardment of Munda, enemy resistance to the drive on the airport was localized in two centers about a thousand yards apart astride the Munda trail. A rainy period had set in and to all the other discomforts sustained by the combatants was added that of mud. Meanwhile important changes in the high command were taking place. On July 15th, Rear Admiral Theodore S. Wilkinson relieved Rear Admiral Turner as ComAmphiForSoPac, and on the same day Major General Oscar W. Griswold assumed command of the New Georgia Occupation Force from Major General John H. Hester, USA, CG 43rd Infantry Division.

Two days later the general informed Admiral Wilkinson that he was planning a new drive to capture Munda and requested that a naval bombardment of the Lambeti Plantation be undertaken in advance of the troop movement.

On the same day the 172nd Infantry pushed its way to within 200 yards of the southernmost center of enemy resistance near Lilio. On the right the 169th

Infantry, facing the northern enemy strong point in more heavily wooded terrain, was unable to gain. During the day, the 161st Infantry of the 25th Division came ashore and went into position on the right in support of the 169th. That night the Japs made two slashing conterattacks from their southern strong point, one against the 169th and the other against the Laiana beachhead. Both were thrown back, whereupon the enemy withdrew along the Munda trail.

The Japs and the jungle had to be blasted nearly every foot of the way to protect our troops from unseen ambushes. Our artillery would lay a barrage in front of our men as close as they could without firing upon our own troops, but at times the shells fell short, killing and wounding many of our own men. One of the most distinguishing features of the battle for Munda was the great proportion of shell shock and war neurosis cases that resulted. One colonel was relieved of command of his regiment when he sent 360 men to the rear after one day's fighting—he considered them ''war nerves'' cases.

In that manner we pushed forward with the main drive. When the going became tough, 50 yards per day was a good record. An average of 100 yards per day was thought to be excellent.

Great work was done by our Air Force. Army, Navy and Marine bombers and fighters bombed and strafed with devastating effect. Close air support for ground troops was started during the Munda battle, later to be developed to a high degree of perfection. One incident in particular was an outstanding example of air-to-ground co-operation. The enemy was preparing for a last ditch stand by the airfield. They began to prepare their troops for a desperate attack. Marine dive bombers came over and dropped their eggs with superb accuracy. Not one bomb landed outside the target area, which only measured about 200 yards.

The bombing had the effect of disrupting the Japs' plans and forcing them to advance into our positions before they were ready, whereupon we reaped a bountiful harvest.

During the campaign the Air Force reported the destruction in combat of 259 Jap fighters, 60 twin-engine bombers, 23 dive bombers and 16 float planes. Marines claimed 187 of the planes and the Army, Navy, New Zealanders and AA the rest. Our losses consisted of 94 planes of which 34 were Marine. Nine hundred and fifty tons of bombs were dropped. Jap shipping attacked by our aircraft included one sea-plane carrier, one oiler, 4 destroyers, 6 cargo vessels and 9 barges destroyed; and 7 destroyers, 9 cargo vessels and 3 sub chasers or corvettes damaged.

Following a period of regrouping, our forces advanced from 200 to 500 yards all along the line on July 25th. The 43rd Division approached Munda along the south coast and to the east of the airfield; the 37th Division drove from the seaward along the northern end of the field; and the 25th Division was deployed in assembling areas along our northern flank. Progress was retarded by the thick jungle, the weather and stout enemy resistance.

The conclusion of the New Georgia Island operation was reached early in August when the Munda airfield was captured following a campaign marked by the co-ordinated use of infantry.

On August 2nd the left flank of the 43rd Division finally pushed across the Lambeti Plantation and reached the east end of the airfield. Two days later the northern flank of the 37th Division spearheaded by elements of the 148th and 161st Infantry broke through to the western shore 600 yards north of the airfield, completely severing communications with Bairoko. By 1500 on August 5th all major organized resistance at Munda had ceased, two days less than a year after the first landing of the Marines at Guadalcanal and six weeks after the invasion had begun.

The Navy Seabees began work on the airfield even before the Japs had stopped fighting. They worked at one end of the strip while the Japs fought at the other.

Munda was a bitter pill for our higher-ups to swallow. This "quick stroke" at the Munda airfield took five weeks and the combined resources of the Army's 43rd, 25th, and 37th Infantry divisions plus the Marines and Navy help. Admiral Halsey wrote:

> Our original plan allotted 15,000 men to wipe out the 9,000 Japs on New Georgia; by the time the island was secured, we had sent in more than 50,000. When I look back on ELKTON, the smoke of charred reputations still makes me cough.

Perhaps the answer to Halsey's statement can be found in the spirit of the Japanese Imperial Marines who constituted the toughest opposition to our fighting men. Many of them were found wearing trousers that were still neatly pressed, and their arrogance was expressed by the Jap officer who remained in his foxhole at one end of the airstrip accompanied by two privates. Although he was surrounded by two Army divisions, when asked to surrender several times during the course of an entire day, he replied defiantly, *"Do* YOU *surrender—Yanks?"*

6.
BOMBS, BULLETS AND TORPEDOS

THE RUSSELL ISLANDS were a tropical paradise. Although we were but a matter of an hour's flight away from Munda, where we had already tasted of the hell of war, it seemed far distant from our little island.

Yes, we callled it paradise, simply because we found some reminders of the civilization we had left. Cold water, fresh eggs, iced grapefruit and tomato juice and hamburgers—sometimes even ice cream.

Long before we had been sent to the Russells the fame of their genuine hamburgers and cold chocolate milk had reached us. Two of our own pilots returning from Guadalcanal with replacement airplanes had "engine trouble" as they neared the Russells and landed. After a few hamburgers and some nice cold chocolate milk their engine trouble seemed to miraculously clear up and they proceeded on their way. A transport plane even flew up from the New Hebrides and took fifty hamburgers back.

Joe's Place, where many of these mouth-watering tidbits could be had, proved to be a small building. A lunch bar at the far end had stools for six customers. To the left were four long tables. You could order hamburgers, cold tomato juice, cold grapefruit juice, chocolate milk or lemonade. At various times of the day you could get a light repast in the form of hot-cakes or ham and eggs.

Scuttlebutt had it that Joe Hayden was a chief petty officer in the Seabees and used to be connected with a famous string of roadside restaurants near Boston. He had suggested to the Navy that they procure ownership of a herd of seven thousand cattle that grazed throughout the Russells and set up a slaughterhouse. Besides Joe's Place there was a Good Humor wagon to be towed behind a jeep or tractor, ringing its bell for all within earshot to come and have a free doughnut, piece of cake or lemonade.

Green grass carpeted the ground between coconut trees, and was kept closely cropped by the scattered remnants of the herd of cattle which had been raised by plantation owners before the war. The area sur-rounding the neatly kept bivouac and the landing strip looked like a city park located in the midst of a plantation.

The weather did not seem as humid as in the other islands of the Solomons. Perhaps the level land per-mitted the sea breeze to sweep away the moisture-laden air. The sun, though, was just as brilliant as on any of the other islands five degrees south of the equator, making the plentiful shade of the palm trees very welcome.

Long to be remembered by men who served in the Russells were the mahogany and teakwood buildings they lived in. Even the docks were built of these heavy and expensive woods. The doorstep of my hut was made of a piece of mahogany. All of these woods would have fetched a fancy price back in the States. We had Dallas huts to live in with wooden walls and windows of mosquito netting. We had a table, the usual canvas cots and a luxury almost unheard of—electric lights.

Hughes, Leach and I bunked together in a hut down in a hollow at the base of a small ridge. Back of our hut was a tiny marsh with huge lilies growing in the fertile mud. These plants grew leaves large enough for Dorothy Lamour to use as a wrap-around sarong—provided she didn't mind exposing her knees.

The Russells proved to be an idyllic place for a group of resting warriors, but even there we participated in several flights. It was from the Russells that most of the fighter escorts for the bombing missions to Kahili came. Nearly every day there was a strike. It was after one of these hops that we realized more fully that we were engaged in a war with no quarter asked or given.

Hughes told of seeing a Corsair pilot bail out of his airplane. Then a group of Zeros made runs on the helpless pilot as he dangled in his parachute. Only two American pilots were near enough to try to drive the Zeros away, and they nearly lost their own lives doing it.

I learned of other incidents in the fighting that had taken place near the Russells about three months before. On June 7th, a lieutenant named Sam Logan of VMF 112 (better known as the "Wolf Pack") was swinging downward in his parachute when a Jap Zero, out of ammunition, made repeated dives at him, trying to slice the hapless pilot with the propeller. He succeeded on the third pass and cut half of Logan's foot away.

On that same day Gilbert Percy of the Wolf Pack bailed out of his plane near the water and fell 2,000 feet into the sea without the chute opening. He survived the fall although he sustained a broken pelvis and other injuries including wounds from fragments of 20-mm shells.

It was during those hectic days that seven Japanese planes were shot down in fifteen minutes, plus one more probably shot down, by James E. "Zeke" Swett for a new world's record on April 7, 1943. He was later awarded the Congressional Medal of Honor for the deed.

All of the excitement and famous achievements were not made by aviators, however, because when the hunting was lush during the early part of July, a battery of antiaircraft manned by Marines at Rendova Island shot at a covey of seventeen Japanese attack planes and knocked down sixteen of them. Furthermore they only used 84 shots to do it— another record!

A part of our relaxation came late in the afternoons when those of us off duty played volley ball. At night, every night, we went to the picture show.

In spite of the old and the bad movies that were shown overseas, I never saw one bad enough to make more than ten people leave. In the past I had sat on the ground, carried my own box to sit on, walked a half mile and sat through rainstorms to watch movies along with a few hundred other men whose daily lives were highly dangerous.

Although I had been through quite a lot to see movies, there is one night that sticks to my memory. The movie was called *Hollywood Canteen*. It was new to most of us, because we had left the States before its release. The first reel was met with enthusiastic approval as evidenced by the howling of the wolves on all sides of me whenever a pretty girl appeared on the screen.

Then the blast of the air raid siren came. Nobody stirred. We continued to watch the picture show. An officer yelled to "stop the machine" and walked out on the stage. "Unless you respond to the air raid warnings the movies will have to be discontinued. Everybody clear the area. You can come back after the raid if it doesn't take too long."

A few hundred feet away the engines of a Ventura night fighter roared into a take-off, and its running lights showed above the tops of the palm trees while we sought cover.

"I sure would like to see one of those boys shoot down a Jap bomber," I said to a dim form seated to my left on the roof of a foxhole.

"You should have been down to 'Guadal' a few weeks ago. A P-38 night fighter flown by an Army lieutenant shot down a Jap plane in flames. After the bomber had dropped a couple of bombs we heard this P-38 take after it and all of us watched the sky.

"It was like having a grandstand seat. We saw tracers up there, some being absorbed by an object and some seeing to pass right through and keep on going. Then a little spot in the sky burst into flames and a big ball of red and white fire fell in an arc, until it went out of sight below some trees.

"Everybody went wild. We got out of the foxholes and jumped up and down and shouted to each other and clapped everybody on the back. None of us knew what we were doing for a minute, we were so happy. It was just like watching the school football hero take a fumble from his own goal line the length of the field for a touchdown. For the next few days there wasn't a thing on that island the pilot couldn't have had if he wanted it."

We waited for fifteen minutes. Then we heard the engines of another night fighter taking off.

"The radar must have picked up quite a few targets tonight," one of the shadows beside me commented.

A half hour later the siren blew the "all clear" and we rushed back to our seats in a hurry lest someone else would beat us to them. But just when the second reel was beginning to roll, the siren wailed again.

"There's a bogey seven minutes away and heading right for us," someone yelled.

We obediently left our seats and scattered all over the nearby hillside. I began to get a little worried, because the report sounded as if the plane meant business. I was none too happy with the crowded foxhole available near me.

"It'd be just our luck to get back here in the rest area and have a bomb fall on us," I forecast morbidly.

Searchlights sprouted and waved in the night sky.

"Turn off those lights, you damn fools, and maybe the Jap might not even see us under this hazy sky," a shape muttered nearby.

In spite of the many times I had seen them, the searchlights never failed to incite a strange feeling. The long fingers of light were cut off about three thousand feet above the ground by the film of clouds and haze. We could see the lights of the other island apparently cut short and then continue upward like a series of long dash-marks.

The sudden unmistakable moan of a diving airplane whined in our ears. There was a mad scramble for the foxhole. I got in, but was so near the entrance no logs protected my head in case the bomb should hit and explode in the tops of the trees and scatter its shrapnel below.

"The son-of-a-bitch snuck up on us!" a sweating body next to mine exclaimed.

"Where'n the hell are all our night fighters?"

BA*Loomph* came the sound of the exploding bomb from far away.

The Jap's engine became inaudible and there was silence. Then came another engine with a lower, more powerful roar.

"Sounds like one of our night fighters is right on his trail."

His noise also faded away. We could only imagine the intense drama of life and death going on in the skies so near.

The "all clear" sounded.

As we watched "round three" of *Hollywood Canteen* a very distant and soft, subdued roar came to our ears, almost imperceptibly at first.

"Rain!"

The curious scattered noise of hundreds of tiny fists pounding on the palm leaves told us it was almost upon us. Water began to splash into my face.

I stood up and unfolded my poncho and handed one end to Hazlett. The poncho was a square piece of water-resistant fabric with a hole in the center where the head was supposed to go. We now used this sheet to cover three of us—Hazlett and I at the ends and Hughes in the middle. We held it up to our chins and tried our best to tuck it over our shoulders, but only the man in the middle was very well protected.

Although it began to rain heavily, only a few men left. The men stayed although they had no protection at all and were soaked as thoroughly as if they had been doused with buckets of water. Others with foresight had brought ponchos and were sharing them with their neighbors, and still others had brought ponchos and were letting their neighbors get wet.

Finally the time came for us to leave our island of comparative peace where we had been able to catch up on our letter writing and checker playing. We had spent less than two weeks there, but we had a war on our hands to be fought a little more viciously. We were ordered back to Munda.

The feeling of camaraderie is probably stronger between the Marines and the Seabee than any other two branches of the service. They both possess a mutual admiration for the other. They both are the first to land. The Marine fights to enable the Seabee to operate his tractors without getting shot at too many times, and when things get hot the Seabee takes care of himself. Even when his only offensive weapon is a bulldozer, the Seabee has been known to attack Jap caves and foxholes and bury their occupants.

We knew the Seabees had been working constantly at Munda, but we didn't dream they could possibly make so many changes in such a short time. They had doubled the width of the runway, and they were still working on it. They had converted the roads into scenic smooth-surfaced drives, moved the pilots' ready tent and the operations and intelligence office across the strip to the base of Kokengolo Hill into lengthy Nissen nuts. Even SCAT was trying to go high hat.

They had tried to disguise Dysentery Chowhall under an expanse of camouflage netting. I never did learn whether the camouflage was to trick the Japs or to fool American and New Zealand pilots, who had previously eaten there, into believing something new had been added to their chow.

The arrival of my squadron's own ground echelon containing the reliable mechanics who had worked on our planes at Hawaii, Midway and the New Hebrides was almost like getting a new lease on life.

The Japanese seemed to be informed of the new personnel that had arrived, for, when the night came, with it came the Jap bombers. Up on the hill we were gratified when the bombs dropped far away, but we also realized they had hit close to the new bivouac area of our enlisted personnel.

The next day we learned that the bombs had indeed fallen close to our men. One of them was a sergeant called "Hollywood" Summers because he claimed to be a former actor and possessed a beautiful singing voice. He had found a ditch to lie in but had tried to rouse some of the other men to warn them of the raid, when a bomb exploded and a piece of shrapnel got him a short distance above the eye. It had hurt him severely and he began to act strangely after that. He told other hospital inmates he could see chipmunks dressed in tuxedoes dancing around his bunk to the tune of "Yankee Doodle." He was finally sent back to the States and received a medical discharge.

Our quarters on the hill now consisted of a Nissen hut lined with a double row of cots. There was a table upon which several games of poker were destined to be played, but which held at the moment a portable hand-winder with several phonograph records, all in the hot jive style. There also sat the remains of two bottles of whiskey. These possessions belonged to the pilots that we were relieving.

Back of our hut a Marine masseur was located

across the sidewalk, ready to give relaxing massages to any pilot. There was one large bomb shelter for our hut and the others nearby. It was lined with benches and the strong logs overhead were much more comforting than the fragile foxholes we'd had before. On the other hand a direct hit on the shelter would wipe out most of the pilots on the island and render it immediately vulnerable to air attack until replacements could arrive from the Russells, Guadalcanal and the New Hebrides.

One of our first days back at Munda gave a portent of the excitement we faced.

I was in a division assigned to provide air cover for a surface force unloading supplies at Vella Lavella. Our altitude was fifteen thousand feet. Major Pierre Carnagey was the division leader.

We received a radio report that some bogeys were coming our way and were given a bearing to fly on. Soon Leach thought he saw them, but Pierre didn't, so Leach took over the lead of the division. The planes turned out to be F4U's heading in the opposite direction. At this point Carnagey left our formation, being unable to keep up with our furious pace.

Leach, R. A. Schaeffer and I flew on and then we heard words over the radio and knew there was a fight taking place not far away. We turned back and headed for the north tip of the island to intercept Jap planes as they flew for home, but we never saw any.

We saw some barges in Warambari Bay below us, filled with troops, but by radio we were told they were friendly, although that area was supposed to be the last center of Japanese resistance on the island.

Leach dove on the barges to take a closer look, Schaeffer and I followed. Then we dove again. This time I lost sight of the other two planes, which seemed to melt into the sea with their blue coat of camouflage.

When I came within sight of the partly built airstrip I could see several airplanes patrolling the sky, but none were my lost companions. I saw something else, too. Along the shore near the strip, orange flames disappeared into a tower of black and gray smoke. Some of the Japs had apparently penetrated the defenses and placed a bomb where it would do the most damage to an LST.

My fuel supply was beginning to run low from the fast flying of the past few minutes. I called the destroyer base and notified them I was returning home. All the response I got was static.

Nosing down into a gentle dive, I utilized my altitude to gain lots of speed. Kolumbangara lay directly ahead. I would have to fly around the island with its massive cap of clouds. The most common route home was around the southern part.

"I haven't ever been around the northern part of the island," I said to myself. "This is as good a chance as any to look it over. Besides I might surprise a Jap barge."

I angled off to the left to hit the island a little left of center.

Over the radio I heard a patrolling Corsair call out, "I see a bogey about eight miles from Konundrum Point."

Picking up my mike I radioed, "This is part of Diamond two, my position is approximately where you report the bogey."

"Plane that just radioed position, wag your wings."

I stuck the stick to the left and pressed left rudder, then to the right and pressed right rudder, five times.

"I recognize you, Corsair—out."

"Thank you and out," I replied.

Looking up and backward I could see four Corsairs begin a turn away from me. At that moment I was thankful I was not a Jap.

Soon the coral-lined shores of Kolumbangara flashed past my wings at 180 knots. I swept low around the island at fifty to one hundred feet, peering up the breaks in the coral reef which would indicate the mouths of streams. "What ideal places to hide barges the Japs have," I exclaimed to my 2,000-horsepower Pratt and Whitney Wasp. It answered with its welcome, steady drone.

Ahead of me the island continued in a curve to the right. Suddenly, I saw an object just offshore. I applied throttle and zoomed upward. I could see one or two ships. From fifteen hundred feet I lowered my nose and dived on them. Then I saw they were two barges, side by side. I put the pipper of my gun sight on the nearest and fired a few rounds. The tracers drooped and plunged into the side of the barge while others sent splashes of water skyward, short of it. The drop of the bullets was more than I had anticipated. I raised the pipper and held the trigger down. Every two or three seconds I released it for an instant so the guns would not jam from overheating. I raised my sights slightly and continued to fire on the second barge.

The barges were now very close and I jerked back on my stick with my heart in my mouth, for fear it was too late. My wings skimmed over the top of their stacks, missing them by what seemed inches.

One of the barges had a dirty rusty color that made it look as if it had been shot up before. The other seemed to have some bundles in the bottom which were beginning to send clouds of smoke upward.

I gained more altitude for my next run so I could come down at a steeper angle and hit less of the side of the barge and more of the inside. Again I continued my fire until the last moment and pulled out in the nick of time. Looking backward, I watched a tongue of flame and smoke billow. Then a small explosion shot the flames into full-blown life.

Staying low over the water I barrel-necked on around the island looking into each hidden cover. Then, I saw another barge ahead of me. Pulling the stick back I zoomed up to one thousand feet. When the barge was about to pass out of sight underneath the plane, I went into a dive.

As soon as I started downward I saw a splash in the water beside the barge. "Now, what the hell is that? Is it a fish splashing the water or someone on board the barge throwing bundles over the side?"

Then I realized that it was neither of the two, but was somebody on board throwing himself into the water. Another splash alongside the barge and farther from shore, another between the two, then one just off the stern, two on the other side, one near the bow and one more on the side closest to me.

"Looks just like a bunch of rats abandoning a sinking ship. At last, I've got a real chance to finish a few Japs off."

I lined up my pipper on the gunwale of the barge and opened fire from over 1,500 yards. As I moved in closer I saw bullet splashes in the water among the swimmers. I moved the rudders and walked my bullets back and forth from bow to stern. It looked like a bubbling kettle of molasses around the barge. I lifted my point of aim into the barge.

The barge came up to me so swiftly I barely came

out of my dive in time to miss the stack. The shoreline was just a couple of seconds away. I saw the palm trees looming up and pulled back hard on my stick, fully expecting to take part of a tree with me. I heard something "tick" against the lower surface of my wing.

Banking to the left I headed back to the water, where I could make a landing if my engine should happen to conk out. My gas gauge showed it was getting very low. As I rounded the shoreline I looked back and saw a small column of smoke rising from the barge.

Upon arriving at the ready room I gave my report to the intelligence officer. He showed me pictures of Jap barges until I recognized the type I had shot at. It was about 75 feet long and had a small wheelhouse on deck with a stack sticking from the top of the house, capable of carrying up to one hundred men.

Major Carnagey came up to me. "Glad to see you back Zed."

"Yes, and I'm glad to see you. The last sight I had of you was when you were leaving our formation."

"I couldn't keep up so I followed those Corsairs Leach led us to back toward Vella. We jumped a formation of twenty-five Vals and fifteen Zeros."

A wave of indignation swept over me at being cheated out of such an opportunity. "Did you get any, Pierre?"

"I pumped some slugs into a couple of Zeros on the way down in a dive, but they both split-S'd and got away, although they were smoking. About that time some Zeros got on my tail and were shooting me full of arrows. Finally, a couple of Corsairs came to my rescue and drove them off. I scooted for home as fast as I could go.

"If you guys had just turned around when I did we could have really mopped up on those Japs. You would have had the sun at your backs and a couple of thousand feet altitude advantage. Each of us could have gotten at least one Jap easy on the first pass. One Corsair perched on the tail of the Val dive bombers and shot four of them down in succession. As soon as he got one, he just moved on up the line."

Army and New Zealand P-40's and Marine Corsairs had accounted for six dive bombers and two Zeros for sure plus several probables. The Japs had been repelled, except for one dive bomber that came in low and dropped his bomb on an LST, killing sixteen men and wounding several others. Most of the men and matériel happened to be at the end where the bomb landed.

We Pilots couldn't kick, however. We were all back alive.

It was only the next day that Okie McLean's and Ace Newlands' divisions were scrambled. Half an hour later we saw some Corsairs fly overhead and each did a slow roll. One of them did two slow rolls. It was the prohibited victory signal. Prohibited, because at Guadalcanal a few weeks before an Army P-38 pilot, while performing the victory roll, scooped out at the bottom and crashed into the landing strip, scattering pieces of P-38 for half a mile. Our boys had done them at a safer altitude, however.

One Corsair flew over all alone, waggling its wings, and then headed out to sea to make a water landing.

"How many did you get, boys?" we asked as the exultant pilots came into the ready room.

Each pilot told his story to intelligence.

"They told us over the radio that it was a small

bogey. Then when we approached their location the bogey was announced to be about ten planes. A few minutes later they said it was over thirty planes and that they were scrambling some help for us.''

''We poured on the coal and got all the altitude we could. The fighter director put us right over them. There were sixty Zeros! The thing that saved our necks was our altitude advantage. We attacked out of the sun and most of us got a Zero on the first pass. I doubt if they even knew we were around.'' Okie stopped talking and Hazlett began.

''The sky seemed to be full of airplanes. Everywhere I looked there was Zeros. Koetsch took one of them and I took the one behind. He went down in flames. Then I buzzed up to gain altitude right through the middle of them. Zeros were split-S'ing and zooming every which way. You've never seen anything like it.''

''I took about twenty quick pot shots as Zeros crossed in front of me. If only I could have made every bullet connect, I would have knocked down at least twenty-one airplanes. Everything was happening so fast I didn't bother to look to see what happened to the ones I shot at, I was too busy shooting at others.

''It was every man for himself after we hit that formation. I saw some arrows going past, so I dived down and got away. Then I went out to the side and climbed up and made runs on the Zeros as they headed for home.''

Ace Newlands said, ''It looked to me like the Japs were bringing a group of their new pilots out for a familiarization hop. That was the screwiest formation I've seen in all my flying days. Zeros looping and slow-rolling and having a regular tail chase. I can't see for the life of me how they kept from having a dozen mid-air collisions.

"They seemed to be good flyers, but as soon as we hit them they seemed to lose their heads. I saw a Zero tailing an F4U, pouring bullets into the tail assembly. Another F4U and I shot it off. It sure made a pretty sight—*poof!* It blew up and went down in a big ball of flame. The U kept on going for home."

"I'm afraid you boys gave the Japs a bad impression of life in the South Pacific," I remarked.

When all was said and done we learned that six Zeros had been shot down for sure along with at least two probables. Planes damaged weren't even counted. Witt had shot down two Zeros and had joined Newlands in shooting a third. Pankhurst, Hazlett and Koetsch had also scored

It turned out that the pilot of the F4U with the Zeros on his tail had been Jules F. Koetsch, our boy form Brooklyn. Koetsch never failed to get some arrows in his tail when he went on missions. Even if nobody else got hit, he usually came home with at least one hole in his plane.

Koetsch had made a safe water landing not far from Munda. He came into the ready room wearing his shorts and shoes and carrying his unopened parachute, soaking wet. Above this array rose his red-haired barrel chest; his face with its huge red mustache and topping it all was his balding head where the hair should have been located—but wasn't.

Someone was shaking me gently. "Wake up, Zed—you've got to fly." I opened my eyes into the glare of a flashlight. "Where does Yeager sleep?"

I sleepily pointed to a bunk across the aisle and

down two. "Right over there," I replied.

I yawned and cursed the war. The luminous dial of my wrist watch showed it was 0330.

My heavy field shoes pounded on the wooden floor so I raised to my tiptoes to walk the four or five steps to the rear door which led to the lister bag. I washed my face to help wake myself.

Over at Maudie's Mansion pilots were busy eating their morning Spam and dehydrated eggs.

"Our destroyers had a fight last night up The Slot near Vella Lavella. One of them had its bow blown off. It is your job to be on station at 0515 and keep any enemy air attack away. Their position is 320-degrees and forty miles. Take off as soon as you're ready."

We were taken to our planes, started them and taxied to the take-off position in the pitch-darkness. I lined up with the runway as well as I could. The nose of my plane blocked out all the lights except those about fifty feet ahead.

How black the sky was. There was no horizon, nothing provided by nature to tell me whether my wings were level or whether I was upside down, in a dive or a climb. The stars were invisible, blocked out by the black clouds of an impending storm.

Well, mankind had devised instruments to meet an occasion such as this. I pulled out the knob of my directional gyro and the knob that would start my artificial horizon working. Immediately, the luminous broken line of the artificial horizon representing the relation of my wings to the ground tilted at a thirty-degree angle. It was broken.

I knew that I couldn't depend on any of those instruments. They had been too badly beaten up in rough combat. They were just like the engines that partially failed in flight often and the machine guns that usually jammed after a few rounds. Yet here I was, all ready for take-off into instrument conditions—with no reliable instruments. By the time I was airborne and tested them in actual flight, I would probably be dead before I learned they weren't working. It was a dilemma, but there was only one answer that would carry out the mission of protecting the men and ships.

My throttle moved forward and the engine roared smoothly into life as I fed nearly two thousand horses their oats. The whistle of the wind past the open cockpit increased, the lights rushed by on each side faster and faster. I put the stick forward and lifted the tail off the ground. The nose went down and I could see what was ahead of me now, except what was hidden by the small round bump of the nose. My speed went up to sixty-seventy, eighty, then ninety knots and I brought the stick back, holding back pressure because the Corsair likes to hug the ground.

The bumps stopped, the noise of the engine faded a half tone. I was in the air.

Watch out for that tree off to the right! I tilted my wings to the left and the momentary green reflection of my running light came back at me as it glowed against the top of a tree. I had just missed it. The wind had drifted me farther to the right than I realized. My stomach was tense. I retracted the wheels and went higher than any trees or hills and began to breathe easier.

I joined into close formation with three other planes. It is safer to fly extra close at night so your light will reflect and reveal the plane you are flying wing on. Then you can judge its position and attitude. If you get too far away and just see its lights you may get hypnotized by them and accidentally run into the plane without realizing it.

I tucked myself under the wing of the other plane like a baby chick under its mother. With one of the quick looks around that I used to prevent myself from getting hypnotized by constant staring at the same object, I saw the eastern horizon appear, as the earth turned enough to let the rays of the sun bounce against the particles in the atmosphere. It grew into a dark orange streak in the direction of Guadalcanal. We fled from the dawn as we departed on our compass heading, flying toward the position of the damaged ships.

As we retreated from the rising sun, its golden-yellow light crept down the division leader's tail and jumped the vacuum in between to my section leader's radio aerial, then down to his fuselage, suffusing the bottom into wings of gold. Then it pounced upon me and made me squint when I looked backward.

We were flying in the light, but down below, everything was still in the bottomless void of the night. The black ink slowly began to diffuse into different distinguishable intensities of opaqueness. We were at fifteen thousand feet now and had long since been breathing from the life-giving oxygen bottle.

The sea below had turned into a gray mask. The mountainous land that we had passed was still dark in shadow as we looked backward across the expanse of liquid yellow.

No longer were we flying so close together a wing walker could cross from one side of the formation to the other. We had turned off our lights and moved apart into battle formation for we were now in enemy country.

As the light increased at 0515 I saw the white wakes

of several ships, twenty thousand feet below. We went into a dive to get a better view and saw they were destroyers. One had her bow blown off!

We droned around in the sky for over an hour waiting for some Jap planes to come in for an attack. We still had enough gasoline for a good fight before heading for home. If worst came to worst we could fight for a while and then land at Vella to refuel. The new strip had been declared open for emergency landings, which meant that there was a good chance of cracking up if you had to land there—but you also might land safely, provided no tractor was in the way.

We were getting to the point where we thought we wouldn't see any action, when the radio crackled. "Tallyho from Diamond one." Witt and I climbed fast and headed in the vicinity of Diamond one.

"They're turning back, they're turning back," came from the earphones.

"Resume stations and patrol," Cat base (the destroyers) told us.

I cussed. Witt and I had never seen the two formations of Zeros and Vals consisting of about five planes each.

"Look at the rafts in the water." I heard this interesting bit of information over my earphones and looked from my high perch above the sea, but nothing could be seen. We went into a dive. Far below we saw two objects that looked like boats. Our curiosity satisfied, we climbed back to that block of the heavens assigned to us to patrol.

When we returned to base we learned that an Army pilot had shot down one of the Zeros, and a Marine from VMF 213 had knocked down another. The

Zeros and Vals had hightailed it for home before any of our planes in substantial numbers could get a crack at them.

That night I learned some of the lowdown on recent happenings from the accumulated information that each pilot had been able to gather during the day. It was always at night, when we were sitting around or getting ready for bed, that I heard the unofficial side of each pilot's activities, what he had seen and done and what he thought.

Jones struck the first chord of interest that evening. "I sure saw a lotta Japs in the water today. I guess they were the only ones left of the sea battle last night."

"How many did you see?" I asked, all ears.

"Oh, I counted about eighty and I might have missed a few."

"I counted seventy-eight," Carrell said.

"I would have liked to have gone down and strafed the whole damn bunch," Jones told us. His sentiment was echoed by several others that had been on the hop.

"There were two whaleboats left near the Japs."

"Witt and I saw the boats but we were too high to see the men in the water. Why did the Navy pull a stunt like that for? The Japs will use those boats to get to land."

"I flew so low over those Japs that when each of them saw me heading for him, he ducked under the water and stayed there until I had passed over. I'll bet that more than a few drowned themselves doing it," Major Sapp told us, lighting a cigarette in a contemplative mood. "I'd have gone down and strafed, but somebody called up and said there were some Americans in the water too."

Another pilot entered who had been shooting the bull with some Navy officers. "I just heard that some PT boats went out and picked up thirty of those American sailors out of the water. They tried to rescue some of the Japs but they shouted something that sounded like 'Kow-we, Kow-we.' (The word was probably *Kowai,* a Jap ejaculation of fear.) It was a weird sound. As soon as our men tried to pick up survivors, someone in the water blew a whistle, the chanting stopped and all the men swam away from the boat.

"They finally managed to get fifteen Japs into the boat and brought them back with them." The pilot paused and then added the terrible news: "One of the Japs asked a sailor for a drink of water and when the sailor turned to go and get him some the Jap pulled out a pistol he'd hidden and shot him in the back!"

Caught between the jaws of the huge Allied vise, Munda on one side and Vella Lavella on the other, without any strong air or surface support, the Japanese on Kolumbangara found themselves in a precarious position, to say the least.

Partly responsible for their discomfort were the Motor torpedo ("They Were Expendable") boats, which were found to be well adapted to the purposed of blockading the island, especially after a 37-mm cannon had been mounted on their bow.

Every night except when our destroyers were on the prowl up The Slot, the MTB's patrolled. They were subject to more than usual hazards because of the waters studded with coral reefs, which were incorrectly charted much of the time. Moving at high speeds in strafing runs against barges, some of the MTB's ran aground and had to be destroyed. In one night two PT's piled up on a reef while attacking 3 enemy barges. One of them went up on the reef to the stern, the other put 40 to 50 feet of reef astern before it stopped. They destroyed at least 12 barges during September and damaged about 10 others.

Although they were frequently fired on by shore batteries their natural enemy was the Jap float plane which constantly harassed them and succeeded in damaging four of our boats. One Jap plane was shot down by Pt 156, however.

The PT's found they not only had to fight the Japs but the Americans too. One tragic mistake was made when one of three approaching Corsairs failed to receive the recognition signals of four PT's at dawn of September 30th and strafed PT 126, killing two men and wounding one officer. The PT fired back at the Corsair and shot it down, killing the pilot. Some us claimed that if the Japanese would quit interfering and would stay clear of us Americans, we would kill each other off—by mistake.

When the showdown came, it was not the PT boats (they were inadequate to the job) nor the airplanes (they didn't fly at night) that were called upon, but the destroyers and cruisers of our Navy.

It was thought that the Japs would seize the opportunity afforded by the moonless nights of the 1st and 2nd of October for evacuating their troops from their impossible position on Kolumbangara. Barges and heavy units of the Jap navy were expected to be used, so our task group under Rear Admiral Aaron S. Merrill included cruisers.

Nightly sweeps of the area had been made by our destroyers on the lookout for barges. A group of enemy destroyers, apparently under orders to use caution in support of the evacuation and to offer direct support only when there was light opposition, were kept informed by Jap float planes as to the strength and location of our ships. The Tokyo Express presented our destroyer commanders with a carefully calculated dilemma. The commanders had to choose nightly whether to try to surprise the Express and let the barges escape or fire on the barges and warn the Express of their location.

As anticipated, the attempt at complete evacuation came on the moonless nights. On the first night the striking force composed entirely of destroyers was supported and covered by Task Group MIKE containing cruisers. The destroyers were under the command of Captain Cooke in the *Waller*, with the *Renshaw, Eaton* and *Cony*, and Commander Chandler in the *Saufley* with the *Radford, Grayson* and *La Vallerre* (the latter destroyer commanded by Lt. Comdr. Robert L. Taylor). This force was supported by Task Group MIKE, Admiral Merrill in the *Montpelier* with the *Denver* and four destroyers, the *Ausburen, Claxton, Dyson* and *Spence*.

There was no lack of targets that night. Both groups made contact with enemy barges ranging from 200 to 75 feet in length. The larger one was the shape of an LST, but cut down lower on the water. Out of an estimated 35 barges at least 20 were believed sunk. The water was thick with bodies. One group was convinced they had killed 1,000 Japs alone.

The next night the covering group did not accompany the modified force of destroyers. They sank an estimated 20 of the large barges, some of which were towing canoes and rowboats.

More barges were sunk the next two nights.

Almost every night our forces were confronted with torpedoes or bombs or the threat of enemy ships.

A Japanese prisoner said that 10,000 men had been evacuated between September 28th and the 2nd of October. During the height of the evacuation our forces destroyed some 60 barges besides damaging many others. Earlier claims of 3,000 to 4,000 enemy dead were later scaled down to about one-third those figures. As they had in February at Guadalcanal, the Japanese managed to get away from Kolumbangara with large numbers of men.

The New Zealanders, under the command of Major General H. E. Barrouclough and Brigadier L. S. Potter, had pushed the 500 to 700 Japs remaining on Vella Lavella to the extreme northwest corner of the island where the Japs were hemmed in upon a narrow strip of land between the 35th and 37th Battalion Combat Teams. A prisoner said they were well organized, but were short of food and tired of fighting. Many of them wished to surrender but were prevented by their officers.

Admiral Wilkinson decided to send a force to intercept the Tokyo Express, which might be expected to complete the evacuation of Kolumbangara or the forces bottled up on Vella.

A bright half-moon was overhead on the night of October 6th and visibility was excellent. There were a few scattered squalls, a calm, smooth sea, with a long swell running. The wind was westerly, force one.

Nine Jap destroyers, three PT's and six SC's were estimated in the Express that night, which passed through Bougainville Strait at about 2200. The three of our destroyers on hand to break up the evacuation had called for reinforcements and were joined by three others, among which was the *LaVallerre*.

Before the reinforcements could arrive, the *Self-ridge*, *O'Bannon* and the *Chevalier* engaged the enemy, zigzagging and firing torpedoes and guns. Their excellent aim caused one Jap ship to blow up with an explosion so violent it was seen by the reinforcing ships, still many miles away. Another target exploded and others escaped, smoking.

Two small high-speed targets approached the *Chevalier* and were fired upon by machine guns while the main batteries were brought to bear on some Jap destroyers which the first enemy group had been trying to protect. Two or three minutes later she was hit by a torpedo. Two concussions followed, the explosion of the torpedo and almost simultaneously what was believed to be the explosion of the No. 2 Gun Magazine. All personnel on the bridge were stunned and the forward speed of the ship was threatening to submerge the vessel like a submarine. The entire bow forward of the bridge had been blown off.

The *O'Bannon* was close behind and was unable to avoid collision with the aftersection of the *Chevalier*. At 2305 she rammed the *Chevalier* in the after engine room, penetrating ten or twelve feet. This stopped the *Chevalier's* diving motion and according to her commanding officer probably prevented her from going under immediately. The *O'Bannon's* bow was deflected to the starboard, but she was able to go ahead (after backing clear) at one-third speed to screen the damaged ships. In the meantime the *Self-ridge* had been busily pursuing the superior enemy force alone, shifting its fire from ship to ship and damaging them all. Then followed an action appropriate only to the crossroads of Torpedo Junction. At 2304 one torpedo was seen porpoising 2,000 yards on the port beam on a parallel course. One minute later two torpedoes approached from 30 degrees on the port bow. The captain ordered left full rudder, but countermanded this order when a torpedo was reported close on the starboard bow and ordered right full rudder. He rushed to the starboard but couldn't see anything because of personnel crowding the bridge windows. He hurried back to the port windows in time to see a torpedo wake crossing the bow from the starboard and passing about 25 yards away. Another torpedo wake was seen about 400 yards away. No other torpedoes being reported from the starboard, left full rudder was given and an effort made to locate the torpedoes reported on the port side. She had swung left when she was hit on the starboard bow and about the same instant suffered another very probable torpedo hit on the portside.

Her bow was sheared off and everything forward of the bridge was wrecked.

This ended the action. Only 11½ minutes had elapsed from the moment our group fired their torpedoes to the torpedoing of the *Selfridge*. The *Chevalier* was torpedoed, rammed and sinking, the *O'Bannon* limped with a badly damaged bow, and the *Selfridge* had her bow sheared off.

The crippled force of three destroyers was left in command of the field of battle. All the nine ships that had been able had fled except for two that circled a burning ship. These fled at the approach of the reinforcing destroyers.

The *O'Bannon* picked up 16 officers, 234 living and 7 dead enlisted men when the *Chevalier* reported she was unable to remain afloat. Total casualties on the

Chevalier as reported by Captain Walker were 1 officer missing, 2 officers wounded, and 53 enlisted men dead or missing. Most of the injured had fractured arms or legs and a few suffered from fuel oil poisoning.

The *O'Bannon* left two motor whaleboats in the water for the use of the survivors who might have escaped observation, then retired alone at 0130.

The *LaVallerre* made an unsuccessful search for more survivors, then was ordered to remain behind and sink the *Chevalier* after the other vessels had retired. After a careful search of the wreck by a boarding party, a torpedo was fired from 2,100 yards and the *Chevalier* blew up with an explosion that sent a cloud of black smoke towering over 500 feet. Her severed bow was located a mile away and was sunk with depth charges.

The *Selfridge* painfully made her way back at five knots. She transferred all wounded to the *Taylor*. Her casualties included 13 enlisted men dead, 36 missing and 11, including one officer, wounded. She was screened in her retirement by the *Ralph Talbot* and *Taylor* and later joined by the *LaVallerre*. Fighter plane cover arrived overhead by 0515 in the form of our Corsairs from Munda.

The New Zealanders met only abandoned equipment and dead Japs at Vella Lavella. Four hundred Japs were thought to have been taken off the island during the night. At 0900 on October 9th the leading companies of each combat team joined together. The task had been completed.

An important offensive base had been secured at a cost of less than 150 killed. The airstrip at Vella was in use within six weeks after the first landing and within two months could accommodate almost 100 airplanes in the next campaign against Bougainville.

The success of the strategy of bypassing enemy strongholds, then blockading and starving them out, and the principle of seizing unoccupied territory and building an airstrip on it, soon to be repeated often in the South and Central Pacific, were worked out in the Vella Lavella campaign.

We pilots were very poorly informed about anything that we didn't see with our own eyes. The only knowledge we gained was from scuttlebutt and occasional bulletins. The only time we knew there had been a naval battle was when we heard rumors or saw the wreckage.

That's the way it is in war. Nobody really knows what is going on except in his own tiny sphere. The generals and admirals know what strategy and tactics will be used, but the intimate life on the battlefield is hidden from them, except for what they might see during a tour of inspection. The soldier in the fox hole knows how many Japs he and his buddy killed the night before, but is unaware that a barge was destroyed. The aviator knows that he covered a task force, but doesn't know it contained New Zealand troops.

Of all the unreliable reports we received, one turned out to be the truth. We were again relieved from Munda and sent back to the Russells. After ten days there we retraced our route back to the New Hebrides.

We had 22 Jap scalps to our credit plus eight or more probables with the loss of only one man, who we still hoped would turn up someday. It was the best record of any squadron in the islands at the time.

The boys of VMF 215 were at Espiritu Santo, receiving replacements and training them for the next combat tour. They seemed to have the knack of acquiring adventures on the most routine flights. I heard R. G. Newhall tell about their trip from Guadalcanal to Espiritu Santo.

"I was aboard one of the three SCAT planes with eleven other pilots. About an hour after take-off we ran into a severe weather front at 10,000 feet, which was very dark and turbulent with rain. We entered it and encountered a gust of extreme violence which forced the nose of the plane up in spite of the efforts of both pilots. The plane went up until it was inverted. The twelve of us in the cabin found ourselves suddenly hurled to the roof for several seconds. The pilot recovered by pulling the C-47 through the rest of the loop, then rolling out.

"He told us afterward that his speed was about 250 mph. We recovered at about four or five thousand feet. The flight was completed under a low ceiling and we arrived well shaken and one hour late!"

Following two or three days of shell hunting and boating in the country-club atmosphere at Espiritu, arrangements were made to fly us down to Sydney, Australia, for seven days of rest and recreation, stopping overnight at Tontouta, the airbase at New Caledonia, en route. Meanwhile, we procured our gear from storage and were busy washing and ironing the clothes we were going to wear.

7.
HEROES IN THE MAKING

SYDNEY LOOKED AS large and as spread out from the air as Los Angeles, California. The houses seemed closer together with fewer vacant spaces between the suburbs. The roofs presented a much more colorful spectacle because of the predominent red tile.

At the SCAT office we were greeted by a Marine major and given a copy of our orders authorizing seven days' leave. We piled into the back of a truck and drove into the heart of the business district where we pulled up alongside the Red Cross Service Bureau housed in the Davey Jones Department Store. After listing our names, ranks, home addresses and other information, we were informed that housing accommodations were extremely scarce, but that some had been saved for us.

Some of the men pooled their resources and rented mansions for the week. Gher, Moore, Hazlett, Koetsch and I went to a private home. Our rent was two pounds per person for the week (each pound worth $3.26 in American money). The family also owned a taxicab, which was a considerable advantage in view of the shortage of transportation.

New to us were the methods used by the Australians to help relieve their gasoline shortage. Some cars had a charcoal-burning apparatus attached to the rear, giving them only 30 per cent as much power as regular gasoline. Other cars carried large gas-filled balloon bags on top.

Prices had nearly doubled since the war began, but they were still about half those in the United States. One could get a lovely steak dinner in beautifully appointed restaurants for $1.50.

It was all like discovering a new life. The cool weather of early springtime, the hot baths, luxurious theatres, good food, soft beds with pillows, and the friendly, beautiful girls—all proved just about more than we could take in such a concentrated dose. Jules Koetsch (a woman hater) was nearly kissed (on his bald spot) when one of the prettiest girls in Australia chased him onto a balcony. She thought he was cornered, but he performed a Doug Fairbanks and escaped.

Some of us went to Katoomba, the resort in the Blue Mountains sixty miles from Sydney. It was somewhat reminiscent of Zion Canyon National Park in Utah, except it was not as large nor as colorful. Nevertheless it felt wonderful to be near mountains not covered with jungle and humid hot air. Then too, there was the Taronga Zoo to see. It contained the koala bears that looked like living "Teddy bears," the ostrich and the kookaburra (a bird with a snout longer than Durante's and sounding like a laughing jackass). There were some very interesting museums with unusually complete collections from the South Pacific. I learned more about the native culture of the Solomon Islands than I did while in the Solomons. A headhunter's hut with its rows of skulls had even been reproduced. (The hut was later reproduced for me in a jungle clearing at Vella Lavella at Alligator Lake, the site of an SCR 270 Search Radar installation. The radar men had a cap on a Jap skull on one side of the entrance and a native skull on the other side wearing a bandanna.) We went swimming at Bondi Beach, which had the largest amd most frequent breakers of any beach I had seen. Sailing in Sydney harbor in a forty-foot cutter occupied one afternoon for some of us. At night there were always parties, dancing, or movies to attend.

Before we left for Australia we were told, "Those Aussies will do anything for a Marine, because they believe Marines saved Australia from invasion by holding the Japs at Guadalcanal." The welcome was not as we had been led to believe, but it was still very hearty on the part of all the people.

The Australian and New Zealand soldiers have proved themselves to be as tough, quick-thinking and as fine soldiers as there are anywhere, whether they serve in the desert near Tobruk or the jungles of the Kokoda Trail of New Guinea. One of the greatest Australian generals of World War I, Sir Iven Mackay, listed his occupation as schoolteacher and put his soldiering under the title of recreation in the Australian Who's Who.

Our seven days of recreation passed all too rapidly and the little band of Marines were once again assembled for the trip to the airport and the war ahead. Bedraggled and hollow-eyed as some of them were from riotous living and too little sleep, they all felt they had won "the battle of Sydney."

Sailing down the shores of Turtle Bay in the New Hebrides, several days after flying from Australia, Hughes and I espied a native village and guided our outrigger kayak to the shore. We were after native souvenirs and wanted to take pictures.

One thatched hut after another was closed, but as I passed the windows I could distinguish the eyes of someone peering from the dark recesses inside. Quite by surprise we came upon a black woman smoking a pipe and spreading wet clothes out in the sun to dry.

I offered a package of cigarettes. She hesitated, wondering what I was trying to bargain for. Then she saw the camera and understood. After taking her picture and not finding any of the other village occupants willing to expose themselves, we embarked and continued on.

Soon we saw a group of men; apparently they had been working in the coconut plantation. We headed toward shore to take a closer look at them, but when they picked up clubs and rocks and made threatening gestures, we decided otherwise.

The head of a giant turtle broke the surface of the water thirty feet in front of us, then submerged. It was at least as large as both my fists. I steered while Hughes grabbed a paddle all ready to conk it the next time it came up. The head broke the surface to the side of us several feet away and then disappeared.

We landed on the shore across the bay and walked on the premises of a Frenchman's plantation. We knocked on his door but apparently he was not at home, so we talked to some Tonkinese laborers out on the porches of their small homes. They were seated around bowls of rice, eating with their fingers.

Up the shore a few yards, I saw a native. I approached him with a package of cigarettes in one outstretched hand and a camera in the other. He retreated into a hut, after muttering an unintelligible word. I went into the hut somewhat hesitantly—then I heard what he had been trying to tell me all along.

"Me sick, me sick!" I laid the cigarettes down to cheer him up and again beat a hasty retreat at the heels of Hughes.

Farther upshore we found a group of Army artillerymen getting ready to do some practice firing. It was almost laughable to see the large number of jeeps and trucks they had. If it had been the Marines, they most probably would have been on foot. The Army was noted for its plentiful and usually excellent equipment. They had nearly 100 new trucks parked under the palms near our airfield that had been there for weeks—apparently forgotten. At the same time we Marines were hard up for transportation and suffered a shortage of trucks.

When the Army boys began to fire a 50-caliber machine gun, suddenly, out of nowhere it seemed, a little black native boy about four years old, absolutely naked, began to run from the scene, as frightened as he could be and crying accordingly.

VMF 215 had gone north for their second combat tour while we went to Sydney. I had promised George Sanders to take his kayak up to the Frenchman's plantation on the other side of the airbase to store it. I. E. Moore and I met a squall as we sailed and the little kayak raced before the stiff breeze with the water foaming from her bow. At the Frenchman's (who was making a small fortune doing laundry for the neighboring servicemen), we put the boat in storage. As we came out of the boathouse, I saw the most primitive natives of my experience.

There were two of them, men dressed only in G-strings and beads. Their hair was a faded red where they bleached it with lime. Their teeth were a mottled black from chewing betel nuts.

With my eye on some beads they were wearing I said in my best pidgin English, "Boy, you belongum long bush?" (Do you live in the interior?).

The men grunted and motioned over the mountain. "Kaorti," one replied. I presumed this to be the name of his village. "How much?" I pointed to a string of beads.

"No savvy."

After some gesturing and fruitless conversation I went to the French overseer of the plantation. " 'No savvy' meant you could give what you wished," he told me.

We gave the natives an assortment of silver coins and got the beads. I wanted to try to bargain with them, because I'd heard they enjoyed it, but Moore paid the money he had in his hand without question, so I followed suit.

As we were leaving the plantation to hitchhike back to base the Frenchman called us back and took us to his house. A large Frenchwoman appeared and they rattled off some French phrases. Then they gave us several handfuls of minute, beautifully colored shells their natives had laboriously gathered.

"I will make a bracelet for *mon cherie*," I responded.

Our skipper, Major Volcansek, was taken from us to be given a job as operations officer. Major Carnagey was assigned to be executive officer of VMF 214, next in command to Boyington. Our new commanding officer moved into the job from executive officer. He was Major Al Gordon, a graduate of Annapolis and a great favorite with all of us.

Fifteen new pilots were assigned to us, because the Marine Corps had decided to enlarge each squadron so each man wouldn't have to fly as much and so that each loss would not be felt as severely as when there were fewer pilots.

We held a big party at the Frenchman's as a farewell to our outgoing members and a welcome to the new. It was a huge success, with many cases of beer available. The best part of all was a barbecued pig the Frenchman had prepared, complete with a wonderful sauce and "millionaire's" salad made from hearts of palm.

I brought my accordion to that party. I had bought it in Honolulu and had been tormenting the boys ever since, except when we went into the combat zone. Our Montana cowboy, Turner, had brought his guitar. We sang:

> "Bless 'em all, bless 'em all
> The long, and the short and the tall.
> There'll be no promotion,
> This side of the ocean
> So cheer up my lads, bless 'em all."

We followed this with:

> "Glorious, glorious—one keg of beer for the four of us,
> Sing glory be to God—that there are no more of us,
> For one of us can drink it all alone—that's all."

Now I am not a drinking man, but when we began to chug-a-lug and Craig thrust a full bottle of beer into my hands, it was up to me to drink it down without a pause. I had never liked beer beyond the first two swallows. I determined to do or die. I couldn't weaken before my friends. They began the drinking song and I took a few deep breaths in preparation and with the same weak feeling in my stomach that I had when I used to get stage fright in plays and when I sighted my first Zeros.

> "Here's to Zed, he's true blue,
> He's a good fellow, through and through,
> He'll drink whiskey, he'll drink rye,
> He's a drunkard, so am I,
> So drink, chug-a-lug, chug-a-lug,
> So drink, chug-a-lug, chug-a-lug,
> So drink! One, two, three, four, five, six, seven, eight."

I had already disposed of half the bottle at the count of five, but from there on every swallow hurt me. Tears came into my eyes. I felt I couldn't possibly do it.

"Eight and a half, nine, nine and a quarter, nine and a half, nine and three-quarters," I nearly had it down, two more gulps would do it.

*"Nine and seven-eighths—*TEN!" And I finished amid their cheers and laughter.

We knew that to the north the stage was being set to deal a knockout blow to the mightiest Japanese base of all in the South Pacific—Rabaul, the former capital city of the Australian mandated territory.

Supplies and reinforcements poured from Japan through the valves of the heart located at Truk, the mightiest and best-protected Japanese naval anchorage in the Central Pacific, 830 miles north of Rabaul. At Rabaul the Japanese commanders routed them to the Solomon Islands, less than 200 miles away.

The Solomons were included in what the Americans chose to call the South Pacific, commanded by Admiral "Bull" Halsey. It was our aim to work up the right flank by way of various islands of the Solomon group to the focal point of the infection, Rabaul, and either invade or by other less costly methods neutralize the stronghold.

However, equipment and men were also being poured into Rabaul from its left flank, from the Philippines to the Celebes, New Guinea and then to Rabaul. Allied Army forces had crawled part way up the protruding "finger" of New Guinea that pointed Australia-ward, to start blocking that artery. This combat area had been designated the Southwest Pacific and was under the generalship of Douglas MacArthur, who outranked Halsey.

While we were in Sydney the newspapers had headlined that Lieutenant General A. A. Vandergrift's Marines on November 1st had landed on the shores of Empress Augusta Bay on Bougainville, the largest island in the Solomons. They had also made landings on the Treasury Islands only 30 miles from Ballale and 40 miles from Kahili. I learned that Marine paratroopers had gone ashore on Choiseul by boats the night of October 27th with the mission to raise all the hell they could to make the Japs think they were the main landing. After about five days on the island they had been evacuated with few men lost.

Other newspaper items told about the Big Three Conference in Moscow and a young ace of the Army in New Guinea named Bong with 19 planes. I also learned the statistics of November 2, 1943, the date the Army's Fifth Air Force attacked Rabaul from New Guinea to do what they could to prevent a heavy

Japanese attack on the Marines invading Bougainville.

The B-25's caught a lot of ships in Simpson Harbor and claimed to have destroyed or damaged 114,572 tons of Jap shipping. The fighter plane cover and the bombers claimed 16 planes destroyed on the ground and 69 enemy aircraft destroyed in combat.

The bombers went in at a low level, which is an invitation to suicide for their crewmen. In some cases, however, the low-level attack is actually safest, because ground fire has only a short time to get on the target.

A total of 44 American airmen were killed or missing and nine bombers and ten fighter planes never returned.

In another month and a half it would be Christmas, 1943, and we were off for Vella Lavella, landing on Munda on the way to discharge mail.

What a tremendous improvement the Seabees and the Army engineers had wrought at Munda! The runway was a wide, long stretch of gleaming white coral, rolled smooth. It looked to be the best landing field south of Pearl Harbor and capable of accommodating large numbers of planes. But despite all the tearing and ripping the Seabees had been doing, I noticed that they had overlooked Dysentery Chowhall.

Two new fighter strips had been built during the month we had been away from the area. They were located at Ondonga, about six miles from Munda and closer to Kolumbangara. We flew over and saw they were side by side with only a narrow lane of trees to separate them. I was glad not to be flying from that base, because I thought the traffic pattern must really be something to see. Army and New Zealand pilots were based on one of the strips flying P-39's and P-40's. Navy pilots of VF 17, flying Corsairs, were on the other.

The 35 enlisted men of VMF 215 who had arrived first to take care of the planes at Munda had each lost nearly 20 pounds after four weeks and had to be evacuated to the Russell Islands where the rest of their ground echelon was located. They were not able to get their long-awaited rest, however, for on the day after their return, orders were received to move to Ondonga to make ready for operations when the strip opened. All those who were in too poor physical condition were given the chance to remain behind and rest up, but all wanted to go with the squadron. Permission was refused two men, who were sent to the hospital instead, to join after they had recovered.

The 120 enlisted men with two officers embarked with all their squadron gear and arrived at dusk on the 26th of September. There were no docking facilities and when the LCT ran aground sixty feet from the shore at high tide, all the men worked four hours in water up to their waists manhandling cargo. Even the jeeps and heavier equipment had to be carried to shallower water by hand.

The Japs speeded up the difficult unloading job by intermittent shelling from Kolumbangara and two air attacks. Our men completed the task in record time and the LCT returned to safer waters for the night.

It was too late to make any attempt for shelter for the men themselves, so they threw themselves on the open ground in utter exhaustion, regardless of the danger from enemy shelling.

The next morning a certain amount of order was achieved. A temporary mess served field rations, and tents were hastily pitched in what proved to be the start of a torrential downpour which churned the camp area into a sea of mud and thoroughly soaked all the gear. The foxholes that had been dug hurriedly filled with water.

It took guts, will power and hard work during these trying conditions, but the men were not lacking in any of these. They continued to work cheerfully through those rainy days, shoveling coral and hauling logs in the backbreaking task of making a camp out of a quagmire, and through it all the Japs shelled the area nightly and made numerous air raids.

When the first airplanes arrived at the strip, these men were ready to take care of them. They were the 36 F4U's of Navy Fighting Squadron Seventeen (VF 17)—the only squadron in the Navy at the time that was flying the Corsair and who unknowingly were destined to become a recordbreaking outfit. They arrived on the 24th of October for six weeks of combat.

Working 24 hours per day in shifts, the enlisted personnel of VMF 215 made 98 per cent of the planes available for combat at all times, although the planes were constantly on combat missions and in need of much repair work after such missions.

The Navy pilots gave the mechanics a good share of the credit for the success of their tour. By having almost every plane in commission each day they were given extra missions with many additional combat hours in the air. They shot down forty-eight enemy planes in six weeks.

The squadron had twice as many planes and nearly a third more pilots than Marine fighting squadrons were allowed at that time. Many of the Navy pilots had their own personal airplanes, flown by nobody else. They were equipped with the latest and newest Corsairs which had the new bubble canopy for better visibility, wing-spoiler and raised tailwheel for safer landing characteristics, and the shorter propellers were an innovation of themselves. The Corsair had been designed with inverted gull wings in order to use a 13-foot propeller—the largest made for single-engined planes. Someone had tried one of the 10-foot props from an F6F on an F4U and found it gave about ten knots more speed!

Throughout these months of Munda-Ondonga operations the enlisted men serviced and repaired about fifty-six planes every day and still maintained a high squadron morale despite sickness and difficult operating conditions. Over 85 per cent of the men were hospitalized at one time or another or under treatment for various ailments. Eleven had to be evacuated from the area. When in the final two weeks a certain amount of fatigue and lassitude became apparent, hopes of relief lent new energy to the men. The value of knowing when they expected to be relieved was incalculable for morale.

Our DC-3 left Ondonga behind and soon we saw the fighter strip at Vella Lavella, where we were to spend our next six weeks of combat. The location reminded me of Munda, for here too you could take off and almost immediately be flying over water. That's the way we liked it, for there was a better chance of surviving a forced landing at sea than on land.

A belt of ground varying in width from ten to fifty feet separated the landing strip from the water. The belt was covered with large coral rocks and coconut logs. Although narrow, it proved wide enough to aid in the killing of several pilots.

These men on Vella Lavella were some of the pilots
who had furnished air cover for our troops when they
had landed on Bougainville on November 1st. I was
anxious to learn what had happened when the
Americans had dared to approach within 225 miles of
the great naval base of the Japanese at Rabaul, New
Britain, with its five airfields and swarms of bombers
and fighters. They had gone ashore within 50 miles of
the five Jap airfields on Bougainville, which had been
so formidable when we had departed from the area.

It was 130 nautical miles from the airstrip at Vella to
the intended place of landing on Bougainville. Our
naval forces had to have air cover against a possible
attack by Japanese planes at dawn. To furnish this
cover the pilots had to get out of bed at 0330 and take
off at 0445 in the darkness of the pre-dawn.

That morning the new skipper of VMF 215, Lt.
Colonel Williamson who had replaced Major Neefus,
led his division off the ground at 0445. Captain
Donald Aldrich of Chicago then took off, followed by
Lieutenant Keister. Over the radio, Aldrich heard
the tower announce that an air raid was in progress
back at the field, which still had its runway lights on.
He looked back and saw two fires burning, one near
the middle of the strip and one about five miles away
in the jungle. He thought the Jap bombs had started
the fires.

It was not until the airplanes returned from their
mission that the missing parts of the story were unfolded. Lieutenant Crill of VMF 212 had started to
take off, but when he was partly through with his
take-off run his plane angled off the runway, crashed
into a parked Ventura bomber and burst into flames.
It was 0500 and another explosion was seen to occur
in the jungle by the airborne pilots. At the same time a

condition red was called and a Jap bomber dropped six bombs in the water less than a mile off the strip.

All the pilots returned from the mission except two—Lieutenants Keister and Kross. Their buddies were sweating it out, for they knew that one of them had crashed into the jungle. They didn't know whether the other would ever come back. Finally, when it was nearly 0930, they saw a Corsair come in and land. The pals of each missing pilot waited in suspense. Kross greeted them with a smile of wonder at the tense atmosphere. Keister was declared missing in action.

Two days later Captain Jack R. Jordan took off in the direction of the hills one mile north of the strip. It was pitch-dark. There was a brilliant flash of red in the jungle and a fire burned fiercely. Pieces of his plane were scattered over a wide area. His watch was found; it read 0445.

Almost at the same time of Jordan's crash, Lieutenant Newhall attempted to make his predawn take-off. He narrowly escaped death. His plane ran off the runway and he guided it back on before running into obstacles. The plane was only slightly damaged. He said that lights on jeeps and trucks all along the strip had dazzled and deceived him so that he was unable to judge his take-off path accurately.

It was two days later, on November 5th, when one of 215's pilots who had been shot down on November 1st returned to the fold. It was Robert M. Hanson, soon to be rated one of the highest of the ranking aces. He was rather happy. He had shot down two Zekes (Zeros) and one Kate (torpedo bomber). He reported to intelligence:

"Flying in Captain Warner's division on a patrol over Augusta Bay, I became low on oxygen. I motioned to Captain Warner as my radio was not working and we started down from 20,000 feet to 13,000 feet. I saw a flight of six Zekes coming out of a trough in the clouds from the direction of Kieta. I also saw about twenty to thirty planes following this flight.

"I picked one of this first flight that seemed to be diving for the beach at Augusta Bay. I tailed in behind him in his dive and gave him a burst. He seemed to try to pull away to the left, but I think he had too much speed to maneuver. I gave him another burst and he started smoking and burst into flames. He slowed down and as I passed over him, pulled his nose up and snapped a few tracers at me but missed. Then he fell off and down, burning as he went.

"I banked to the right, then left and got in position behind another Zeke. When I was sure I had him in my sights I gave him a long burst. He smoked slightly, then exploded. I pulled up in a *chandelle* to the left and climbed to 8,000 feet. There I saw about six Kates above and to my left. I had enough speed to make a low-side beam run on the nearest. He peeled off to the right as I shot. I saw no smoke or damage to this one. After I pulled through this run, I ended up above the remaining planes and to their left. I started a fairly low, high-side run on the left plane of the formation. In the middle of my run, they dropped their bombs in the water of Augusta Bay. I finished my run on this left plane and all but the one I shot peeled off to the right. After this first long burst the Kate nosed over very slightly. Then his dive became steeper and steeper. He did not burn or smoke. I followed him down until he crashed in Augusta Bay. Then I pulled up and right to chase the other Kates that had peeled off my first run.

"Then, I realized that my engine was dead. I had no power and lost speed rapidly. I knew I would have to make a water landing. I believe that on my first pass at the Kates, or when I followed the one down to the water, a rear gunner must have damaged my engine, although I saw no tracers.

"I headed toward the task force, which consisted of six destroyers and eight transports. I made a deadstick water landing about six miles southwest of the Magine Islands in Augusta Bay. I was about five miles from the task force.

"I crawled out of my plane, which sank in thirty seconds or less. When I inflated my old, inferior life jacket, it deflated almost at once. I then broke out my rubber boat, inflated it and started paddling for the destroyers. I paddled with considerable effort because I knew they were due to leave soon. I was also singing, "You'd Be So Nice to Come Home To.'

"A flight of two TBF's flew over me about eight times. I had my dye sea marker out, but they did not see me. I paddled to within 250 yards of the destroyers, when they finally identified me and picked me up. I was on the water four and a half hours. It was the USS *Sigourney* which picked me up at 1805. They pulled out about five minutes later for Tulagi!

"We were at sea until the morning of November 3rd. I had some very welcome meals, noting the conspicuous absence of Spam. The eggs, steak and ice cream were a real treat. I went on shore at Tulagi, caught the ferry to Guadalcanal and reported to ComAirGuadal. I was treated very well and drew some gear, which I had lost. After receiving proper permission I ferried an F4U back to Vella Lavella."

Lieutenant Petit of VMF 215 entered a cloud bank

and was never seen again, raising the losses even higher.

It did not sound too good when we heard about all the crashes resulting from predawn take-offs. All those accidents were called operational losses, because they were not the result of actual combat. It was constantly my fear that I would die in one of those useless operational accidents instead of in combat.

If the Army Air Force in Europe was losing many planes operationally, the cost to the United States in lives and matériel would be staggering, for they were taking some very high losses in combat at that time. In the Pacific we were losing as many pilots in operational accidents as we were to the enemy, because about 40 per cent of the pilots shot down by the Japs returned to their squadrons after some harrowing experiences.

Second Lieutenant Kenneth Duval had gone down off the coast of Choiseul Island. He tried to swim to shore, but the wind and the tide were against him. Conserving his water, he floated on the ocean in his one-man rubber life raft for eight days. He still had two drinks remaining when he was fished out of the ocean by the USS *Apache*. It was not until he was rescued that he learned how lucky it was that he had been unable to swim to shore. He would most certainly have been captured by hundreds of waiting Japs.

Just three days before our arrival, Lieutenant L. B. Hazelwood of VMF 215 made a strafing run on Kieta Harbor on the coast of Bougainville. After a wingover, he was shot down and crashed.

Aldrich with five and Spears with four kills now led

the list of victorious pilots of VMF 215. Major Owens and 1st Lieutenants A. R. Conant and R. M. Hanson had three confirmed kills apiece.

Even though all the pilots claimed they hadn't seen a Jap plane for many days Vella was certainly not all flowers and honeysuckle.

I talked with some of the enlisted men about the high mortality rate of the field.

"There is always a cross wind," one of them told me.

Another man with a bronzed, glistening, sweating back, whose name I cannot remember, said, "These planes are beat up terribly. It's a wonder some of them get off the ground. We are starting to get a few of the newer jobs now, though. What makes me mad is that we enlisted men worked hard to recondition some of the planes for the pilots of VMF 221 who you relieved; then the Navy squadron came up from Ondonga and picked out eleven of our best planes, which included some with the new type greenhouses we had just got. The Navy got all our best planes and in return they gave us ten of their planes that had to be overhauled and repaired. That really burned us up, but there isn't a damned thing we can do about it as long as the Marine Corps is under the Navy!" This man's eloquent expression, punctuated by swear words of unprintability, were accented by the swearing of the others in hearty approval.

"How's the chow up here?" I asked.

"Oh, the food is rotten—mostly Spam and bully beef. We eat at the New Zealanders' mess and they don't like to coddle their men in the least."

"You pilots of 222 are lucky," one of the men informed me. "Our planes are situated at the west end of the strip, where most of the take-offs are made. VMF 215 and 212 have their planes near the other end and have to taxi the length of the field lots of times to take off. You're liable to take off from one direction and land in the other. We've been keeping our fingers crossed ever since we've been here for fear somebody is going to have a collision. Anyway, things are better here than they were.''

Gunner George Schaefer had preceded us to Vella to make advance arrangements. When George asked for instructions concerning our squadron, he found the colonel very much surprised for he hadn't even been told we were coming! When we arrived, the pilots of Major Nathan T. Post's VMF 221 packed their gear and waved farewell to us as they rode back to the strip to take off in the SCAT planes that had brought us. They had shot down 72 Jap planes and lost two of their own pilots. James "Zeke" Swett with 18 planes and "Murderous Mannie" (Harold E.) Segal with 12 planes led the scores of "The Flying Falcons." They arrived at the strip just in time to see the transports leave. No one had told the SCAT pilots they were supposed to take a load of fighter pilots back with them!

Our tents were much the same as we first had at Munda, with the addition of electric lights. There was a large shallow community foxhole nearby, which was next to worthless. We immediately began to strip the newly vacated tents of their extra boxes to make shelves for our own use.

We began to live in comfort, considering we were in the combat zone. The chow was better than expected; although the cook didn't have much to work on he did a good job. The messhall had an ice flake machine and when it was not broken we were able to have cold water, lemonade or chocolate water for every meal. It was a godsend to us. Next to letters from home a cold drink was the best morale builder in the tropics. Under the care of the 37th Seabees and Acorn 35 we were equipped with mattresses two or three times thicker than those we had used before and were able to drive on good roads and fly from a fairly good runway.

There were two tents near the west end of the strip where planes were kept. The pilots on scramble alert stand-by duty could sit on the broken-down canvas cots out of the hot sun. Some Army P-39 pilots flew up nearly every morning from Ondonga and took turns with us Marines on all-day scramble alert. At night they would fly back to their base. Their airplanes lacked the range for the escort mission up to Bougainville, so they did not have much else to do on those days but fly up to Vella. They had to take off before dawn, however, to arrive in time. Sometimes they were used for strafing missions because they packed a 37-mm cannon, but most of the targets were out of range for them.

I was on alert duty one day and talked to them. "Only two more flights up here and I'll have earned another Air Medal," one of the Army flyers told me.

"How many have you earned so far?" I queried.

"I've got my fifth cluster coming up."

"Do you mean to tell me that you get air medals just for putting in so many flights?"

"Oh, I haven't been actually awarded that many yet, but we get an Air Medal for every five combat missions and a Distinguished Flying Cross for every twenty missions."

"Well, if that doesn't beat all. Nobody in my squadron has got a medal yet, no matter how many planes he has shot down or how many missions he has flown. I always thought a guy had to shoot down about ten planes to even be considered. In fact, I thought that shooting down enemy planes was considered just a part of our normal duty and the only way you could get a medal would be to do something above the call of duty such as volunteering for some dangerous mission.''

This question of medals was a sore spot with Marine and Navy flyers. We delighted in clipping short items out of the newspapers telling about Army flyers such as the one with a Silver Star, DFC with five clusters and the Air Medal with twenty clusters. We exchanged tales of Army flyers getting lost on hops and being forced down out of gas, then given Silver Stars for their trouble when rescued. Marine and Navy pilots in such circumstances would run the risk of getting courtmartialed for getting lost in the first place.

Ordinarily, though, we never thought of medals. If somebody managed to get several Jap planes he considered himself lucky and was considered so by the other pilots. Sometimes we even acknowledged that he had skill and a certain amount of guts, if his victories hadn't come too easily.

My old friend George Sanders was always getting some kind of an expedition on his mind. The newest was a souvenir-hunting trip over to Baga Island, where he had spotted a Zero in the water next to a barge. Using his connections we got an LCVP for the trip. George persuaded Lieutenants Sampler, Chandler and Hanson from his squadron to go with us and I got several pilots from my squadron.

Late in the day we returned to the dock laden with

brass binoculars, compasses, Japanese sailor hats, and a blackened skull.

The first enemy plane seen in the vicinity for several days had been shot down by Major Sapp that day. "Mother" Jones, Sapp's wingman, swore that Sapp never tallyhoed the solitary bomber to let anybody else know of its presence until he had a running start on them. Then every plane in the sky started for the poor lone Jap. Sapp beat them all to it and had the two-engined plane smoking downward before the next man got there.

VMF 215's six-week tour was nearly up and an unlucky one it had been. They had lost several men and didn't have many enemy planes to show for them. However, they had done their job of protecting our fighting men on Bougainville well and their value was not to be judged by the mere number of planes downed.

I figuratively crossed my fingers, hoping their bad luck would not fall upon us after they left.

8.
VELLA LAVELLA

WE HAD ONLY been on the island of Vella Lavella for five or six days when we had the first serious accident.

"Major Sapp's division has been assigned the pre-dawn take-off," George Schaefer told us one night when he made the rounds of the tents. After he left, one of the new pilots in the squadron, Lieutenant X, came over to my tent to "shoot the bull" with his good friend Charles P. Lassiter, a tall Atlantan with the strength of a young bull. I didn't pay much attention to Lieutenant X, except to say hello to him. I was busy writing letters home. I didn't know then that that was the last time I would see him alive.

I must have slept particularly soundly that night for the first thing I heard was the predawn roar of an airplane as it took off. It was followed by two more which passed with a raucous thunder and a flattening of the sound as each plane left the ground. Immediately came the rising crescendo of the fourth plane. I was wide awake in my cot, tense, hoping that all of them would get off the ground safely.

The snarl of the engine grew into a thunderous roar as it approached. Then suddenly there was a silence. Absolute limitless silence. There was only a crunch—no explosion—before the complete silence. There was just the black night outside, no longer dominated by the full, throaty, thundering roar of a 2,000-horsepower engine, guided by a small, handsome, pink-cheeked lad. A cold, icy hand clutched my heart for the space of one beat. Toward the strip a red haze was rising above the edge of the hill.

"*Fire!* My Gawd—he's on fire!"

I slipped my shoes on and ran to the hill with two or three others pounding along beside me. We stopped. The orange and yellow flames rose high into the air and the smoke disappeared into the sky. I wondered if the soul of the pilot was intertwined among swirls of the smoke. Silhouettes of men were standing around the fire and lights were driving toward the spot.

"The poor bastard!"

We turned and walked back to our cots.

"Who was it?" two of the men in my tent who hadn't bothered to get out of bed, asked.

"I don't know except it is the fourth man of the division. I hope Sapp's division didn't take off before the other squadrons."

The fire caused the full warload of the six machine guns to explode. Sometimes they would go off in a long burst and other times just a few sporadic shots. The bullets only traveled a short distance when they were set off in such a manner. Many of them spluttered around in a mad whirl in the fire like a pinwheel. Some rose into the air like hot coals.

When the runway was cleared again, the rest of the dawn patrol planes took off. I succeeded in dozing off to sleep again.

Not far from the control tower, midway down the strip, lay the smoking remnants of the crashed airplane. Only the wing tips, the tail and the engine remained. The rest of the plane had melted down into rubble. Some of the metal was still hot at 1000. They had already gathered up what little was left of Lieutenant X.

It was worse than I thought. The plane went off the runway, passed behind the tower and hit an antiaircraft emplacement. It had killed an enlisted man who had been on watch at the AA gun and badly scared the rest of the crew who were asleep in their dugout. It had gone over on its back and skidded to a stop in flames among some large coral boulders twenty feet from the water's edge.

I remembered Lieutenant X. He had only been with our squadron three weeks—quiet, smiling and friendly to everyone, with a rosy-cheeked cherubic face. He had been in other crashes bad enough to kill most pilots, but he had led a charmed life and walked away from them all—until now.

Ten hours after he died we held his funeral at a small cemetery up the road a few miles. A New Zealand and American flag hung side by side from a pole in front of the burial grounds.

The little body now reduced to four feet in length had ridden on a stretcher in the back of the bumpy truck with some of us pilots, who had to stand there and watch the remains of our buddy jiggle up and down over the rough road and red stains appear on the white sheet that it was wrapped in. It was hard to believe that all that was left of Lieutenant X was in that sheet.

A couple of our pilots carried the stretcher over and laid it beside a shallow hole in the coral. There were other holes already dug in anticipation of the men they were to receive. Sergeant Axel Larson of our squadron was buried nearby. He had been crushed between the wing of a ground-looping plane and a truck shortly before we pilots arrived.

There was very little ceremony, but about all that would have been appropriate in the combat zone. A Catholic priest muttered some phrases and the body was lowered into the pit by Leach and Hazlett. The American flag was pulled off to be used again later.

We put our caps back on and the bugler blew Taps as we saluted.

I looked back as we drove out of the cemetery. The New Zealand caretaker was shoveling the clean, coral earth.

Patrolling over Cherry Blossom (the code name of our Torokina beachhead) became very boring. It was littered with clots of small landing craft with others standing by offshore. There were several other craft present also, destroyers and LST's. The presence of so many targets made the continuous patrol necessary but nothing much tried to come in during the daytime, at least while I was around. We chased a few snoopers sometimes, but the radar usually lost them before we were able to get to their position. Sometimes we watched SBD's bombing Jap troops to help our ground forces. When we saw them strafing we experienced a great desire to go down and augment their firepower with the 24 machine guns of our division, but that was their pie. Our job was to stay up and patrol, so we just watched. After each bomb dropped, all the trees seemed to move momentarily and flatten out from the center of the explosion. After a second they would spring back.

To relieve the tedious patrol we would sometimes swing wide on a turn and fly over Mount Bagana, overlooking Augusta Bay. This live volcano rose from the surrounding mountaintops like a monarch among the rabble. Symmetrically sloping sides narrowed at the top to form a beautiful peak. When seen from the air the top was not sharp and pointed, as I had expected, but leveled off to form a large crater. From 15,000 feet I looked downward. Inside the crater rose a small cone, and inside the cone was another crater which led deep into the bowels of the mountain and from which tons of volcanic ash were spewing forth. I hoped to see great fires, but they must have been too far down. There was a mysterious-looking lake resting within the perpendicular confines of an adjacent extinct volcanic crater. Another lake lay at the foot and between the live and the extinct volcanoes. We followed along a plume of smoke which appeared to extend in the direction of New Guinea for 75 miles.

We were flying six, seven and eight hours per day all too frequently. After sitting in the cockpit for three hours I always began to get very tired. We usually flew four hours from the time we left Vella to patrol over Cherry Blossom until we returned. We would fly one hop in the morning, then another in the afternoon. It was on the second flight that I became really tired. At about the sixth hour of flying during the day I began to meditate on the relief that bailing out would give me. I would twist sideways to the left and to the right. I would raise my seat as high as it would go until my head touched the plastic canopy, and I would lower the seat until little more than the top of my head could be seen. Sometimes I would fly near one of the other pilots with my seat down as far as it would go. He would look over and see my plane flying close to him with an apparently empty cockpit! I would curl my left leg around the control stick and try to raise my weight off my seat with my elbows. Most of the time I took my feet off the rudders entirely and did my flying on the patrols with the stick alone.

About the time I felt I couldn't stand sitting any longer we would arrive back at our base and another Marine Corsair was saved!

The night after Thanksgiving (which we celebrated with a wonderful unexpected turkey dinner), Dr. Killjoy (George Schaefer) came along to tell us what was up for the next day.

"Do we have the predawn take-off?" we asked.

"Why of course you have the predawn take-off. It's about time, don't you think?" George answered.

"Are you serious, George?"

"Of course I'm serious, why shouldn't I be serious?"

I felt the same as if I had been handed a letter edged in black. I slept lightly that night. I not only wondered if I could keep the plane going straight down the runway, but I hoped that when I ducked my head down to retract the landing gear I could keep from diving into the water.

We began taking off at 0445 the next morning while the night was pitch-dark. Flashes of lightning flickered for bobtailed instants in the clouds, the first I had seen in the tropics. A complicated maze of airplane lights, looking like red, white and green dots, was ahead of me. I followed the plane from the next revetment out. I knew it was Steve Yeager on whose wing I was to fly.

The puzzle began to unravel as the planes took off one by one. As soon as Yeager started his take-off I taxied out and lined myself up carefully with the lights, although I couldn't see very far ahead, to know for sure that I wasn't headed wrong. I wouldn't know that until I got the tail up. When I saw Yeager's lights rising into the sky I muttered a quick prayer: "My Father in Heaven, see that I don't do any damage to matériel or personnel, including myself, these favors I ask in the name of Jesus Christ, Amen."

I shoved the throttle forward easily and pulled back on the stick to hold the tail on the ground so I would continue to roll straight, until there was enough air passing to make the rudder effective. I moved the stick forward and lifted the tail up. I had been wandering to the left slightly. I pressed a little right rudder. The air whistled ever louder past my open cockpit, I thundered between the two rows of lights at 100 miles per hour, pulled the plane off the ground smoothly and heaved a sigh of relief—so far so good. I gained a couple of hundred feet in altitude, then reached down to raise the landing gear. It was an old-type plane and I had trouble with a homemade safety catch that had been installed on the lever to prevent accidental retraction while on the ground. I had to lean forward until my hand wasn't far from touching my feet and my head below the rim of the cockpit. As soon as I was able to pull the handle, which took only a few moments, I straightened up and the plane gave a spurt ahead when its wheels came up. I saw I had gone into a dive. The lights on the island were close to my own altitude. I hauled back on the stick and watched my altimeter jump from about thirty feet into a steady increase.

I flew straight ahead until I had everything well under control. Then I began a slow turn to the left, checking on my instruments and watching carefully for the lights that would warn me of the location of approaching planes. I kept a close watch on the white speck ahead of me that looked no larger than the head of a pin, for I knew it must be Yeager. He went into a left turn and I could see his red wing lights. I then turned sharper than he did so I would have less distance to travel to catch up.

Yeager went below two red lights and then clung to them—that must be Morris and Lassiter. I also crossed below the lights and gently nudged forward into position close to Yeager's wing. If I had gotten much closer, we would have been flying cheek to cheek. Flying formation at night in an F4U is no cinch. The wings are contructed at a tilt, which gives the appearance that the plane is banking when seen at certain angles. It is particularly deceptive at night. I stepped down far enough so that I could see the lights on both wing tips at the same time, to enable me to judge more accurately.

Below us a powerful searchlight was directed parallel to the water and another pointed vertically into the sky. They had learned from previous crashes they should give us visible indication which direction was level and which was straight up.

Halfway between Vella and Bougainville, as we approached the Shortlands, it was light enough to see the other planes, so we opened our formation wider and turned out our running lights.

''Bogey's at four o'clock up,'' Steve's voice boomed over the earphones.

I looked and saw four planes, which began to climb and thus revealed the distinctive twin tailbooms of the P-38. One of them started down on me from behind. I waggled my wings and continued to fly battle formation. He zoomed past and turned in front of me, leaving his surprisingly turbulent slip-stream behind to jounce me around badly.

We arrived over Augusta Bay and patrolled at 10,000 feet. From that altitude the sunrise was beautiful; stringers of red clouds floated like veils past the dull sun. The smoke plume trailing from the volcano pointed like a dagger for sixty miles toward Rabaul, as if the Almighty were trying to indicate our next main objective.

A strange feeling came over me as I watched the massive darkness below change into dancing sunlit shadows, with the volcano smoking so proudly and our ships and men down there fighting for their lives. Men who were trying to take back from the Japs this land that they never wanted to see again, even on an all-expenses-paid tour. I felt as though I had just come through a long, dark cave and was almost to the entrance when I burst out into the sunlight as the gloom fled from the land and the water.

Down there below me I could see the velvety jungle that covered several thousand natives and close to 40,000 Japs. I wondered what my chances of coming out alive would be, if I were ever forced to parachute down. At least we had a coastwatcher on Bougainville again. While we were stationed at Munda, all the coastwatchers had either been captured or been evacuated to prevent their capture.

The Japs had threatened to kill and burn the villages of any native who helped an American flyer. They had carried out their threat too and killed entire families for good measure. Some of the coast natives captured downed American flyers and delivered them to the Japs. Most of the natives, especially those farther in the bush, would just keep away from the Japs. The natives around Kieta had been helping the Japs wholeheartedly ever since November 1942. Under the influence of a Japanese resident of

Bougainville named Tashira, they had called them-selves the "Black Dogs" and raided inland native villages, raping, murdering, burning, and stealing. They had teamed up with the Japanese to wipe out the last of the remaining Europeans and Chinese, a project in which they were only partly successful.

My best chance would be to contact only one na-tive and get him to help if he would. If several of the villagers knew somebody was hiding an American they would get frightened and turn him in to the Nips. Some pilots had saved their lives by secretly moving from the hut the natives took them to for the night and hiding in the bushes. That night a Jap patrol came outside the hut with bayonets ready for action. One of the natives had turned informer.

The Japs had most of the natives thoroughly frightened and willing to do anything to avoid bloodshed and trouble. After all, the Japs seemed to be winning. They saw only yellow soldiers day in and day out. Why didn't the white man come and kill the Jap if he was so strong? The natives had seen the white man's thunderbirds; some of them had had their relatives killed by them; but the Japs stayed on.

Before returning to base, Morris led us up to Buka Passage at the far end of Bougainville. I recognized the Chabai airfield, which we had strafed a few days before with Al Gordon's division. We were near it when I saw a boat anchored offshore from the airfield. Suddenly Morris peeled away into a steep dive, and simultaneously black balls of smoke with fiery centers appeared at our altitude, but a thousand feet to the right.

The following minute was nearly the death of Mor-ris and me. It was my duty to follow him, so I kicked rudder and shoved the stick over and followed him

down, turning on my guns and gun sight on the way.
"What the hell are we going to strafe, the boat or
some shore positions?" I asked myself.

I could see that the ack-ack was much more accurate than I wanted it to be. Exploding shells appeared
just short of Morris' right wing—*puff, puff, puff*.

I was suddenly struck with the horror of having
entered into a situation which I could not get out of.
True, I could dive to the left and away from shore, but
only a few seconds more and I would be on the target.
I wouldn't turn away now, though any second might
be my last.

The large balls of black smoke began to fall behind
Morris. Already they were stabbing at me. I diverted
my gaze from the boat toward the shore and saw fiery
bursts appearing in a thick curtain to my right.
"Thank God, they're short, so far," I breathed,
wondering when they would correct the range.

Morris was firing his guns now. I flew through the
smoke trail left by his chattering machine guns as
Morris pulled up and into a left turn. I concentrated
my attention and my pipper on the boat which was a
mass of smoke in the center, framed by wooden ends.
I pressed my trigger and the tracers shot forth in long
streaking sparks and entered the middle of the
smoke. I kicked the rudder gently and watched the
tracers walk back and forth on the near surface of the
dense cloud—a fraction of a second rest for my guns
and then I pressed the trigger again and held it down.

I stopped firing and pulled back sharply on the
stick to leap-frog over the boat. Then I pushed forward and dived down to the top of the water for my
getaway. I climbed just high enough to drop my left
wing in a turn without it striking the water, then
swung to the right and junked up—then down. A

feeling came upon me, an urge of the instant. I jerked the stick back abruptly, kicked left rudder and looked backward. Small geysers shot up from the water twenty-five yards behind my plane as exploding shells and shrapnel sprayed the waves. Down went my nose as I dived again.

As I circled to join Morris, I became worried. What if Yeager and Lassiter had tried to follow us? They would be dead pigeons by now. I looked at the sky and saw two planes waiting for us to come up. They had been too far behind to join when we went into our dive. I looked back at the boat—sixteen clouds of smoke still hung in the air. The boat itself was not visible, because of the amount of smoke and flame pouring from it.

Back at the base, Morris barely mentioned to intelligence that we had strafed a thatch-roofed boat, which he hoped was a Jap admiral's. No wonder he didn't think much about the strafing, he hadn't even known he was being shot at until he was ready to pull out of his dive!

"It looked like the Japs were throwing all the AA shells they've got at Buka Passage at you two. They were just missing Morris and then they dropped back and had the right lead for poor ol' Zed. I sure thought he was a goner," Yeager told us.

"I saw a trail of black puffs follow you all the way down, Zed," Lassiter told me. "You would just leave a spot in the sky and a split second later an AA shell would explode there."

Evidently some of the 40-mm AA batteries were not giving me enough lead, and others had the right lead but were cutting their fuses too short.

I didn't find a scratch on my plane, but Morris found a hole the size of a quarter where AA had pierced his. It was located just 12 inches behind his head!

The next day I was put on scramble alert duty for a while and met my college friend Joe Lambert, from Lehi, Utah. He was flying P-39's. He had been forced down and made a water landing at night near Guadalcanal a few months before. Joe had survived the crash, but almost got drowned swimming to shore in a heavy surf. The only chance he had to get a Zero was ruined when he was all ready to open fire and his engine quit on him momentarily. He was out of fuel until he switched to another tank. Joe wanted to spend Christmas at home with his wife—she lived just around the corner from me back home.

"You'll sure be able to tell P-39 pilots back in the States," he told me. "They will all be walking around with P-39 cramp." I didn't know what that was until I saw some of the P-39's taxi by. Each of the pilots had his neck tilted forward in his low cockpit so that he could see better. I couldn't help but admire the ease with which the P-39's could taxi, take off and land. With their tricycle landing gear, they seemed as easy to steer on the ground as an automobile.

As we drove along the edge of the runway at noon for our next mission I heard an unearthly screeching and scraping din. I looked over my shoulder in time to see a P-39 go sliding past flat on its belly—an emergency landing. Luckily, the pilot had remembered to get rid of his belly tank.

We took off and when unable to find the task force we were supposed to cover, Yeager led us to Bougainville for the second phase of our mission. We had a field day strafing all the buildings and huts between Kieta Harbor on the Northern and Kahili on the southern part of the island.

We hadn't arrived back at the base very long when some of the fellows watching from Vulture's Hill began to yell. We ran out and saw a parachute floating down. A dark object dangled from the shroud lines, oscillating far worse than the pendulum of a grandfather clock. The man was hanging limply and we knew he smacked the water hard when he hit out in the bay. Two Corsairs and a C-47 circled the spot.

We conjectured who it could be and decided it was probably a pilot from VF 17.

I began talking to one of the fellows from 215, who would leave the island when the C-47 arrived. He told me they had lost two pilots doing the same kind of wild up-hill-and-down-dale strafing we had just completed.

Major Gordon and Johnny Morris landed. It was they who had been in the two Corsairs. They had also been strafing at Bougainville and found the Japs ready and waiting for them. Evidently they had arrived about five minutes after we left, through no fault of their own. Captain John Fitting of Chappaqua, New York, was the one in the parachute. Morris' plane had a hole through the fuselage about eight feet back of his head.

The next morning Morris, Lassiter and I went over to the tent hospital to see Fitting. He was a good-sized man, well liked by everyone. I could remember him as one of my gunnery instructors at Miami, Florida, a year before. He was new in our squadron and it was his first tour in combat.

We found him propped up in bed with a plaster cast around his chest. His large eyes had the lids dropped halfway down. "I feel dopey," he told us. "They gave me some pills a little while ago and I feel dizzy. I can't breathe very deep and my left arm pains me so much I can't move it."

Two or more gun emplacements near Kieta had put two holes in his left wing, one of them over a foot wide and a smaller one back of it. His left aileron had been practically shot away and it took all his strength to hold the stick over to keep his wings level. His plane had started on fire but he purged his wing tanks with carbon dioxide, dived and put it out.

At 5,500 feet over the bay he lowered his wheels to test the plane to see if it could be landed. When he put the flaps down they threw the plane out of kilter and rolled it over; he pushed the stick forward, unbuckled his safety belt and fell out.

The stabilizer must have hit him as he couldn't remember anything from then on except swallowing a lot of sea water, thinking he was going to drown and that he was too tired and that he hurt too much. He couldn't even remember opening his parachute. Only half of his life jacket inflated. Fitting was about to go under in the heavy seas for the last time when the crash boat arrived and Doc Brittingham grabbed him. It took three men to pull him into the boat. Doc gave him something and he threw up about a gallon of sea water.

When we walked down the aisle and out of the hospital I looked at a young kid Fitting had told us about. He was a Marine raider just evacuated from Bougainville. Blood was soaking through five different bandages on his naked body, making a dull red tinge in the center of each. His skin had a mottled, half-transparent waxy and surprisingly yellow look, probably from eating the atabrine we were given daily to suppress malarial symptoms. He lay there with his arms at his sides and his eyes closed. They thought he would die. He was only eighteen.

On the other side of the aisle there were five burned sailors swathed in bandages from head to foot, except for their faces. A powder explosion in their gun turret had got them—one of those accidents that happen in war or peace.

The daily news bulletin that evening said that another pilot had bailed out near Vella Lavella and was rescued. Also, a Navy VF 17 pilot had been shot down by a new AA position at point Dog near Augusta Bay. The Japs had noticed the pilots liked to take a short cut home over that strip of land and had secretly moved up a 40-mm AA gun. Other Navy pilots kept the Japs away from his position in the water until a Dumbo (PBY) landed and rescued him. A cannon from shore opened up on the Dumbo and came within thirty feet of it, but the plane got away.

We had forgotten that Christmas was not far off, but several packages came in the mail to remind us. I didn't wait until Christmas to open my packages despite the instructions on the outside. There was no telling whether I would still be alive by then, so I didn't wait. One of the packages contained several pounds of pine nuts from my Uncle Joe. Nobody but Al Gordon and myself had seen any before. The other fellows began to chew the nuts, shell and all, until I showed them how to crack the shell between the teeth and get the cream-colored nut meat inside— after which my pine nuts disappeared rapidly.

It kind of made me homesick to get back where it snowed. I imagined Uncle Joe out on the farm with his wife, all alone now that their youngest son had joined the Army Cadets. I laughed when I remembered how Uncle Joe considered Italian Balm good for all ailments. If it was an earache, Italian Balm was the thing, and corns or just plain sore toes received the same treatment.

Some socks and handkerchiefs from Charlie

Lundgren and his family were of military color, I was happy to see. I could use them on my next trip to Sydney. Charlie had come to America as a penniless Swedish immigrant while a young boy. He raised sheep and through hard work had become one of the richest men in town. An explosion around a campfire had cost him the sight of one eye. He used to have pillow fights with me when I was little and always gave me a two-dollar greenback every Christmas, enough to last me for weeks in those days.

There was a shaving kit from my Uncle June and his wife. It was too good for the tropics, but I planned to use it in Sydney.

While I was opening my presents, I heard a crash and ran to the rim of the hill. An F4U was standing on its nose almost vertically. The pilot climbed out and slid down with an unhappy smile on his face.

Later that night, some of the boys produced some whiskey and wine, and became happy enough to start singing. Without waiting for them to request me, I got my accordion out and tried to accompany them. The first was sung to the melody of "The White Cliffs of Dover."

There'll be Zeros over, the hills of Rendova, for tomorrow is another day.
There'll be love and laughter, and children ever after, we return to the U.S.A.
The Jappies have lost their sleep, the Marines are now in their way.
We keep them on their feet, and on their corns we'll stay.

The next song, sung to the tune of the "Road to Mandalay," was:

Take me somewhere east of Ewa
Where the best ain't like the worst
Where there ain't no Doug MacArthur
And a man can drown his thirst.
Where the Army takes the medals
And the Navy takes the Queens
But the boys that take the rooking
Are the United States Marines.

Chorus:
Hit the road to Gizo Bay
Where the Jap fleet spends the day.
You can hear the duds a-chunkin'
From Rabaul to Lunga Quay.
Pack a load to Gizo Bay
Where the Float-plane Zeros play
And the bombs come down like thunder
On the natives 'cross the way.

In the air to Tonolei
Losing Corsairs all the way
You can hear the pilots cussin'
You can hear the gunners pray.
On the road to Munda Bay
Where the Haps and Tonys play
And the flak comes up like thunder
From Vila 'cross the way.

The next song was sung to a tune that must have
originated with the words:

Friggin' in the riggin', friggin' in the riggin';
Just a friggin' in the riggin', cause there's nothin' else
     to do.
Oh, the first mate told the sec'nd mate, the first mate
     told the sec'nd mate,
Oh, the first mate to-ld the sec'nd mate, that there's
     nothin' else to do.

About the time that I cleared a space on my cot large enough to permit me to go to bed, the fellows began to leave and the local public relations man entered. He was a Marine sergeant who wanted to interview Foxworth about the Air Medal he had received a couple of nights before.

Robert F. Foxworth from Tennessee was still feeling gloriously uninhibited. He began to bawl the correspondent out for not printing the truth about our planes.

"And why don't you guys ever tell the people about the faithful wingman who has never shot down a Zero, which is a matter of luck in meeting one where you have the advantage, anyway," Foxworth continued, flipping a fly away that had drowned in his cup of cheer. "He sticks by you through thick and thin, but never gets a medal and the people in the States accept him as common as if he was a bloody P-boat pilot.

"When I go back to the States and I stand up there to a bar side by side with a blessed instructor, who has never been out of the States and we both order a drink at the same time—the instructor will get his immediately 'cause he's been at the bar so many times the bartender knows him, while a half hour passes before I get mine—after I've been out fighting my blessed head off for the whole kit'n kaboodle.

"I think that I should have been awarded the DFC the day I left the States. Anyone who does his duty out here should have one. Doing your duty is plenty hard enough all by its lonesome."

"If a woman walks up to me with my little Air Medal after looking at some Army SCAT pilot with all his DFC's, Silver Stars, Air Medals and Oak Leaf Clusters—who has just got through flying 100 hours in the combat zone—and asks what I have done, I wouldn't slap her or anything for comparing me to that Army pilot, I'd just turn on my heel and walk away without saying a word!

"I remember once before when I was interviewed after shooting down my third Zero, the correspondent wrote up his little say. He said I saw a Zero in a corner of the sky. Now how in the hell can a guy find a corner of the sky? There isn't any! If I coulda' found a corner of the sky during that fight, I'd have got into it and stayed!"

The correspondent who had been listening, but not taking any notes, now defended himself. "I would get courtmartialed if I wrote that our planes were inferior to the enemy's! It isn't a matter of me having guts, but the news would be stopped before it was released and I can do more good out than in the brig. I've been a newspaperman for seventeen years and I have also been on eleven missions as the tailgunner in an SBD, so I can sympathize with you, but there isn't much else I can do."

Yeager now spoke up. "The Army gets the Air Medal for either five or ten missions, I don't know which, and the DFC for thirty or so. We might get an Air Medal for three Jap planes and about 200 hours of combat."

It was Foxworth who had once made a pass at a Jap pilot in a parachute without shooting at him. When he came back for another close look the Jap pilot slipped out of his parachute harness in terror and fell several thousand feet into the sea.

The next day we were down at the strip when we heard one of those God-awful crashing and screeching noises that had become so familiar. I looked up from my game of checkers just in time to see an SBD slide to a stop in a belly landing. As soon as they opened the field again another SBD came in all shot up. They had been bombing the Jap AA position at point Dog.

Through sometimes costly experience we had learned there is little use trying to knock out AA batteries with strafing raids. Time and again we had strafed gun positions and silenced them, only to have them talk the very next day, sometimes with a fatal effect. The only sure way was to plant a good-sized bomb on them.

Major Boyington's outfit VMF 214 had relieved VMF 215. They had lost one of their pilots, named Kesseler, who had made a strafing run with the rest of his division at the same location near Chabai where Morris and I had met such withering ack-ack. After the run none of his division could see him so they decided he was a goner. The very next day, however, he was rescued after making a crash water landing near Vella Lavella and drifting over to Kolumbangara. He had rigged a sail on his small rubber boat and was making good time for his home base at Vella when picked up.

That Chabai location was restricted from then on, because we thought it was a trap, baited with barges and boats.

The weather became so bad on one hop early in December that I lost Morris even though I followed him in the take-off. Once he got off the ground I lost sight of him. We returned to base and pancaked. The clouds and rain squalls of that day were only the forerunners of a frontal area that provided such poor visibility for the next six days that all flying had to be canceled. We still had to go down to Squadron and be on hand at all times even though we felt sure we wouldn't fly.

The immediate objective of our troops on Bougainville was to build an airfield from which our planes could protect the men and installations and also launch attacks against Rabaul. We pilots had watched the jungle disappear and the wide "dirt road" appear bit by bit until December 10, 1943, the great day the field was ready for use.

Most of the pilots wanted to be the first to land on the new conquest, but ordinarily we lesser mortals were but pawns in the hands of the higher ranking officers and had to do as we were told. Major Robert Owens had been the first to land at Munda. Now the first landing at Bougainville was made by an SBD pilot who came in before the field was completed and made a belly landing, very unofficial. A new squadron in the area, VMF 216, was assigned to be the first up there and carry on the local patrols and scramble alerts, until the rest of us came up to help. They had 17 F4U's and felt fully capable of winning the war by themselves.

The landing strip at the Treasury Islands was also completed about this time. While it was still good enough only for emergency landings, one of the pilots from Vella had made a forced landing and had flipped over on his back when his plane hit a rough spot. Some Seabees rushed up to him as he lay unconscious upside down, hanging by his safety belt. They didn't bother to take him out of the wreckage, which has a nasty habit of catching fire—instead they stole his goggles, helmet and gloves, for souvenirs!

On December 11th it was my turn to fly. Major Marion Carl, the C.O. of VMF 223, led two of his divisions off at 0500. Major Gregory Boyington's division took off, followed by Benjoe Williams' and then ours.

It took us over an hour to fly up to Cherry Blossom, because we were bucking a strong headwind. We arrived at the strip just as a beautiful orange sun lifted itself from the sea to the east, revealing a curtain of filmy finery at the far end of the airstrip where a rain squall was expending its force.

We zoomed over the strip and peeled off in right *chandelles*. As I came around in my landing approach I felt confident that I could land without mishap, because of my success at Munda. This field was reported to be about 4,200 feet by 100 feet. I pulled the nose up as I came in and stalled the plane in on a three-point landing. It was a good landing, but I dropped it in farther than I had expected.

The plane swerved slightly to the right and I gave left brake to correct it, but it kept right on going, seeming to skid on the wet iron Marston landing mat. I received a brief scare for I was sliding to the side, but when I had slid to the edge of the strip the plane responded to my efforts and headed back for the center. I sighed with relief.

If a wheel so much as left the iron Marston mat the soft, fine black volcanic sand at Bougainville would drag the entire plane off and probably flip it over. There was also a rather deep ditch dug near the edge of the strip to carry off excess water and cause things to be more dangerous.

I couldn't see any visible signs of the battle for the beach that had raged six weeks before, perhaps because the Seabees had scarred the earth and changed it about so much that shell marks became indistinguishable. Long lines of Marine raiders walked along the edge of the strip and rushed up to the planes and the pilots to look them over. What tickled me more than anything was the joy the men displayed to see our airplanes present to protect them from the Jap air hecklers.

A couple of Seabees came into our tent to visit us. One of them was an old ex-artilleryman of the First World War, the other a young kid—still sporting fuzz. "A few days ago, the Japs tried to land reinforcements up the coast," they told us. "We sent up a group of Marine Raiders and wiped nearly a thousand Japs out."

"If you want to make a yellow Jap turn white and his teeth chatter, just mention 'Marine Raider' to him," the oldest man told us. "The Japs are smart and tricky, but yellow. On our initial landing some water-cats (amphibious trucks) were left on the beach while the Marines pushed forward. They left some of the crews behind to guard them, but when they returned to the beach they found the Japs had infiltrated behind them, killed the crews and pried the treads off a long line of vehicles."

"I went to a Jap body and started to get a souvenir when a sniper shot at me. As soon as I heard that bullet sing over I jumped over a log and fell down an embankment and never ran faster in my life."

The intelligence officer had come in with the first wave and encountered a crossfire between two Jap 77-mm cannons that caused several casualties. One small Marine crept and crawled forward and threw a hand grenade smack into one 77-mm position and then rushed them with his rifle, in spite of machine gun and rifle fire from other Japs. He was going to be recommended for the Congressional Medal of Honor, the officer said.

According to the intelligence officer, the aviators and the Marine Raiders were winning the war on this part of the world. The Raiders led a hard life. They were on their own the minute they set foot on the shore. They plunged straight into the jungle without hesitation, seeking out the Japs. For three weeks they remained in the front lines without any hot food—only the crackerlike rations. Much of that time they spent in water up to their necks in their foxholes.

Sometimes a patrol of two or three Marines were landed up and down the coast to make a reconnaissance of Jap activity. A few of these Marines met two full Jap battalions equipped with heavy artillery and mortars. Our men had a time getting out alive, but they made it.

So far, over 2,000 Japs and 200 Marines had been killed. The day before, 12 of our men had been killed on hill 1000 by a Jap ambush. A few of the Japs had been shot to help compensate for the loss, however. Dogs were being used to warn of Jap locations and had saved many lives.

We were told about a Jap who yelled to a Marine, "Did you have a good time in Auckland?" Strange to say but the Marine had been there only a few weeks before.

The real opposition was furnished by the Japanese Imperial Marines—the pick of the Empire. One of the Jap Marines killed had measured 6' 4" in length and weighed 257 pounds.

The Japs liked to get our men mad by yelling, "Marines eat K rations!" The Marines shot many a Jap for this and then Jap machine guns would open up on the Marines—give and take! I heard that the enemy painted natives green and used them for snipers because they were more accurate shots than the Japs.

We all had the idea the Japanese were beginning to starve to death on Bougainville and that their chief diet was fish heads and rice. That appeared to be a false impression, because the Marines captured supplies containing meat, potatoes, fruit and other food, proving that the enemy had been eating better than our own men who carried only emergency rations.

Those Raiders were so bloodthirsty that when they returned from the front lines, they had nothing to do except stick around the landing strip waiting for us pilots to crack up! Up in the front lines they had been extremely trigger happy. Nobody dared to move at night for fear of getting shot by his own men. They liked to take a razor blade and stick it in a tree trunk, so that when a Jap sniper tried to climb one at night he would let out a scream. Then a Marine could creep out of his foxhole and finish the job.

And through it all we pilots took turns maintaining a constant aerial umbrella over the beachhead. No longer did we have to fly four hours to have a two-hour patrol over the position, for now we could take off and be on station within fifteen minutes.

9.
MID-AIR COLLISION

TWO DAYS PASSED, two days without an accident in my squadron, although a plane cracked up every day at the Torokina airstrip on Bougainville.

Then a terrible thing happened. Idly we stood on Vulture's Hill at Vella Lavella watching the planes pass over the strip and break off. We laughed and wisecracked as we guessed how many planes had been wrecked at Torokina that day. We watched four F4U's fly over in a right echelon in the usual close formation. When they reached the break-up position the plane next to the leader suddenly peeled away to the left.

Instantly there was a burst of flame and later the dull thud of a crunching explosion—the sound of stepping on a tin can and crushing it. Two pieces of metal flew outward and up. A wing fell off and came fluttering down. One plane was completely enveloped by long red tongues of flame and a mass of black smoke. A burst of flame came from the other plane too when it began its spin, but the flames disappeared. The plane spun down slower than I ever thought possible. We could see that the pilot of the burning plane didn't have a chance to get out so we concentrated upon the one that did.

"Bail out!"

"Jump!"

"Oh God! Get out! Get out!"

We shouted futilely to the pilot in the eternity of watching the spinning Corsair plunge inexorably downward in its death struggles. My muscles were taut. I was conscious of holding my breath.

A small figure seemed to be moving in the cockpit. The collision had occurred at the low altitude of about 1,000 feet. Now it was almost too late for a man to jump—and live. Then we saw it! An object came arching from the cockpit trailing a web of silk. The web turned into a small pilot chute at the top and in less than two seconds the main parachute mushroomed out into its snowy fullness.

The pilot swung from left to right in a terrific oscillation that threw him parallel with the ground. Then he swung downward to return, but the ground came up violently to stop him. The plane crashed an instant later, nearly on top of the pilot.

An exultant cry of relief escaped our lips. Someone beat wildly and unknowingly upon my back and yelled hoarsely into my ear, *"He made it! He made it! By God, he made it!"*

I ran for the wreckage the length of the landing strip away. Two tall columns of smoke bent by the breeze towered into the sky. The one on the left was black and came from the burning mass as if it were providing a solid stairway to the heavens. The other was a milky white.

The colonel was at the scene when I arrived, directing the fire-fighters as they sprayed small streams of water upon the flames. Fifty-caliber shells began to beat a rapid tattoo, yet still the colonel remained. Several men were looking at the remnants of airplane, when tracers whined closely overhead from a fresh outburst. We ran for cover and sprawled flatly on the slanting shoulder of the runway while the bullets pinged and spluttered a few yards distant.

When things quieted down we looked at the pieces that had been symbols of the marvelous ingenuity of man, but were now reduced to a more frightful sight than a charred and fallen tree. The back half of the plane that had carried the parachuting pilot was almost completely intact. It had been severed from the front part, which lay burning several feet away. Always in crashes, it seemed, the Corsair had the habit of breaking and crumpling in two just aft of the cockpit, which was good for the pilot as long as the cockpit itself was built strong enough to remain intact. The other plane was a flaming and smoking wreckage.

"His plane only missed him by twenty-five feet," one of the men told me. "We had to pull the parachute out of the flames. We dragged it away from the fire with the pilot still attached and found we were dragging him along on his face and scratching his nose pretty bad. He was unconscious, but came to as they were carrying him away to put in a jeep. The other pilot's body was thrown about a hundred feet from his plane—his head had been severed from his body."

I recognized the number on the plane and knew it was one from my squadron. "Do you know who they were?" I asked.

"Somebody said one of them was Witt and the other was Lieutenant Y, but I don't know which one it was who got it."

Witt was one of the new boys in our squadron, who had joined shortly before we left Hawaii for Midway. He always wore a silk scarf around his neck. We liked to kid him about trying to look like an aviator. None of the rest of us wore one.

Lieutenant Y was one of the new, new pilots who had joined us at Espiritu and was on his first tour of combat. Just the night before, he had kibitzed a checker game between Yeager and myself. He was the quiet type, but very likable. He had the same physical build as Robert Hanson, who was soon to become a leading ace.

I knew who it was who had got killed, because I had seen a jeep rushing past with Witt in it. I thought at the time he looked dazed. He was pale and kept staring straight ahead. I hadn't associated him with the accident, because I didn't expect the surviving pilot to be conscious.

Four hours later we buried Lieutenant Y—near Lieutenant X and Sergeant Larson. I was surprised at the number of graves that had been filled during the three weeks since our last visit to the cemetery. We gently laid some fresh palm leaves over the graves of our men.

To complete the day of disaster, 75,000 gallons of 100-octane gasoline burned up at the PT boat base about ten miles up the coast at Lambu Lambu Cove. Several men were killed and others injured. We could see the smoke billowing up from a great distance.

A couple of days later, Morris and I visited Witt at the canvas-roofed hospital. He was occupying the same bed Captain Fitting had recently vacated. Gunner George Schaefer was in the adjoining bed with a bad tropical ulcer on his leg.

Witt had been leading the formation. When they arrived at the break-up point he saw the way was not yet clear, so he decided to make another circle of the field. Lieutenant Y had peeled off at this spot and pulled in front of Witt's plane. Nobody knew of any reason why he should do that, but I personally believe he must have been blinded by the sun momentarily and thought Witt had already peeled away. Witt's propeller struck Lieutenant Y's plane near the cockpit.

Thinking a plane from another formation had zoomed into him, Witt pulled up and pushed his throttle forward, with no response. He didn't know then that his engine had fallen off. The plane began to spin. He thought about trying to pull it out of the spin, until he saw flames. Luckily, his hood worked easily when he slid it back. He worked fast, disconnecting himself from his oxygen and radio apparatus and the safety belt. Jumping out and sliding off the wing, it seemed to him a long time before his groping hands found the rip cord. Actually, he was working very fast. He looked down and saw the ground so close he wondered if he was above 300 feet—the minimum distance it takes a parachute to open.

The parachute jerked him violently when it opened and flung him in a breath-taking swing. He grasped a riser to try to stop the swing and hoped to run in the direction of the swing as he hit the ground. He was unable to do this, because a few seconds later he hit the ground traveling sidewards and backwards. Then he woke up in sick bay.

While we talked to Witt, eight Marine Raiders were brought into the hospital from Bougainville. One had his leg chewed nearly off at the thigh by machine-gun bullets. He had been hit two days before. His buddy had been hit in the back about the same time. Together they had managed to drag themselves to safety.

When the pilots returned for the night, we learned

that tough Bob Wilson from Warren, Minnesota, had played the return engagement of a pilot who had a slight accident at Torokina the previous day. He ran off the steel matting and the sand flipped him over on his back. His head and shoulders were submerged in the large ditch, containing water. He was nearly to the point where he would have to start breathing water, when a group of men lifted the plane up so he could get out.

Hobbs had spent part of the day with some Raiders. They had invited him to eat with them. They roasted a stolen pig on a grill that had been stolen from the radiator of a tractor. The rest of the meal consisted of potatoes; both food items were "damned good" according to Hobbs.

"How about getting Jap souvenirs?" Hobbs asked.

The Raider lieutenant answered, "In the first wave we used to kill a Jap, take his flag out and go on and kill some more. I personally gave away twelve flags. When we came back with more time on our hands we found that the Seabees had stripped those bodies bare.

"There was a bunch of pillboxes and nothing short of a direct hit from a 75 mm would do much good, so we had to use Cats [Caterpiller tractors.] The operator would head it straight for a pillbox and then lay down. We buried at least 50 Jap pillboxes that way. After a half a day the Seabees would dig them out and proceed to make their runway. One Seabee found a live Jap in one of the pillboxes and captured him, using a pickax to do it."

"How about me buying some souvenirs from you either for money or whiskey, whichever you choose?'' Hobbs asked one of the Raiders.

"I don't need any money up here," the Raider answered, "and I make my own whiskey." He pulled a bottle out of his pocket, one day old. The Raiders made their whiskey in a day and then let it age for about 30 minutes. It was real powerful rotgut, for when the Marine took out the cork the bottle nearly exploded.

Hobbs gave the Marine a cigar. The Raider really weakened over that cigar—it was the first he'd seen for months. Hobbs was to take him some more cigars soon and the Raider had a nice Jap flag with blood on it for Hobbs.

"Kitty" Hobbs told about an incident that backed up what I had previously heard, but hadn't been willing to believe completely. A heavy artillery barrage of about 7,500 rounds of 75 mm and 155 mm had practically annihilated a Jap battalion a few days before. They had lost over 1,000 men. After the bombardment, the Marines found 800 Japs wandering around acting crazy, apparently shell shocked. Marines, like the Japs, don't take prisoners.

The Marines had not felt kindly toward the Japs ever since Wake Island, but their feelings kindled into a fiery blaze when their major had been captured by the Japs. They heard his yells of agony, strong at first and growing weaker and then none at all. When they were able to, they captured the Jap position and found their major. He was tied to a tree, naked. He had met a merciful death, but not in a merciful manner. The Japs had not touched him above the waist. They had cut slices from his legs, buttocks and pulled his guts right out.

We now held about 15 square miles of ground—mostly swampy. Many lives had been saved because it was swampy, for when bombs and shells struck they penetrated the ground easily and the explosion was confined and deflected in an upward direction, leaving a large hole but not doing much damage outside of the immediate vicinity.

Nearly fifty thousand troops occupied our beachhead. A broad highway led toward the front lines, carrying a constant stream of vehicles and lined on both sides with lots of tents and foxholes. Instead of a scene of death and destruction, Bougainville, the springboard to Rabaul, and our Little Anzio, with its background of jungle and smoking volcano, looked more like the celluloid jungle home of Maria Montez.

The night of December 16, 1943 we were told there was going to be a fighter sweep over Rabaul from 1000 to 1025 the next morning. Over eighty Army, Navy, Marine and New Zealand planes were to participate.

We were all anxious to go on this strike, because it should meet up with a large number of Jap planes, and, since there wouldn't be any bombers to protect, the pilots could fight the Japs all over the sky to their hearts' content. Williams, Morris and Okie rolled dice to see whose division would get to go. Okie won the roll.

The next day things popped 475 miles to the northwest, but not nearly to the extent we expected. New Zealand P-40's were supposed to set the pace for the fighter sweep. They were at the lowest altitude, because their planes did not operate efficiently higher up. They set the pace all right. So fast did they bat-eye to Rabaul that they arrived far ahead of all the other planes. As a result, the P-40's were pretty badly shot up.

The New Zealand wing commander cussed the Japs when he was over Rabaul and hurled taunts at them. "Tojo eats Spam, Tojo eats Spam," he yelled over the radio.

Boyington, whose home was Okanogan, Washington, and with three children to his credit, tried to encourage the Japs to come up and fight by saying, "Gee—I wish we had some good airplanes instead of these P-40's," and, "I sure wish we had more planes up here!"

Few of the pilots made contact with the enemy. The planes they saw were low and they left them for the P-40's to handle while they kept their altitude to cover them. Many didn't know that anybody had made contact until after they had returned.

Two P-40's went down off Cape St. George. One of them was the New Zealand wing commander who had been talking over the radio. One P-40, while landing at Torokina, hit a tractor, killing a Seabee, although the pilot escaped injury. Another plane crashed at Torokina while landing and an F4U came in all shot up. The pilot had lost a lot of blood from a bullet crease above his ear, but landed safely.

The P-40's had knocked down five Zeros. Moore of VMF 214 fought seven Zeros and got two.

Five days before Christmas, Morris, Yeager, Koetsch, Hazlett, Virgil Teeter, Gunner Saint the sergeant major, and myself went up to the trading post to buy some native souvenirs. I invested in a knife made from bone of a wild pig and used by the natives for opening coconuts, and a stone adze which had been used by the grandfathers of the present-day natives for cutting trees, and looked like the head from an American Indian tomahawk.

A couple of the natives thumbed a ride back with us. Along the way we met natives who would hold their fingers up in a V-for-victory sign or else wave hello. One of the natives with us was named Jacob. He was thirty-eight years old, married and had five children, the eldest of whom was eleven years old. He was from Munda.

A New Zealand soldier who was also riding in the truck with us knew Jacob. "How many Japs have you killed, Jacob?" he asked.

"One."

"How did you manage to do it?"

"Jap he come 'long village and demand food. He no get food so he go into our gardens. At night while he sleep we get ax and kill 'im."

"Where is Gordon? I haven't seen him for days."

"Gordon went to Choiseul to spend Christmas," Jacob replied.

The New Zealander told us that Gordon acted as a scout when our troops landed on the island. He was partly New Zealander and very intelligent. He had been away to school, spoke perfect English and was considered to be a doctor by the natives. Gordon had killed so many Japs he had lost count long ago. He was only seventeen years old!

The other native who rode with us was named Samuel. He was also from Munda and had come up to Vella for the holidays. He told us the Japs didn't do anything to the natives. All the women, children and old men hid in the bush and most of the young men worked for the Japs and then reported all they saw happen and the location of all the gun positions to the Australian coastwatcher on the island.

The news sheet told us about the Army making a landing on the island of New Britain, near Gasmata. Someone said 125,000 men had landed there and that was one reason for the diversion raids we had been staging upon Rabaul from its right flank. Beer issued to me on an earlier occasion was put to good use. I used four bottles of it to bribe our parachute man, Jeffries, to make a double-thick sponge-rubber cushion for my parachute and for one of our ordnance men to file the trigger sear on my pistol so it would have a lighter pull and to clean the barrel, which had become rusty in an amazingly short time. I was getting prepared for our dangerous raids on Rabaul.

The beer also served another key purpose. I had an arrangement whereby the colonel and I shared the manually turned ice cream freezer at the messhall. Of course the colonel was not aware that I was in on it. With the help of a couple of bottles of beer to bribe the messboys, who were custodians of the freezer, we whipped up several batches of ice cream the last two weeks of our stay at Vella. Because I furnished the beer, Levine did most of the procuring of the ingredients, then Lassiter and I would help him turn the crank, using chipped ice and salt from the messhall. There was always enough ice cream to fill up everyone, and even Li'l Red Dog—the Irish setter pup that Jules Koetsch had bought in Sydney—had a dish.

This dog was not the only member of our squadron who had joined us at Sydney. Pappy Reid had bought a large Irish setter. The Australian owner had sold him claiming the dog was only a year and a half old. I asked Reid why the dog had gray hairs if he was so young. He looked more like fifteen years old! Reid named the dog Sid, but most of us just called him Big Red Dog.

Shortly before we left Vella, the public relations officer had a picture taken of Sid wearing a baseball cap decorated with a single Jap insignia of the type we sometimes put on our planes whenever we shot down an enemy. To go with the picture he invented an exciting write-up about how some Marines were walking down the road when a ferocious Jap dog that had been left on the island attacked them. To the rescue dashed heroic Sid and launched a counterattack on the "ferocious" Jap dog, causing him to retreat with his tail between his legs.

Actually, the "ferocious" Jap dog was the same dirty, brindled-gray, partly bald dog I had seen around our hut on several occasions. He was such a thin, dispirited and altogether mangy-looking cur I felt pity for him. We made the mistake of petting him the first time he came around, not knowing he had been with the Japs. He found it difficult to take the hint he wasn't wanted after that—no matter how uncomfortable we made it for him. Big Red Dog would make him stay away though and Red lived just across the path and a few feet up the hill from our tent.

We began to bomb the shipping in Simpson Harbor at Rabaul and the five surrounding airfields regularly. We were the first to subject it to an all-out aerial assault. I had been up to Rabaul once, but the bombers had gone into a cloud as they went into their bombing run and my division had lost them. Nothing happened of interest on that raid except my engine conked out on me briefly, just when I was directly above the city of Rabaul.

My squadron was the only one to make contact with the Japs from our base. Jones knocked down two Zeros and Okie got one. Jones led Okie on a run on two Zeros. They dived from 15,000 feet to 8,000 feet. Then Jones got his sight on the lead Zero and poured lead into it. Okie took the second Zero and both Japs were well taken care of.

"That was the purtiest sight I've ever seen—when I saw Jones' Zero blow up into nothing. One minute he was there and the next second he wasn't!" Okie told us.

That action took place between an extinct volcano rising from the sea, named "The Mother," and the city of Rabaul. It was exactly the spot where Morris and I had been only a few minutes before.

Jones later saw five Zeros chasing a lone F4U. One of the Japs was almost within firing range. Jones dived down and shot the tail off the end Zero.

"I never did know what happened after that to the poor bastard flying the 'U'," Jones told us. "I got really scared about that time; there was Zeros all over the place. I got pot shots at six or seven that went flitting by and then I got the hell out. After that I saw two Zeros on the tails of two F4U's way down at about 5,000 feet. I looked a little later and saw the U's on the tails of the Zeros. I'll be damned if I know how they managed to do it."

We heard about some Zeros chasing some P-40's which had to fly up canyons and duck over hills to get away. Six F4U's chased one Zero all over the sky without success. The Zero would wait until the U's were almost to open fire, and then go into a loop or a split-S or some other maneuver which our planes could not follow.

Okie got on the tail of another Zero, but it got away from him by ducking into a cloud. All in all, our squadron shot down three of the six planes accounted for.

Three P-38's cracked up when they landed at Munda. Two F4U's from VMF 216 and two P-40's with New Zealand pilots failed to return. No bombers were lost. Two pilots were seen in their life rafts by fighter planes. When the fighters began to run low on fuel, two Lockheed Venturas that were on duty especially for the purpose relieved the fighter planes in circling the position of the downed airmen. Dumbo was notified to come up and rescue the pilots, but was not at the base at Torokina that day because of bad weather and did not go up until the next day to pick up the pilots. They were never found.

It was only three more days until Christmas. Shortly before bedtime we learned there would be a big Rabaul strike the next day—our last day of flying before being relieved. It would be a climax to our second six weeks of combat duty.

Robert Foxworth, the tall lean young pilot with a broken front tooth; Robert Dailey Jr., of Flandreau, South Dakota, a lad with a wife back in the States just about to have a baby; Henry Huidekoper from Washington, D.C., an insurance man with black hair and dark eyes; and James A. Walley of New Orleans, who used to run an antique shop—were all from VMF 213. When their squadron went back to the States they had been transferred to our squadron.

Their division had been split up when they joined VMF 222. New, inexperienced pilots were teamed with men who had been in combat before. Foxworth and Dailey were due to return to the States after the present tour.

When they learned of the impending strike, Foxworth and Huidekoper came over to our tent. It was our turn to fly and their turn to stay at Vella Lavella. "Why don't some of you boys let a few of us go in your place tomorrow?" Foxworth asked.

"No sirree," we chorused.

"Surely you wouldn't want to go up to Rabaul among all those Zeros and get shot at tomorrow. We're willing to take your places."

"Nope!"

"You surely don't want to deprive us of a chance to get our picture in *Life* magazine with the rest of the aces, do you? It's our last chance to run up our score."

"We've got to get a start ourselves," we answered.

They found a division that was willing to let them take their place in the raid the next day, but first they had to find out if their own division leader, Bob Dailey, would go. They hadn't intended that he should go, but Teeter, one of the new men in the squadron who was in their division, wouldn't fly on anybody else but Dailey. Consequently, they reluctantly asked Bob if he would go on the mission, although it was one he wasn't supposed to fly.

"Sure I'll go," Dailey told them.

Immediately the fellows tried to talk him out of it. Foxworth said, "You've got too much to live for— you've got a new pup and you're practically through flying out here. Now me, I don't have a blessed thing to worry about. I might get married when I go back, but I'd rather tangle with Zeros over Rabaul than the wildcats back home!"

They couldn't talk Dailey out of going with them, so it ended with the division that was supposed to go in the first place making the run.

I didn't sleep too soundly that night, but I slept. I did not worry so much about getting shot down as I did about cracking up when I landed at Torokina. I could still feel the sensation I received of applying brake to keep from going off the runway and getting no response. I hoped I would get a chance at a Zero, but my main hope was that everyone in the squadron would come back safely.

No longer was I concerned so deeply about getting some Jap planes for myself. Instead, what mattered was whether my squadron got some. I was pulling for our team now where formerly I had been pulling for myself alone. Any score was a credit to all of us in the team and not entirely to the man who made it.

My fears proved groundless on December 23, 1943, when I came in with a nice three-point landing at the Torokina airstrip. At the ready tent we waited for a couple of hours. The heat was high and the atmosphere vapid. We had the usual beads of sweat forming on our arms and faces and running in streams from our foreheads.

As I looked around at the pilots I saw Stacey of VF 33. I hadn't seen him since September when I was on my way for my first combat tour at Munda. He had recently been to Auckland, New Zealand, on leave. He had one probable to his credit.

I said hello to Foulkes, a husky, good-looking fellow who had joined our squadron at the rest home at Waikiki Beach and had transferred to another squadron.

There too was Major Pierre Carnagey. He had been in VMF 222 for months until eight weeks before when he was made executive officer of VMF 214. Only four hours before, his squadron was getting briefed on the strike and they couldn't find him. I told them where he was—in VMF 222's ready tent asleep on a cot. They cruelly awoke him to the world of reality—the last time he was ever to wake up again.

Brubaker was standing by a truck talking rather

earnestly with three of his squadron mates. I was about to say hello to him, but he seemed too busy to be interrupted. Only ten days before, Brubaker and I had introduced ourselves across the mess table when I had heard him talk about getting permission to go on night patrol in a PT boat. As we talked he warned me that casualties had been piling up with the PT boys and it was entirely possible we might never come back from our nighttime adventure. One of the stories he told made me a little less eager to go. About the time that VMF 222 had arrived at Munda one of the PT boats was sliced into two parts by a Jap destroyer. The night was so black they hadn't time to get out of the way despite their own high maneuverability. The destroyer must have been doing over 35 knots when it hit them. Undoubtedly the Japs thought there could be no survivors because they had fired a few shots into the flames of the wreckage and kept right on going. The skipper of the boat and ten men lived through the wreck. The skipper, a good swimmer, had actually towed one of the injured men close to three miles to an island, much of the time pulling with the enlisted man's life jacket strap between his teeth. After about a week they were finally rescued by some friendly natives. Brubaker heard that the skipper is the son of Ambassador Joseph R. Kennedy.

A few days after meeting Brubaker I gathered my poncho, Mae West, knife and pistol and met him during a heavy tropical shower to begin our escapade. Both of us had the next day off duty and the PT boys had promised that we would get a chance to help lambast some Jap installations. When we arrived at the dock there was a message for us. The transportation to the PT base would not be able to arrive that day and it would be necessary to postpone the trip until later.

I did not know when I saw Brubaker talking so animatedly that our little adventure together was going to be postponed permanently.

It was nearly 1045 and take-off time, so all the pilots began walking to their planes lined up along the taxi strip which ran the length of the runway. The airplanes formed a double column, nose to tail, like a herd of elephants. The two columns contained over 100 fighter planes and extended over half the length of the runway.

A jeep passed by and stopped. It was Major Max Volcansek, our ex-skipper, who had been made operations officer at Bougainville. Major Marion Carl was in the jeep with him. Carl was going to lead the fighter sweep that was scheduled to arrive over Rabaul an hour after the bombers had left.

"Wish I was going with you," Volcansek told us.

As we parted I said, "I'll get a Zero for you today, Major."

"Good luck," he shouted as he started the jeep and pulled away.

The planes at the head of the line-up started their engines, taxied out and took off. We were near the middle of the line and didn't start ours for a while so that we could have all the fuel we possibly could to fly on. Although an airplane was taking off every few seconds there were so many it would be half an hour before the last plane could take off. Each pilot taxied out promptly and lined himself up with the runway without delay. He would begin his take-off while the plane ahead was only halfway down the strip.

The B-24's arrived on time, but circled too many times to give the fighters a chance to rendezvous with them. Each circle took about five minutes and cut down our gasoline just that much. One circle would have been sufficient.

We stayed below oxygen level and below the bombers, traveling at only 140 knots until we neared New Ireland, when we took our places above the bombers. Morris' division, in which I was section leader that day, was to provide close cover for the first formation of 12 Army B-24's. Williams' division was to provide the close cover for the rear formation of the same number of B-24's. Some F6F's and F4U's were about 1,000 feet above us acting as low cover, some F4U's above them as medium cover, and some P-38's on top of the stack as high cover. We started out with 48 fighters covering 24 bombers, but several of the fighters and one of the bombers had to return to base for various reasons on the way.

I had been worrying slightly whether or not I would be able to tell when Johnny Morris wanted me to scissor with his section. When the time came, though, I had no trouble at all in recognizing Morris' intentions. We were nearly to New Ireland and could expect attacks from Jap planes at any time. I saw Morris start a turn in my direction so I turned toward him and led my wingman, Lassiter, beneath the other section. After a few seconds delay, I waited until I saw Morris dip his wings to head back in my direction and I immediately followed suit. We had a smooth scissors working as we left the water and passed over the coast of New Britain and flew up the Warangoi River.

Bogey reports began to come in over the radio. Our scissor increased in intensity as we applied more throttle to make harder targets for the Jap Zeros and Tonys to hit. At the same time we hoped to utilize our extra speed in getting some of the Japs as they came in toward us or the bombers.

Far off to our right, near the water's edge, we saw the Jap airfield of Rapopo. A few minutes later Tobera passed beneath our starboard wing, then Vunakanau. We passed almost directly over Keravat, the airbase on the far shore of Cape Gazelle, and began a turn to the right before we reached the ocean on the far side of the peninsula.

The turn was the most dangerous part of the scissor. Morris worked it right though and neither of us was left in an exposed position wide of the bombers. It was all simply a matter of anticipating when and how fast the bombers would make their turn. I had to keep one eye on Morris, one eye on the bombers and one eye on Lassiter, and use another eye to search the sky for Jap planes. The failure to learn the correct technique of a weaving turn had cost many a fighter pilot his life when he discovered too late that he was too far from the other planes to save himself from the Japs.

The sun was almost directly overhead and I couldn't see a thing above me. The scratches in the surface of the plexiglass canopy, caused by mechs wiping dust off with a dry rag, diffused the sun over a wider area, making visibility even worse. I could never have seen a Jap coming from that angle even if I used a monocle with a Polaroid lens that I had constructed for looking into the sun.

When I was on the left side of the bombers and getting ready to turn back and cross them again on my scissor, I suddenly saw a plane come diving straight down out of the sun at one of the lead bombers. I wrapped up my turn to get back toward them as another plane made a beautiful overhead run on the same bomber with his nose pointing straight down. A couple of seconds and another Jap Zero made his run. *Zip, zip zip!*

I watched the last Zero go down in his dive far below until he began to make a left turn heading across my bow and away from the bombers about eight thousand feet below me.

For an instant I didn't know what to do. Should I leave the bombers and go after the Zeros? I might get sucked away from the bomber formation and out to where I would be cold meat for the Japs. In spite of this, my desire to get a Zero was so great it would have sent me diving for the Zeros except for one unforseen factor.

I flung my plane over and stood it vertically on the left wing, all ready to plunge down on the Japs. I looked, but I couldn't find them. Their camouflage had caused them to fade into the ground. That settled all questions of pursuit.

By now, a thin film of clouds had forced the fighter above us to drop down. The bombers were climbing slowly upward and we were being compressed between the bombers below and the fighters above like a Dagwood sandwich in a vise. The F6F's and some of the F4U's were at our altitude. I cursed them roundly as I dropped closer to the bombers to avoid mid-air collision.

The formation became a rat race. Lassiter and I would zoom up and hop over the bombers and hurriedly duck down on the other side of them to avoid crashing into other planes. All the while we had to watch out for Japs.

In a few minutes the clouds disappeared and our formation expanded.

We were heading for the shipping in the harbor. Off

in the distance I saw about thirty Zeros in groups of twos and threes or singly darting hither and thither. A few came within a couple of thousand feet of me and then would zoom up and away steeply, trying to lure some of our fighter planes away from the bombers.

There was a feeling of suspense deep inside me that cannot be described. I never knew for sure whether the sky was clear or full of Zeros. Things could change so rapidly and there were so many blind spots in my fighter plane. Any second I might feel the thudding of a 20 mm, but when I looked behind there was nothing close enough to worry about. I would then whirl about and look in the other direction and all the while something might be coming at me from below or from the sun. I would check constantly to make sure Lassiter was still with me.

As the tempo of the raid increased and we came within sight of the ships in the harbor, Morris' section disappeared. I twisted my plane left and right trying to see behind me and find Lassiter, when I realized that I was all alone. I had drifted quite a distance from the formation looking for Huck.

Instantly a feeling of desperation came to me at being alone and I dived to gather speed and move toward the bombers. Then I pulled up and over them and continued to weave.

I looked down. In front of my port wing was the city of Rabaul and its crescent-shaped harbor with several volcanic cones rising into the sky around the rim of the harbor.

Six black puffs appeared, mushrooming in the sky as from nowhere. Ack-ack! I flew off to the right side of the bombers because I knew the AA would be directed at them. Within the space of moments a curtain of antiaircraft fire sprang up. It was the most intense heavy-caliber barrage I had ever seen. Most of it seemed to be off the port wings of the bombers at 12,000 feet. A multitude of lights around the harbor kept blinking at me as I gaped into the maws of the cannons.

Without warning a huge puff of dense white smoke with streamers exploding from the center burst forth 300 feet above and to my left. Each streamer was led by a red dot of hot metal—white phosphorus. Forty seconds later another aerial bomb of white phosphorus broke farther to my left and higher. Closer to the bombers, a brilliant red glare shone in the middle as it exploded.

Four more phosphorus bombs had been dropped, all farther away, when I felt my plane jolted downward as if it had dropped into a deep vacuum. I kicked rudder and shoved the stick over to make a fast getaway. Looking backward, I saw the crooked tentacles of white smoke and hot metal reaching out to clutch me in their hellish grasp. Ack-ack exploded close and threw my plane higher in the air. A plane left a long dark smoking arc as it fell flaming into the sea and sent up a towering splash. Zeros above were sparking tracers toward our planes. A bomber began smoking. More aerial bombs burst close. The Japs were making a veritable Hell in the Heavens.

A large ship in the harbor, only slightly smaller than some of the passenger ships of the steamship lines, was untouched one minute and pouring a stream of smoke into the air as it spewed up its innards the next. Many bombs fell into the water uselessly, far from any target. Two or three other ships began tossing black burning columns of smoke toward us.

"Tallyho, three Zeros to the rear of the formation,

high." I turned slightly, but couldn't see them. I held a personal grudge against at least one of them for dropping phosphorus bombs at me.

I was scissoring with two F6F's when we got away from the AA. They left and two F4U's moved up. Pretty soon another U caught up to me and flew wing. I was glad to recognize the pilot. It was Lassiter. I caught a glimpse of the U's' numbers scissoring with me and was surprised to see they were Morris and Levine. We were all united again.

Another section of planes came up and also tried to scissor with Lassiter and myself and cut Morris and his wingman out. I wouldn't let them do it, so they came with me in my scissor and tried to cut me out. Morris ignored them, so they went halfway between in their timing and tried to scissor with both Morris and myself. Finally, they dropped behind and joined another lone section in a scissor.

A P-38 with its right engine dead was flying under the protecting wing of one of the B-24's and was joined five minutes later by an F6F that had been shot up. The B-24 looked like a hen protecting her chicks under her wing.

"This is Oboe two one, my co-pilot has been wounded," one of the bomber pilots radioed.

When we arrived near Torokina, we left the bombers and unleashed our engines. Some of the fighters had to pancake for juice (fuel) at Torokina, but the rest of us ducked our noses downward and made it home in jig-time at about 300 miles per hour.

The only boys who scored from VMF 222 were Reid, who shot down one Jap, and Williams, who got two.

"I was back there covering the rear formation," Williams told us, "when I see these three Zeros making runs on the bombers I was covering. I caught on to what their procedure was and found out that I could follow the tail-ender down from 12,000 to 6,000 feet and catch up to him and shoot him down and still not get sucked out very far from the bombers. I waited until three more Zeros made their pass. I don't know where the third Jap came from, but he was there. I followed him down and got him without the others knowing anything about it.

"My guns jammed after that second Zero. If that hadn't happened I could have got at least five planes, because they kept coming down in threes, over and over."

Meanwhile, Reid and his wingman, Jesse Leach, who were both in Williams' division, were having a fight for dear life at the rear of the bomber formation and a few hundred feet below. Several Zeros were making runs on Reid and he was frantically scissoring with Leach. Leach got a good burst into one Zero, but was too busy to look to see what happened to it. Reid shot at several and got at least one. Leach saw it crash.

Leach had been griping and moaning at not seeing a Zero and being the only one of our original squadron that hadn't yet seen one. After he landed, his outlook had changed greatly. "I saw thousands of them bastards and I don't care if I see another as long as I live!"

The fighter sweep had been planned to arrive over Rabaul one hour after the bombers, but the plans were wisely changed and they arrived just as we were leaving and were able to catch the Zeros still in the air. An hour later and the Zeros would have had time to land, rearm and refuel, and if they didn't want to bother about taking off against just our fighters the strike would have gone unrewarded.

Marion Carl was the officer in tactical command of the sweep and led the divisions from his squadron of VMF 223 in the lead. The Zeros were still up in the air, some high and some low, just as they had been after completing attacks on the bombers and the bomber escort. Carl led his group in an attack on the first batch of Zeros they saw. Major Boyington's outfit, which was farther behind, saw planes falling from the sky like leaves. Carl's VMF 223, however, only claimed five sure kills plus several probables. They had been too busy to watch what happened to the Japs they hit. Boyington's outfit then found their opportunity and went to work.

That evening when the score was totaled up we learned that the pilots based on Vella Lavella had shot down 27 Jap planes that day, not counting probables. Most of the planes were claimed by Boyington's VMF 214. Boyington had knocked down 4 planes himself.

My squadron was feeling angry because we had not been permitted to send any of our pilots in the 40 planes on the fighter sweep, but had been assigned to escort the bombers, where there was not nearly as much chance of getting Japs and still a good chance of the Japs getting us.

Carnagey, Brubaker and Foulkes failed to return to base. All that was known was that an F4U was seen to go diving straight into the water during the bomber strike, and during the fighter sweep a Zero and a F4U were seen to collide head on. Foulkes had been on the fighter sweep; the other two were covering bombers.

Back at the tent Lassiter told me how he happened to lose me. "I lost sight of you for a couple of seconds when my wing tip got in the way and I turned in the wrong direction. That left me so far behind I had a hard time to catch up, especially when I had to dodge all those F6F's and F4U's.

"When I got a little too far away from the bombers I saw a Zero boring straight in to get me, so there wasn't anything else for me to do but head for him. I opened up on him and he opened up at me; at the last second we pulled out so we wouldn't run into each other."

"Did you get him?"

"No, I missed him and he missed me. I guess we were both too excited. We decided to call it a draw. That was just before I caught up to you, Zed."

It was the night before the night before Christmas, when all through the messhall there was a big party stirring to celebrate the successful completion of our last day of the combat tour. On the morrow we were supposed to get relieved by VMF 321, by New Year's Eve we hoped to be back at Sydney, Australia, for another week of "rest."

We sat around the mess tables talking while we waited for the night's activities to get under way. Boyington was there, dressed only in his shorts. I noticed that he had the hairy chest and husky build of a wrestler. (I didn't know that he had once been one.)

Boyington to me had been just another pilot. Then I began to learn more about him. He was then noted for several things: 1. His power of absorption. 2. His pugnacity. 3. His being an ex-Flying Tiger of the Adam and Eve Squadron. 4. His score of 24 Jap planes. 5. His log of over 2,500 hours as a fighter pilot, possibly a world's record for wartime.

Back at Munda, when we used to be raiding Kahili,

Pappy Boyington had become famous for some of his conversations with the Japs. The story went that one of his men asked, "Has anyone seen Pappy?" one afternoon during a scrap.

"I'm busy," Boyington replied. "I've got five Zeros surrounded."

"Where are they?"

"Outside this cloud they've got me in!"

At the time of our party, I was only interested in Boyington for what information I could learn from him about fighting. I supposed that at some time in the future somebody would try to write his story, especially if he managed to get three more planes and break the record. I knew that a writer would seize upon any and all details to build up an interesting story and probably varnish it if he didn't think it was exciting enough. Pappy's story, however, did not need to be altered to provide an unusual but true picture of the fightingest American pilot of them all.*

When you're actually associating with such men as Carl and Boyington, Swett, Walsh, Wilbur Thomas, Hanson, Frazier, Foss, Aldrich, Spears, Smith, Bauer, and all the other aces, you do not look upon them with awe. They are just other pilots who sit across the table and eat with you, whom you shower with, get bombed with and sometimes fight with. You are anxious to learn what you can about how each gets his Japs and manages to bring himself back alive.

Boyington was sitting on my right-hand side and four or five of the men from my squadron were seated at the bench facing us. "Tell us how you got your four Zeros today, Greg," one of them asked.

---

*Boyington's story was published in 1958 by G. P. Putnam's Sons, under the title *Baa Baa Black Sheep*.

"Well, I was going along when I saw a Zero below me so I dived from 18,000 feet down to about 6,000 and boresighted him from fifty feet. He went down in flames. I climbed back up and saw another Zero so I popped down and got him before he knew what was happening. Another Zero that must have been his pal went down and circled the plane that had just gone in, so I dove down and opened up at 100 feet closing to 25 feet and picked him off, kerplop! That Zero just turned over on its back and went straight in from about 100 feet.

"A while after, I was all alone, when I saw nine Tonys. I was above them so I dived down and got the closest man. Then I kept right on going merrily on my way. If I hadn't been so low on gas I might have come back at them, but J—— C——, we were all starting for home and I had been using a lot of gas to get these other planes. I couldn't afford to take a chance like that. If they managed to get between me and home I would use up all my gas supply just maneuvering and wouldn't have enough to get home. Besides I said to myself, 'Now Boyington—you've already got four planes, that's pretty good. Now don't stretch your luck too far and go on home!'"

A Jap submarine thought the fight was all over and was surfacing when Boyington approached. He made a run on the sub and pumped some of his remaining bullets into it. He was low on the water as he made his retirement.

"I don't expect any wingman to follow me in a fight," Boyington told us. "In fact a man can take care of himself if he has the altitude advantage to start with. Of course if the Japs have the advantage, a wingman is the best form of life insurance you have."

"You've got 24½ planes now, haven't you,

Boyington? Are you going to run your score up to 27 to beat all the records and then quit?" I asked.

"No, I don't care too much about beating the record. I used to, but now I want to get 33 planes. When I get that many, I'm going to quit."

"Why 33 planes, won't some other number do just as well—or is that your lucky number?" Yeager asked.

Boyington denied that it was his lucky number, but did not tell us any reason why he chose 33 as the place to stop. He probably was so close to breaking the record he no longer thought too much about it. There were still plenty of Zeros left and he still had several days of combat remaining in the tour.

We began to ask questions about tactics and how to shoot Jap planes. He said that naturally some of us wouldn't and couldn't be expected to do as he had. "I have spent four of the best years of my life learning how to kill Japs. I've found out what to expect a Jap to do under various circumstances and I know pretty well how much of a risk I can take. If the results won't be worth the risk, I just past it by.

"I always pick my target and plan my attack before I start on the original attack. I choose one target and stick to it. You can't do much good by spraying lead over a wide area. Another thing—I never open up until well within range, say 50 or 75 feet. Sometimes I get as close as 25 feet before I pull away. I wish to hell they wouldn't put any tracers in my guns, all you need to do is use your sight.

"If a Jap is diving at you it is generally best to pull up sharply. He's going so fast he can't follow you and then you can come down on him.

"If they would just let me run this show my own way I would have Rabaul knocked out in two weeks.

(It was estimated 145 fighters were based at Rabaul's five airfields.) These boys haven't had combat flying and don't know how to make the most of what they've got. Every time I want a fighter sweep, I've got to go down and argue like hell and get permission from two or three different people. By the time you do all that you don't feel like trying it again.

"The strike today was an example. The fighter sweep was planned by the higher-ups to follow the bombing by one hour. Anyone can plainly see that it would be much better if it came shortly after the bombers arrived over the target area."

Boyington was feeling good by now and was working on his third Bourbon and water.

"What do you say to people back in the States when they come up and ask you how many planes you've shot down?" Foxworth asked.

"If a person back in the States came up to me and asked me how many planes I shot down, whether I had one or one hundred, my answer would be the same. 'How many months have you spent in the jungles with the heat and the insects? How many times have you had malaria? How many times have *you* had to stay in a foxhole all night? How often do *you* get up at 2:30 in the morning to go to work?'

"Nothing makes me madder than to have somone ask me a question like that, or 'Well, how are things going out there?' I used to answer such people—now I just walk away or pretend I didn't hear him."

"How about when I go back to the States and stand beside some Army flyer, who is strung from hell to breakfast with decorations, without having ever shot down a plane, while I'm there with my solitary Air Medal with at least three to my credit?" Foxworth asked.

"There's no reason to feel bad about medals even if a man hasn't shot down a plane," Pappy told him. "He's been out there and he's done his duty. It is just luck whether or not you get any Jap planes—a lot of luck along with a little skill."

Major General Ralph Mitchell had sent Boyington a message of congratulations for his excellent work that day.

The party finally started. Each division of VMF 222 had been given three quarts of whiskey by Colonel Smoak. A riproaring time was anticipated by all.

The coke ran out so Doc Brittingham made a concoction out of powdered milk, elements unknown and firewater. Men with any remaining bottles of whiskey were sent to get them to put into the punch.

The master of ceremonies, Foxworth, stood up on one of the tables. Foxy was persuaded to tell a couple of his stories, and then he toasted our skipper, Al Gordon, who said a few words. Other pilots were toasted until the party almost became a testimonial meeting. Even I was toasted and urged to play the accordion.

"I didn't expect to be forced to play tonight, boys," I told them as I dragged my accordion out from under the table. Then I stood up on the bench and tried to play the Marine Hymn. I nearly fell off the bench and my fingers played the wrong notes. I began to botch the sacred tune up terribly so I yelled for everybody to sing. They responded with wim, wigor and witality and I could hit any note I cared to and still not be heard.

Gunner Lou Schaller was then toasted. Our engineering officer from Coronado, California, he had been in the Marine Corps for many years and had a wife and child waiting for him in the states. He told us what his men had accomplished in keeping our planes in good shape.

Joey Craig was the next man toasted. He got up on top of the table. "I jus' want you-all to know that what Lou Schaller said was true. We've got the best kept planes of any squadron up here. This morning I was taking off up at Torokina and when I was just off the deck the engine conked out on me. I managed to get back on the deck and get slowed down pretty well, before I reached the end of the runway, where I had to groundloop to keep from going off the runway and turning over on my back. Well, it didn't do a thing to the plane. I just want you-all to know that what happened this morning wasn't the fault of Lou Schaller. Lou grounded that plane two or three days ago and this morning one of the mechanics who didn't know his face from a hole in the ground put it back in commission, without asking Lou's permission.

"Everybody here knows that our ground crew get some of the worst planes in the combat area to take care of and just when they get them all in good working order we have to move on up and get some more to start over on and they're the best ground crew up here. That's all I've got to say."

A few toasts later and Pankhurst was called upon. There had been about seventy-five men who received their golden wings in his graduating class with him. Over half of them had been killed in combat or flying accidents. I knew he was thinking of those men as well as our lost pilots of 222 when he said, "Here's to our friends who have gone on before. There's nothing we can say which will bring them back or lessen the pain of losing them. All we can do is to go on doing our duty. May we avenge them. Gentlemen, I now propose a toast to our comrades—may they rest in peace.''

By this time all of us were standing—silently. There was a trace of wetness in many an eye as we silently drank. Never had I felt so close to my dead buddies. Never had they seemed to be so much alive and silently raising their cups in an unseen toast with us.

The next morning, Boyington was dressed in his shorts helping Foxworth to drink the last of his beer. We said good-by and piled on the truck to go down to the strip.

Two canoes came by, rowed by eight natives each, as we waited along the strip for our C-47 to come and pick us up. The day before a 15-man war canoe had come by, inlaid with mother-of-pearl. The natives were gathering for the Christmas season near the missionary's house.

When our C-47 lifted us off the white strip of crushed coral at Vella, I looked back and remembered the two lads who were left behind.

10.
DEATH BEFORE DAWN

WE STEPPED OUT of the plane at Tontouta, New Caledonia, fresh from "R' n R" and a gay New Year's Eve in Sydney, and were blasted by the heat of the subtropical climate. Heat waves rose and engulfed us from the asphalt runway as if trying to stifle us then and there to save the Japs the trouble later on.

It was with a feeling of dread that I left the plane. Only eight hours before we had been in beautiful, wonderful Sydney. It was hard to step out of that happy world into the reality facing us. I knew that the combat tour ahead would be rougher than any we had been through, with the possible exception of Munda. And evidently I was not the only one with misgivings. Most of the men remained silent, but Jesse Leach revealed his thoughts when he remarked, "Lord, I hate to come back to the jungle and what's ahead of us after all the fun I had in Sydney."

If only we had known what was ahead we could have left Jesse Leach, Joey Craig and Huck Lassiter behind and saved their lives.

Instead of continuing on to Espiritu Santo this time, we stopped a hundred miles short at a small island named Efate, where our new rear base was to be.

A long string of Dallas huts extended along the

shoreline of the island, nestling under the pandanus trees. Fifty feet from the front doors, the ocean tide deposited its crabs, coral and sea shells. A wide circular coral shelf of reef extended for a quarter of a mile out to sea and dropped precipitously several hundred feet. Every twelve hours we watched the water covering the reef become shallower as the tide went out, until it was bare, except for shallow pools. At the outer edge of the reef you could look into holes and crevices and watch the waves dash beneath the overhanging shelf. This outer edge created a barrier to the waves so that in stormy weather the spray dashed high and all but submerged a lonely sand dune.

I liked to take my flashlight and walk out after dark on the reef when the tide went down, to look at the night life in the water and gather shells. At midnight if the rest of the men saw a solitary light far out on the reef they knew who it was.

Sometimes I would cross the steppingstones leading from one pool of water to another and my light would reflect on a ripple made by a fish or an eel. Many times I could approach an eel hidden in a cave with only its head sticking out with open jaws, the throat moving in and out as it breathed. Some of the eels startled me when they became confused in their directions and swam toward me instead of retreating.

With a long stick I carried to help me cross the pools of water I flipped eels out of the water and watched them wriggle as furiously as snakes. One eel struck at the wooden stick and grabbed it in his powerful jaw and hung on. I carried it to my beach and almost put it in somebody's hut—but I valued my life too dearly to try the trick.

A shaggy dog belonging to one of the men living a

short distance down the beach would invariably join me out on the reef and along the beach. He loved to catch crabs scuttling for cover in the rays of my flashlight and had the technique of avoiding their pincers down to perfection.

Ponds of water only a few inches in diameter would appear empty, but when I put my eye within a foot of the surface I could see various forms of sea urchins looking like tiny octopi, sea cucumbers wafting their tentacles and innummerable bugs and minnows.

There were a large number of pilots commanded by Captain Jack Richards at Efate. These pilots were put in a "pool" as replacements. They had to spend weeks waiting for their chance to get into combat. The time they spent waiting did not count toward the fulfillment of their overseas tour; only the actual weeks in combat were considered for that. They were a disheartened group of lads. They had tried to get permission to form a squadron of their own, but the request had been denied.

Major Boyington had formed his squadron VMF 214 from just such a group of pilots as these men. Because they were replacements whom nobody seemed to want they called themselves "Boyington's Bastards," but later changed the name to "The Black Sheep."

Those of us already in a squadron were continuously afraid we would get sick, be left behind and be put in the pool. Meanwhile, we worked on our combat tactics and broke in the two new replacements, Lieutenants Clyde A. Dingfelter from Corry, Pennsylvania, and Ralph Langley of Los Angeles, both of whom proved themselves to be good flyers.

We had only been at Efate a few days when an

order came that all of us would have to do some night
flying and make predawn take-offs. It came from
somebody high in command.

We would not be considered experienced in night
flying or night take-offs until we had performed several at Efate, no matter whether or not we had from
one to a hundred hours at other bases. Refusal meant
possible court-martial and transfer to the Efate pool.

That order seemed like the voice of doom to us.
Ace Newlands, our flight officer, went to the field
operations officer to see if our squadron couldn't be
exempted from the order, because we felt we had
already proved our ability by coming through our
experiences at Hawaii, Midway, Munda and Vella
Lavella alive. We felt that any further attempts at
practice just increased our chances of not surviving.
Ace came back from his attempts (after telling the
operations major off), and we had to perform more
night landings than had been called for by the original
order.

When we first heard about the new requirement I
said, ''I'll bet we'll be lucky if that order doesn't kill
somebody.''

''What do you mean, you'll bet—I'm as sure as
shootin' that there will be somebody killed. It will
take two or three deaths before they get sense enough
to change the order,'' Gher told me. ''I only hope our
squadron stays lucky and it isn't any of our boys,
especially with these old beat-up airplanes we're
flying down here. I'll bet they've been in every battle
since Guadalcanal. Most of them should be junked.
While we were up in combat the best planes were
back in the states and in the rear areas; now that
we're back in the rear areas, they've sent the best
planes up to combat. By the time we get back up

there they'll probably all be worn out."

"What d'ya wanta do—live forever?" Ace commented.

Two mornings later the first man was killed.

It was 0415. The first airplane had passed directly overhead on its predawn take-off, awakening us all because it was only about 400 feet high. The roar of the second plane approached and it passed above with a raucous racket. The third man then took off successfully and I remembered in my still sleepy mind one other morning, which seemed a long time ago, when I had been listening to our fighters taking off. I also remembered the jolt it had given me when one of them had failed in a burst of flame and smoke. It had been the fourth man.

For some reason now, I became alert, listening to the fourth man. I heard him when he first applied the throttle. I heard him as he came above me. He sounded lower than any of the others had been. The noise of his engine began to fade. Seconds later, I heard the now-distant roar end unexpectedly in an unmistakable thudding crash—that same can-crunching sound I had come to know so well.

I jumped out of bed and rushed outside, looking seaward for flames or a distant glare. There was nothing to be seen except for the grayness of the moonless predawn.

"Where's the crash?" I heard Lassiter's voice call to me from the next hut.

"I dunno."

Other men were standing in front of their huts, lost in their observations without any flames to guide them. I looked at the sea again. There was no horizon, yet the night was not black. Only a vague indistinct band of grayness melted into the void that was the sea—and the darkness faintly polka-dotted with a few stars, that was the sky.

I went back to bed. Nobody else in my hut had bothered to get up. "Couldn't you see anything, Zed?" Morris asked.

"No, it's too dark out there and he didn't burn."

"Who was it? What happened? Was he killed?" These were the questions that came to my mind. I wished that I had happened to be out on the reef; then maybe I could have saved him.

I was shivering and shuddering and suddenly realized I was cold. After curling up on the canvas cot and wrapping the blanket around me as close as possible, I waited to warm up, but I kept on shivering.

After a time, I looked at my watch. It was 0430. I realized I might as well go to sleep and try to forget it.

When I left the hut at seven, I felt a sickening apprehension. Just off the right side of the sandbar out by the breakers I could see a boat. To the right was the tail and part of the fuselage of an F4U sticking above the surface of the water.

Nobody knew the cause of the crash. Some said they heard the engine spitting as it passed over; others said it sounded okay except the plane was unusually low. A couple of days later, Morris was to advance his own theory from his personal experience.

When we had first arrived at Efate, we received a severe mental blow. Gregory Boyington, the Indomitable, had been shot down!

Three days after we had left Vella Lavella, Boyington had sent one Zero down in flames. He left another smoking, but oil covered his windshield and he was not dead sure of that—his twenty-sixth plane. Three times Pappy had leaned forward and tried to wipe the oil away, but the windstream was too much for him and he had to leave the battle and go home.

The planes were grounded for the next few days because of bad weather. When Pappy and his boys took off on January 3, 1944, he was tense. The Public Information people had made him record-conscious. He had carefully checked all his equipment and the fuel tanks of the plane. His boys knew that it was to be the day that their Pappy was going to do or die to break the jinx of the Marine fighter pilots—26 planes. Joe Foss had tied the record made by Rickenbacker, but hadn't broken it. Pappy had one more to go to tie it and was determined to break it. After that, he wanted to go on and get the rest of his goal of 33 Jap planes.

The Japs hit the Black Sheep as soon as they arrived at Rabaul. Pappy's division split and took on twelve Zeros. His wingman, George Ashmun, followed behind as the old maestro tailed in on a Zero and sent his twenty-sixth torching downward. According to B. J. Matheson, who was leading the second section, the last he saw of Pappy he was diving through a cloud with guns blazing after more Zeros, with his faithful wingman still sticking to him.

That was the last view anyone had of Pappy—the way that he would have chosen for his exit from this world, still fighting and killing Japs.

That evening his heartsick friends went out into the face of a storm to search for Boyington, but they found nothing, not even a trace of wreckage. The chill wind that spread from the revetments to the ready rooms when Boyington didn't come back struck us five days later when we finally learned he was lost.

If the Japs had been able to get Gregory Boyington—the man, above all men, who knew what to expect from a Jap in a fight, who had learned during four long, dangerous years how to hate and how to avenge that hate—then what was the chance for the rest of us, who were rank amateurs by comparison? None of us believed he was lost for good. He was too tough, too hickory-like. There wasn't a man alive who could survive whatever was dished out to him as well as Pappy. He had the sturdy body of the wrestler and the keen mind of the scholar with the spirit and tenacity of the bulldog. Every time I saw Boyington, I always seemed to think of a bulldog. Perhaps it was the set of his jaw. Perhaps it was the legend he had built around himself.

I wondered if Pappy would ever be captured alive, should he have survived the crash. If they did get him alive, how would the Japs treat him? Would they gaze at the formidable ace in awe and respect him for his fighting qualities, or would they revile him for the deaths he had caused and give him their special tortures? Would they kill him at Rabaul or would they send him back to Japan for exhibition?

Weeks later our hopes were to be raised when a report came that a friendly native chief had about twenty Allied flyers safely hidden from the Japs. Our hopes were dashed when a later report claimed that Japs had executed the friendly chieftain.

To add to our mental discomfort, scuttlebutt came that VMF 321, the squadron that relieved us at Vella, had lost 13 pilots, of whom 8 were division leaders!

We had expected them to lose quite a few, because many of them were ex-dive bomber and P-boat (patrol seaplane) pilots trying to be fighter pilots and likely to have difficulties changing the tempo of their thinking in accordance with the great increase in speed of the Corsair, not to mention the swarms of Zeros they would meet over Rabaul.

As usual with such advance information, the true picture was not as bad as it appeared. The pilots of VMF 321, commanded by Eddie Overend, who like Boyington had been a Flying Tiger, came back from their combat tour and told us what was going on up north. They had lost six men in combat and two in operational accidents.

I asked many questions from one of their pilots about the conditions at Bougainville and fighting over Rabaul. "The food and living accommodations at Torokina are pretty good," he told me. "You won't need to take your bedding, because there's an Acorn unit there to take care of you. They have big thick mattresses so you can get a little sleep at night. The Lord knows you'll be needing it. One trip over Rabaul is enough to give you nightmares for the next month!

"We've sure been knocking the planes down up there over Rabaul. There have been 360 shot down so far this month and we've lost 62. We think that 20 of our pilots have been saved by coastwatchers."

"How is 215 doing?" I asked.

"They've shot down nearly 60 planes in the past three weeks. One pilot named Hanson claims 20 of them by himself, in only six hops!"

"They sure must be going to town."

"Yes, but they've had their losses. I don't know

how many or who, but I do know that if we had better planes up there instead of some of the beat-up wrecks, our losses would have been lighter.''

"Still flying the same old crates?"

"Oh, we've got a few of the new ones too, but they're getting pretty well worn now and could all stand a good overhaul. A lot of them have water-injection systems, but we didn't have alcohol to use in them so they might as well have left them off and saved all that weight.''

Ace Newlands was a great kidder and tried to start some scuttlebutt that we would have to use 80-octane gasoline instead of 100 octane and that there were eleven engines failures during the last three days. We caught on to that one in a hurry and it didn't get very far, although it succeeded in worrying several pilots until they learned the truth.

More bad news arrived when I learned the fate of "you bunch of high school prima-donnas" Milton Vedder of VMF 213 and Los Angeles, California.

We had all finished our combat tour at Munda. It was Milt's last. He and his mates were due to go back to the States. In those days it was the rule to send the pilots down to Sydney for one final week of "rest" before returning them to the States. Milt didn't want to go to Sydney, he had nothing to go for. His Australian wife, who was pregnant, had arrived in the United States to wait for him at his parents' home in California.

Milt went to Sydney with one of the planes carrying a portion of my squadron. He constantly harped to Gunner George Schaefer that he was afraid he wouldn't get to go home. That was his biggest worry.

Milt had his own philosophy for charting his life:

"I'm gonna go down the middle, George," he said. "I'm perfectly sober right now, so I am on one side of the line."

"How about the times you get drunk, Milt? What do you call them?" George asked.

"That's the other extreme, on the other side of the line."

"Then how do you figure you're going to strike a happy medium and travel down the middle?"

"Well—George, it's like this. When I'm sober I'm on one side, when I'm drunk I'm on the other side, but I average down the middle!"

Milt's predictions, which seemed so cockeyed at the time, came true. He never did return to the States.

The day before he and his mates were to leave for the States, Milt packed his gear and went around saying, "Going home, going home, going home." He was that happy. He had waited an eternity and been through hell to get back home and the moment was now so close and so sure.

Some of the men began to think that Milt had gone off his nut the way he kept muttering "I'm going home" and sitting on his baggage waiting to go, hours ahead of time.

They began to worry about Vedder and some idiot or idiots had the bright idea to chuck him in the hospital. The rest of his buddies took off for home and Milt stayed behind. These well-meaning people through their blockheaded efforts literally murdered Milt, except that they didn't use knife or bullet. They sent him to a New Zealand hospital and he kept acting worse all the time.

All we heard later was that Milt had committed

suicide. His nerves were just too bad—too much had happened to them and in the end he had decided he would never get home.

Only two days after the fatal predawn take-off it became Morris' turn to make his practice run. Morris seemed to be a past master at hairbreadth escapes. While he was an aviation cadet he had bailed out of a burning plane and still bore the scars on his hands. Since he arrived in the combat zone he had crashed in the water once and bailed out once, besides receiving bullet holes a few inches behind his head. He didn't know it, but when he went out in the dead hours of that morning he was going to have another close shave, without benefit of a razor.

The rest of us had already made our required number of take-offs, but Morris hadn't received a plane fit to fly, so he had to be rescheduled.

The planes woke me up when they roared overhead. I couldn't help but listen. One of them sounded very low. I held my breath expecting to hear the engine suddenly stop and to see the sky light up, but the engine kept up its steady racket and faded into the distance. "I'll bet some poor guy is shaking in his boots right now," I told myself.

After I returned from breakfast I found Morris in our hut. He had just returned from the strip. "Do you know who it was that flew so low over this hut on their predawn this morning, Johnny?"

"Yep, Zed—sure do."

"Well, who was it?"

"Gol darn it, Zed—it was me!"

"I was hoping it wasn't. I thought your plane was a goner for sure."

Major Gordon dropped in with a couple of the

other pilots. He said that he saw Morris losing altitude until he could swear the plane was only five to ten feet off the water. He felt sure Morris was going right in. Then he saw him start to climb at the last instant. Morris said his air speed indicator wasn't working right and showed that he was close to stalling, so he put his nose down to pick up some speed. When he heard the air rushing past his hood faster he pulled out of his dive. He looked at his altimeter and it registered about twenty feet. Due to the lag in the instrument and other errors, he could have been higher—or lower.

"It doesn't take much to cost a man his life in this flying game," was Morris' comment.

Every day that we spent in the "rest" area was just so much more time away from home as far as we were concerned. Strange as it may appear, we were happy to receive the dispatch ordering us to Bougainville for our next tour of combat.

Marine Air Group 12 located at Efate gave us the best sendoff we ever had. The commanding officer, Colonel Guyman, had presented our squadron with all the beer we could carry. Our weight allowance on the C-47's permitted us to take along 33 cases of beer, amounting to nearly eighty dollars' worth. There was even a photographer to take our picture. The colonel and the island's two Red Cross girls were there to see us off. The girls gave a carton of gum to be divided among us and cigarettes for those who wanted them.

The crowning gift was a large box full of roast chicken, bread and jam for us to eat during our long overwater hop. Several cases of fresh eggs were lashed on the forepart of the C-47. The pilot told us to leave our luggage at the rear. (That was the opposite of what most of the SCAT pilots told us. Usually we carried all the weight forward that we could, particularly on take-off.) It was through sad experience that the importance of weight distribution had been learned in the service. After several transports and bombers became airborne their noses came up uncontrollably, due to too much weight aft of the center of balance, and they had stalled in.

Only a few weeks before, a SCAT plane had taken off from Espiritu Santo for Efate carrying mostly Army men. It never arrived and no trace was ever found. The consensus of opinion was that someone had lit a cigarette and the fumes from the spare gasoline tanks located in the cabin must have exploded.

Colonel Willis had been sent to Tontouta, New Caledonia, to take over SCAT a month earlier. He learned he was supposed to run the operations, while another colonel would command the SCAT personnel. He saw Admiral Halsey and told him he wanted no divided command and for one of the two colonels to get the whole shebang. And so the admiral told Willis to take over. He tore out all the so-called "papier mâché" auxiliary fuel tanks mounted in the cabin, which were generally leaky. "If we can't get decent tanks, we won't have any," he said.

"But what if they give us a long mission?" he was asked.

"We just won't do it unless we have the necessary equipment; there's been too many squadrons lost in SCAT planes," was his answer.

No longer did the planes have to be loaded to the bulging point. The new policy was to carry a load no heavier than what the plane could support with only one engine working. In contrast to the 23 pilots and their gear of our first few experiences in SCAT planes, we now only had 10 pilots comprising two divisions.

"All right, boys—all together—let us pray," Turner, the lad from Montana, remarked as we turned and started for the take-off. We were all nervous. Practically the only time we felt nervous was when we rode with SCAT, even though they did have a comparatively good safety record.

We had no sooner climbed to a hundred feet, still flying quite slow, when the pilot made a sharp turn to the left. None of us liked that at all. We flew over the sandbar and I looked down at the remains of the wrecked Corsair. Only the part aft of the cockpit was visible; the plane had broken into two pieces when it struck. The front part containing the pilot had been thrown forward—just enough to sink off the edge of the reef into hundreds of feet of water.

We took off at 0830, landed at the bomber strip at Espiritu Santo and refueled, then took off again. We counted many ships in the harbor, including two aircraft carriers and a battleship. It was from Espiritu Santo, our closest base to Guadalcanal, that our first attempt to stem the tide of Jap conquest was launched.

A few hours afer leaving the New Hebrides, we flew near the stretch of water where the giant aircraft carrier *Wasp* had been sunk and the *Saratoga* damaged. A few hundred miles to the north was the place where its sister ship, the *Hornet*, was sunk during the battle of Santa Cruz.

The country around Henderson Field was covered with sheets of water. We landed at 1400, and as we rolled to a stop Hobbs said, "I've never seen so much mud since I left Munda. Don't anybody take off your

Mae Wests or you'll drown!''

At chow that evening I was agreeably surprised to see Lieutenant Cornelius, a medium height, huskily built, lighthaired lad from Durango, Colorado, who had been a roommate of mine when we were flying ''Yellow Perils'' as cadets at Corpus Christi, Texas. I also saw George Petty, one of the fellows I kept bumping into so often all the way through training that we had eventually introduced ourselves to each other. They had flown their TBF's down from Bougainville with another pilot to get 90 cases of beer for their torpedo bombing squadron. An hour later they dropped over to the hut and we had a bull session about what had been going on at Bougainville.

''We had a little excitement up there a couple of days ago,'' George Petty told us. ''Some Army pilots reported seeing a carrier up at Rabaul. Operations immediately organized an emergency strike on shipping. We went up there and couldn't find anything. I think they had mistaken a small island or a cargo vessel for the carrier. We got back so late that most of the planes had to make night landings. Two F4U's collided in mid-air and killed both pilots. One of them was the skipper of VMF 211, Major Hopkins, who had replaced Major Harvey when he was put in Operations. Another F4U spun in and two more of them crashed when they landed. Only one SBD crashed.''

''On the whole we haven't lost many bombers,'' Cornelius said. ''The fighters have been doing a damned good job at covering us and have been losing a few of their own men instead. VMF 215 has set a new squadron record for the number of planes shot down. They've really been goin' to town. They lost Stidger though, when his engine conked out.

"Another squadron up there has really been doing good, too. They have lost three men so far this trip and knocked down around 80 Zeros, Tonys and the new Jap Tojo, which looks like a Zero that has been put in a vise and squeezed together slightly from both ends.

"I suppose you boys are going to relieve VMF 311. They've got a wonderful record, 71 Zeros and lost only one pilot. You should have been there the past few days. We've really been knocking them down over Rabaul. One day we got 35 Japs and lost three of our planes, another time our men knocked down 47 and lost five. Lately though, the score has become more in favor of the Japs. They seem to be catching on. They only lost 32 planes and got 15 of ours the other day."

We were airborne before dawn the next morning and when it became light I could see that we were flying only 100 feet above the ocean. We had encountered a front, and clouds were thick above us. Suddenly we entered a rain squall and bits of cloud flew by and blanked out the water even at our low altitude. Our hearts did a flip-up. The pilot abruptly climbed a couple of hundred feet until we were able to see the water again. We were nearing some mountainous islands and the pilot wisely didn't want to fly in the clouds.

It is impossible to describe the feeling that flight gave me, aside from the weather and scenery. It was with the knowledge of all the losses over Rabaul and the increased resistance the Japs were making that I went to Bougainville. There was only one bright spot: it sounded as if the chances were very good of shooting Zeros.

Almost the biggest thrill in all our flying experiences came when we arrived at Torokina. We flew over the strip at 400 feet. The visibility was so bad we lost sight of the strip a few seconds after passing over it. The pilot turned to the right, then over into an extremely steep left turn. I was on the deck on my knees. I should have been praying at that moment, but I was looking through the low windows at the water, hoping our long wing wouldn't hit and that the pilot wouldn't stall us out at the rate he was pulling us around in the turn. I had never heard of anyone being in a steeper turn in a transport plane at that low altitude.

We didn't spin in but straightened out, and we found ourselves back over the strip heading seaward at an acute angle. The pilot whirled us over into another left turn—even steeper than before. I saw the wing tip clearing the water by some fifty feet or less. The landing strip came into view from out of the clouds. I could see we needed to hold our rate of turn to make the field.

When we arrived at the point where the plane should normally straighten out, I saw, much to my dismay, a tree rushing for us. The left wing would surely hit it! At the last instant the pilot lifted the wing over the tree, both to miss it and to move farther to the right to hit the center of the runway.

Trees swept past the wings and missed only by inches. We touched the ground in a wheel landing, nearly halfway down the strip. The plane had good brakes luckily, and we were able to stop before we ran off the runway.

All during the violent maneuvers the Army nurse on board kept saying, "Don't worry, everything is all right." She wasn't frightened. The truth of the matter was, she didn't know enough about flying to know when we were in danger.

When the pilot walked through the cabin, Turner told him, "For a while there I sure had my molars achewing on my heart."

"You weren't the only one," the pilot replied. "I was plenty scared myself."

"If I had known the pilot was scared too," Jones told us, "I'd have jumped!"

Nevertheless, we were at Torokina fighter strip, Bougainville, ready to start another combat tour, and, for some of us, the last few days of our lives.

11.
BOUGAINVILLE

IT WAS RAINING outside, a fine misty rain. With the usual inexplicable logic exhibited by sheep following a goat, everyone left the cabin of the airplane, except Yeager, the nurse and myself. When they got outside the plane, they huddled under the wing to keep dry!

After a ride of a couple miles in a jam-packed truck, we arrived at the pilots' area and were assigned tents by "good ol' George" Schaefer, who had preceded us by two days to make advance arrangements.

We lived in tents across the road from the messhall, a very handy location. Our tent differed from the others we had used in that it had walls made from mosquito netting, instead of no walls at all. It was also built on stilts two feet off the ground. Above all things the mattresses took our eyes; they were many times thicker and much wider than the pads we had been using.

At evening chow that 2nd day of February, 1944, I was happy to see my friend George Sanders and know he was still alive. He picked his plate up and brought it over to my table and we talked. I learned about how his squadron had lost its men.

"Sammy Stidger practically gave his life trying to bring his plane in to a landing instead of bailing out or making a water landing. He wanted to save the airplane when the motor began to miss. It conked out before he could make it back to the field and the plane crashed and exploded.

"One of the missing pilots was Jack Knight, a big jolly fellow, who was flying wing on me. As we neared Rabaul he dived away and toward home. The last thing I saw of him he was going into some clouds over Duke of York Island. John," George said, "I don't know how I'll ever face his folks, after I tell them what happened."

"Good hell, George, it wasn't your fault. Anybody would have done the same as you and assumed he was returning to base and thought he could make it okay. If we all went back every time with planes that drop out, there wouldn't be any fighters left to protect the bombers."

"Well, it's been worrying me for the past few nights. Of course plenty of other fellows have lost their wingmen. I guess it's just something you've got to expect when you're fighting a war.

"A few minutes after Jack started for home I joined a two-plane section comprised of Dick Braun and E. N. Moore. A Zeke made an abrupt pull-out and settled smack on Moore's tail. I turned toward the Zero and shot him off the F4U's tail, but it was too late. The U went straight down with flames coming out of the wing roots. Then the Jap's buddy settled on me and I had to dive out.

"We got nineteen sures and six probables that day. Hanson got five, and Captain Warner, our Exec, got four. We lost the two men in combat and Sammy Stidger in operations on that hop."

We arrived at my tent and I recognized two pilots passing by. One was D. C. Gill, the only other surviv-

ing Marine beside myself from our original class of
Aviation Cadets at Oakland, California. He was a
short, quiet, shy pilot, a product of the C. A. A.
primary and secondary flying courses before he
joined the service. He now had two Zeros to his
credit. The pilot with him was Coffman, a light-
complexioned slender lad I became acquainted with
during the latter part of our cadet training. They were
both from VMF 212, the squadron that had relieved
mine at Midway.

VMF 217 and VMF 218 were new squadrons at
Bougainville, having arrived only a couple of days
before we did. VMF 218 was an unusual Marine
squadron, because all of their planes were the
newest. Originally the new planes were to have been
distributed equally among the fighting squadrons, but
218 grabbed them and after a while it was decided to
let them keep the planes.

The new planes with the bubble canopies did not
seem to be quite as fast as some of the older type,
because of increased wind resistance. The seat was
six inches higher and six inches farther ahead so that
it gave better visibility, but it also put the pilot so far
ahead of his armor plating that he felt like a duck in a
shooting gallery. Only when the enemy was directly
behind could the pilot feel adequately protected.

VMF 212 and VMF 215 had an arrangement under
which all of their pilots flew one day and took the next
off, while the rest of the squadrons on Bougainville
flew. With the arrival of our squadron and VMF 218
and VMF 217, the system was changed so that half of
every squadron flew every day, with the two halves
alternating days.

The Navy squadron VF 17 was also doing its stuff
at Bougainville. The Skull-and-Crossbones Squad-

ron flying the F4U Corsair were led by Lt. Commander Tommy Blackburn of Chevy Chase, Maryland. Blackburn was friendly, but very aggressive. He fought hard to get good equipment and good tactical positions in the strikes for his squadron. His marvelous maintenance crew kept a high percentage of his planes on the availability list all the time.

Despite all the Zeros the Navy squadron claimed to be shooting down, many Marines were burned up at the very thought of VF 17. The Navy squadron had 52 pilots and 36 planes compared to a Marine squadron's complement of 40 pilots and 18 planes. Blackburn's squadron was assigned positions in the strike much the same as the Marines, but that left him with several planes not being used. When it was too late for plans to be changed, VF 17 would notify Operations and request permission to send up all their extra planes as a roving high cover. The Flying Foxholes of the Army, the P-38's, had been flying so high and roaming so far the strike needed more roving cover.

After VF 17's roving high cover had met with great success, the Marine pilots began to gripe so loud it reached official ears and Marine squadrons got their turn at roving high cover—that is, all but my squadron.

The Japs used to take off and wait near Wide Bay on the far side of New Britain. Then, when our bombers and fighters would come by, ready to start their bombing run, the Japs would jump them. Blackburn advanced the idea of a "Statue of Liberty Play." Some of our fighters were to circle back after the bombing run and surprise the Japs about the time they were getting ready to land. No particularly sensational results came from his juicy idea, however.

The Skull-and-Crossbones had thirteen aces. Blackburn himself had eleven Japs to his credit. Lt. Ira C. "Ike" Kepford of Muskegon, Michigan, had sixteen and was the high-score man for the Navy at that time. He had been a flashy halfback at Northwestern University a few years before.

A race was on between VMF 215 and VF 17 to see who would break the Navy record. VMF 215, "The Fighting Corsairs," broke the record and rolled up an all-time high by destroying 135½ Nip planes before being sent back to rest. When they were sent back a week or so after my squadron's arrival they had created the record of 85½ planes shot down in one month, 104½ planes destroyed in a single combat tour of six weeks, and ten aces in a single squadron, besides their grand total of 135½ enemy planes during eighteen weeks of action.

Our sister squadron had begun its third tour with less planes to its credit and more casualties than VMF 222, but now they had completely outstripped us and it looked as if we could not possibly catch them.

After The Fighting Corsairs left the area, the Navy squadron permitted them to hold the record for only a few days and then surpassed them. VF 17 went away credited with 154 Jap planes destroyed, seven ships and seventeen barges sunk and more combat stories and hours than any other squadron.

VMF 215 had lost 13 pilots in combat and operational accidents, giving it a ratio of slightly less than 10½ Japs planes for each pilot lost. VF 17 had also paid through the nose for its achievement, losing 20 planes and 12 pilots.

I was uncertain whether to feel glad or sorry we hadn't been in on most of the heavy fighting. I knew if we had been, we too would have rolled up a sizable score and we too, unless we were very lucky, would have lost several of our squadron mates in exchange. On the other hand, we were arriving for combat at a time when there were usually only forty or fifty Zeros attacking the strike formation instead of the seventy to one hundred that used to come up regularly, and the Japs now rising to the attack were harder to get.

Don Aldrich of Chicago and Harold Spears of Newark, Ohio, both from VMF 215, were inside my tent talking to Yeager and Morris when I walked in. Aldrich was the second-ranking ace in his squadron with a score of 16 Japs, and Spears was third with 12. Robert Hanson, a comparatively new man in their squadron who had been transferred from VMF 214, had shot down 20 planes during the past few weeks of the combat tour, raising his total score to 25! With still a few days to go it looked as if he undoubtedly would break Rickenbacker's and Joe Foss' and Gregory Boyington's joint record of 26.

"Well, men, what's the secret of your success?" I asked.

"Mainly luck," Spears replied. "But there is a certain amount of aggressiveness necessary also."

Aldrich added, "When you can see a plane you can get without exposing yourself unnecessarily to Japs waiting above—okay. Go and get him.

"Above all, don't get separated from the bomber formation by going out wide and coming in on the Zeros by surprise. The Zeros are getting smart now. They form two or three different groups along the route they think we'll follow; then they change off with each other in staging their attacks.

"The little yellow bastards have been very unethical. Instead of coming in after the bombers, most of them are content to sit up there above us and try to pick off our fighter planes whenever they get the chance. We've got enough planes now so that we can have a roving high cover which ought to have good pickings and at the same time help out the poor devils protecting the bombers. It's a hell of a feeling to sit there in your cockpit and watch the Zeros flying lazily off to the side, doing slow rolls, loops and anything else they can think of. Whenever they want to, they form a regular column and play follow the leader. They fly over you and as soon as one of the fighters gets in an exposed position in his weave, one of the Japs is always in the right position to make a run on him.''

Don Aldrich was to run his score up to twenty planes within the next few days, to rate among the great fighter pilots of this war. He had been wounded twice, but not seriously. After returning to the States he was decorated with the Navy Cross, Distinguished Flying Cross, the Air Medal and the Purple Heart with star. He didn't get the one he wanted most, the Congressional Medal of Honor, although if his achievements had been written up in a more specific form he probably would have. Don's buddy, Harold Spears, ran his score up to fifteen before he was sent back to the States and was given two Air Medals.

They told us about the new type of radio installed in some of the planes. It was called VHF (very high frequency) and was in the same range of frequency as radar. All static was eliminated and the voice was heard very clearly. The disadvantage was that the radio waves traveled only in line of sight. If the pilot you wished to contact was blocked from view of your antenna by your wing, he would not receive the message.

I was appointed Squadron Duty Officer the next day, our first flying day of the combat tour. I was at first angry at being grounded, but consoled myself with the thought it might be for the best and I could learn something from the other men's experiences.

We were to have a busy day getting things in shape for the pilots. In the morning we drove down to Fighter Operations in a jeep, only to find half of the dirt floor covered with water. The shedlike building was built half above and half below ground and protected by sandbags. The operations officer, Major Harvey, was not there so we drove to the ready room belonging to VMF 218, which they were to share with us until we got one built. It was only a bare pole framework covered over at the top with a tarpaulin. There was nothing to put our chutes on and no truck to haul the pilots to the planes.

I rode down to the operations center to the briefing with the four division leaders whose pilots were going on the strike. An Army officer gave the briefing. Evidently the Army, Navy and Marines were each trying to run things. Because the Marines provided most of the cover, it was only logical they should have most of the control.

It was a good thing I took notes at the briefing, because when we returned to squadron I was asked to tell the pilots everything that was said; then Major Gordon added a few points I hadn't covered completely, until everyone knew what was going to happen. I borrowed VMF 218's truck to take the pilots out to their planes, which I assigned after first learning which planes belonged to our squadron and where they were located. Everything went fine until some of the pilots discovered that the new Navy oxygen mask with a built-in microphone (actually the old Army type) had no connecting cord to the transmitter. The pilots of VMF 211 had taken them back with them.

I rushed madly around to all the supply houses in a jeep and learned there were no cords on the island. Some would have to be flown up from Munda.

Our pilots took off anyway, although most of them would have to remove their oxygen masks whenever they wanted to transmit over the radio. Some had planes with the old gray Navy masks and were using throat mikes.

Morris failed to get off the ground because both of the planes I assigned him to fly proved to be unfit. Turner came back when his wing tank purging apparatus sprung a leak and poured carbon dioxide into his cockpit. We had emergency bottles of CO_2 and just before going into action against the enemy we were supposed to release the gas into our wing tanks, supposedly to prevent the tanks from catching fire if hit by bullets.

Yeager soon landed also. He became an odd man in a three-plane division and couldn't get anybody to scissor with him, so he came back all the way from New Ireland by himself.

I waited in a jeep to pick up our pilots when they began to land at 1330. When Levine's plane landed, I saw that the top third of his rudder had been shot away. Another plane came in for a landing with a right aileron shot off and the lower half of the rudder completely gone. It landed on a flat tire.

I crossed each of my squadron's planes off my list as they landed. They all came back!

The men gave their reports in the ready tent. Sapp

had one Zeke for sure and one probable. Wilson one sure, Major Gordon one probable, Levine one probable.

Sapp got his probable off Levine's tail. He got his sure kill when a Jap came up in front of him in the last part of an Immelman. Levine had chased one Zero down in a vertical dive and left it smoking, but didn't see what happened to it after that.

It was VMF 218's first combat flight. They lost two men and got two Japs.

Probably the biggest news of the day was that Hanson, "The One-Man Air Force," never came back. I talked to Spears about what happened to Hanson. He said: "I heard him call me up and say he was going down to strafe Cape Alexander. He wanted to know if it was all right. I told him, 'It's all right with me. You don't need to ask me whether it is all right or not. You've got more planes than I have.'

"He strafed all right. Some ack-ack shot at him and tore off part of one wing. He pulled up low over the water and skimmed along to make a water landing. Then one wing hit the water and he cartwheeled over and over in a big splash of water. Nothing but debris and an oil slick remained. That is why he never managed to get his twenty-sixth plane."

There seemed to be a 26-plane jinx on the Marine Corps. No matter how close, nobody seemed to have been able to surpass the mark. Hanson was lost exactly one month after Boyington and one day before his twenty-fourth birthday.

Robert M. Hanson, USMCR, looked much the same as any other pilot. He was about average height. His hair was rather blond with a tendency toward the brown and if my memory serves me rightly he had blue eyes. When you saw him stripped, you noticed he was more muscular than many of the pilots, but you would never have known he had been the light heavyweight and heavyweight wrestling champion of the United Provinces.

Hanson grew up in Lucknow, India. He was the son of Methodist missionary parents, who still claimed Newtonville, Massachusetts, as their family residence. After gaining fame as a wrestler he decided to attend Hamline University in the United States. In 1938 en route to the States he bicycled his way through Europe. The multilingual youth, able to speak Spanish, German, French and Hindustani, arrived in Vienna at the time of Hitler's *Anschluss*.

At Hamline in St. Paul, Minnesota, he supported himself by working in a cafeteria and evenings as a night club bouncer. He starred during the daytime in football and track. After beginning training in May 1942, he succeeded in winning his gold wings at Corpus Christi in 1943. He reported to his squadron in the South Pacific on October 6, 1943.

In combat, Hanson had performed his duty well but was originally luckless when it came to getting Japs. Then he began to hit his strides and knocked a few Jap planes down, was forced down himself and declared missing in action for a few days. But he returned.

January 1944 came along and with it the opportunity to meet as many enemy planes as he desired, with some to spare. Hanson realized that as a wingman he would never have as much chance of getting Japs and at the same time Jappies attacking from the rear would probably shoot at the wingman first, because he would be closest to them. Hanson must have figured things out for himself because he began to go off all alone to surprise the Japs waiting to pounce on the approaching formation.

Hanson's teammates didn't like him to go away by himself, because their training had been founded upon close teamwork. Then Hanson began to hit the jackpot and rocketed to fame and top position among the aces of the South Pacific. In exactly six consecutive flights in seventeen days he set a record which stands today—a record of twenty sure kills, bringing his total to twenty-five, one short of the existing mark.

Only a few days remained before his squadron would leave the combat zone. He had flirted so often with death he could laugh at her, but this, the third day of February, 1944, she decided to embrace him, and nothing remained behind, only some debris and an oil slick and a record.

12.
BLOODY RABAUL

THERE IS NOTHING like fighting a war to make a boy grow up. Levine, who gave us the impression at first that he needed to grow up, was no longer continually bewailing the fact he hadn't had a chance to fight the Japs. On his first flight from our Bougainville base he returned a wiser and better man. A 20 mm through his right wing next to the fuselage, another cannon shell in the tail and a 7.7 mm through the plastic canopy, which caused some of the broken plastic to trickle down his neck and made him think for a moment that he had been wounded, had converted him into one of the disciples of fighter-pilot doctrine.

His was the same combat metamorphosis the rest of us had gone through. Keen at first to fight the Zeros, no matter how many there were, we all changed after our first real contact with them. We who survived were able to evaluate their dangers and their shortcomings with more accuracy. We became more cunning, ready to strike at their openings and cover up our own. At the same time most of us were able to evade the traps the Japs set to lure unsuspecting fighter pilots away from the main formation.

As usual, Koetsch hadn't neglected to bring home a Jap souvenir from that first strike of his third combat tour. It was a 20-mm cannon hole through his left wing which had put his three machine guns on that side completely out of action.

It was a well-known fact that the strikes on Rabaul served to "separate the men from the boys." We always knew that at least one pilot would not be coming back and that we would be lucky if less than three or four failed to return. If it wasn't a fighter plane it would be a bomber. If not the Jap fighters it would be the intense AA. It was a strain upon everyone to go on those hops and some of the fellows weakened. We heard the pilots of one squadron denounce one of their men. Outwardly he was doing his duty, taking off with the rest of the fighters and returning about the same time. They found out, though, that he purposely became separated from the formation not long after they had passed beyond Bougainville, then would circle for a couple of hours until the planes began to come back. He would join in the race for home unobtrusively and to all observers had been with them all the time. He did that trick once too often, and his suspicious squadron mates purposely checked up on him.

Another favorite trick of the chicken-livered pilots, who were afraid to go to Rabaul but didn't want their cowardice known, was to take off as usual and then, when the strike had gone so far from their base they couldn't possibly get back in time to be sent out again, return and land and report some minor plane trouble to the mechanics, who often were not able to find anything wrong. Sometimes there was something wrong, such as the oxygen bottle being too low on pressure or the electrical gun sight needing a new globe. The pilot would claim he hadn't found it out until after he had taken off.

I had strong fears of going on the strikes, but the desire to get some Japs, coupled with my fear of failing in the performance of my duty, superseded the fear of losing my life. We all wanted to go on fighter sweeps, or as roving high cover where our job was to knock the enemy down or disperse him, but we hated to go just to protect the bombers, for we knew the Japs liked to pick off the fighters rather than take the more dangerous chance of penetrating the fighter cover to get to the bombers. The Army B-24's and B-25's were rarely attacked by the Japs, but the Marine SBD's and TBF's were not completely ignored by any means. We fighter pilots preferred to escort the faster Army bombers. We presented less of a target to the Japanese because of our speed, and these bombers did not go into dives in which they became vulnerable.

Our third night on Bougainville a division from across the path was in my division's tent—Koetsch, Hazlett, Mack, Carrell and their leader Okie. We were holding a regular bull session.

"I don't see how we are winning anything in this war, everyone seems to be out for himself," Carrell said. He then went on to give us his own picture of military life in general. How he got his information, I don't know. "The Marines ordered the P-61 (North American Black Widow, which was then the newest model announced to the public, supposed to be a formidable fighter plane with two 2,000-hp engines and two gunners) and the Army wanted it and got it. Now they're going to use it for a night fighter."

"Wonder where they're going to use it?" Huck asked.

"Probably over Kansas City and maybe as far west as Los Angeles."

"The service is the most disorganized organization I've ever seen," Carrell commented. "Here's the way it works. The Navy orders some Norden bombsights and tells them 'We'll take all you can make.' The Army sees the sight is a good thing and wants some but the Navy has the contracts sewed up and won't give them any. The only way the Army can get any is to say 'I'll give you some B-24's for some sights.' That's the only way we can get B-24's for the Marines and then they can only be used for photographic purposes. They won't give us a B-24 for bombing, 'cause the Army wants all of them."

"If you would go back to the States and if someone came up to you and asked how your equipment was," one of the others added, "you would really get your head in a sling if you told him how poor the condition of our planes and equipment was. The military would probably stick you in a brig on bread and water for thirty years."

"Yes, and if you said anything against MacArthur or any other general, no matter how true, you'd be fried for life," another pilot chimed in.

"It's too bad that we can't tell the American public what is really going on without getting hung for it."

"This traffic pattern is so screwed up that at least two men have been killed in it already. What they ought to do is to have a certain point that all planes must pass over, then make the fighter and the dive bombers stay at their assigned altitudes. Then maybe we'd have some air discipline around here, instead of having to dodge SBD's and TBF's every time we came near the field and vice versa."

"They ought to install a small-pressure gauge on the CO_2 bottles so we can tell if it is good or not. As it is we don't know for sure whether our wing tanks are purged or not. The pilots who think they are, when they aren't, rarely get back to complain. It's just like trying to bring back a parachute that doesn't work," I interposed.

"They ought to put some kind of a guard over the CO_2 bottles," Morris added, "so that when a guy reaches down to purge his tanks he doesn't twist the emergency handle that forces the wheels down. One guy did that the other day over Rabaul and couldn't keep up with the rest. He never got back."

"Nobody will take any action until they get damned good and mad. Then they will go up to the colonel or the general and tell him the story. Then maybe the mud will hit the fan."

"Yeah, like it did back at Munda when Carrell got the skipper's permission and went straight to General Moore and told him about the guns being so rusty and dirty that they would jam after the first couple of seconds. He made things pop among the ordinance men and we were able to depend on having at least one gun that wouldn't fail us."

We heard a loud explosion, but we didn't pay any attention to it. We thought it was just one of our artillery pieces shooting at the Japs. A few moments later there was another explosion. We stopped talking to listen. *Balloom,* BALLOOM, BALLOOM! Each explosion grew louder.

"Bombs!" we yelled spontaneously.

Levine and Hazlett led the rush out the door. *"Somebody shut the light off,"* they bellowed over their shoulders as they jumped down the steps. Meanwhile, I was busily burning my fingers as I unscrewed the light bulb. With Yeager a close second, I ran out the door barefooted and leaped into a foxhole. I rolled aside to get out of the way so Yeager wouldn't land on me. The next bomb burst close and simultaneously with Yeager's entrance.

Only three narrow logs were strung across the width of the slit trench we chose to call our foxhole. And nearly ten of us were trying to crowd under the protection of the logs.

Ack-ack belched and seachlights searched. They picked up the plane at 16,000 feet, a Betty, one of the largest of Jap bombers. Some 50-caliber machine guns sprayed streams of tracers uselessly into the sky. They would burn out after the first two thousand feet.

"The guy who ordered those .50 calibers to fire out there ought to be shot himself," Carrell exclaimed vehemently. It made us all angry, but at that they did as much good as the heavy stuff.

Some pilots came by later on their way to get a jeep and ride around to view the damage. They came back and told us the bomb had destroyed one TBF and damaged four or five others.

I'd put on my shoes and steel helmet a few minutes later, when we had another raid. The bombs dropped a long way off. There was a beautiful large, bomber's moon and a good high cloud cover for him to hide in. We could hear him zooming around up there above the clouds trying to worry us—and he did. Our listening was rewarded when something came whistling down out of the sky. We ran for the foxhole. Nothing happened. Two more whistles came out of the clouds and stopped near us.

"Those are either delayed-action bombs or duds," Hazlett maintained.

"Yes—or else some beer bottles they tossed at us," Yeager answered.

Our ground forces had advanced their lines to the Torokina River on the east and a few hundred yards short of the Laruma River to the west. That formed the width of our perimeter defense and our beachhead extended from the ocean to the foothills inland. Altogether it was about four miles deep by twelve miles wide.

Every night, Marine and Army artillery shelled the pass in the mountains traversed by the Numa Numa Trail to discourage Jap reinforcements. Whenever targets were discovered by scouting Grasshopper planes during the daytime our artillery opened up sporadically.

To the east, however, our men had occasional fights. A few days before, the Japs had got one of our armored tanks on the other side of the Torokina River. Because the Japs usually had nothing to stop them, our tanks roamed at will. They succeeded in disabling the one tank, however. One man was left to guard it while the rest of the crew returned for help in another tank. When they came back they were fired upon by Japs, who had captured the disabled tank and killed the guard.

The Navy and Marines estimated 45,000 Japanese on Bougainville of whom 25,000 were troops in moderately good condition and the others laborers. During January, a total of 368 Jap planes were shot down over Rabaul and we lost 64 of ours. That meant the Japanese had to replace their air force at Rabaul three times during the month. The amount of shipping had dropped to less than half of what it was. The enemy realized the danger their most important base for the Solomons was in and began to make Rabaul a less strategic target by using New Ireland with its base of Kavieng for supplies. It was believed most of their airplane reinforcements came from the Phillippines through the Celebes Islands to New Britain, besides coming down from Japan via the Japanese Pearl Harbor of the Pacific—Truk.

One day 49 Jap planes had been knocked down from over Rabaul, yet the next day they came up and performed aerobatics in view of our bombing formation as cocky as ever!

What kind of effect on the morale of the Jap pilots did these enormous losses have? How did they feel when they returned to their base an hour after taking off to find that half or more of their outfit never came back from the single fight? Scuttlebutt had an answer for this. The rumor went around that the Jap pilots were required to land at airfields different from the ones from which they took off. By thus rotating the bases, the pilots lost track of their mates and never knew whether the missing men were shot down or just at a different airfield.

It was only about three days after they had lost their super ace, Hanson, that the Fighting Corsairs left combat to go back to the rest area, from which the remaining members of the original squadron would leave for the States, having had three six-week tours of combat. They had been commanded on their third tour by Major Robert G. Owens of Greenville, South Carolina, who was credited with shooting down seven Japs plus five probables, and who had survived a crash water landing thirty miles from the Torokina airstrip after his plane was shot up. He took many of my friends back with him, and others who had come in as replacements and had lived through some tough fighting. In their tours they had seen the thickest of the fighting in the Solomons and had witnessed the near death of enemy airpower in the South Pacific, an end to which they had contributed greatly.

My squadron had been at Bougainville for seven

reeling days when we lost Joey Craig.

Joe was flying an F4U with its plastic glass canopy cracked and discolored. There were no replacements so every airplane that would fly was pressed into service, but any pilot flying that particular plane was practically blind on one side. As they were leaving the target of Rabaul, scissoring over the bombers, Craig's wingman, U. V. Johnston, a lanky, frecklefaced replacement pilot, had his throttle jammed wide open. He tried to close it to decrease his speed, for he was running away from Craig. Something was wrong. Johnston couldn't pull his throttle closed at all. He looked back in farewell at Joe and saw that he was apparently safe from the Japs.

Johnston had to land his plane with throttle wide open. He managed to do it by decreasing the propeller RPM and shutting off his engine momentarily with the mixture control on the idle cutoff position. The mechanics found that a nut had dropped off the control, thus preventing the changing of the throttle position.

Joe never came back.

Gunner Schaefer inquired around and learned that another pilot had seen a Zero attack an F4U in a high-side run, from a direction which would have been on the blind side of Joe's cockpit. The Zero hit him hard the very first run and was in turn, but unsuccessfully, hopped by the pilot Schaefer talked to. It was believed Craig went down near the mouth of the Warangoi River. It was the last time he was ever seen.

I had been on several Rabaul strikes when February 12th arrived, a day which I shall always remember.

Schaefer woke us up at 0530 and we went across the street to eat grapefruit juice, toast and powdered eggs. We then drove the carryall to the ready tent and used its lights to illuminate the bulletin board, while the SDO (Squadron Duty Officer) assigned a plane to each pilot.

Okie McLean's division was given the dawn patrol. The rest of us were to stand by on scramble alert until the time came to take off on the daily Rabaul strike.

Huck Lassiter drove the carryall out to the planes we were to fly. I got off the front fender and climbed aboard #835. Huck went on to the next plane, #798. We revved the engines and tested them, then drove back to the ready tent and played checkers while we waited for take-off time. At 0930 we taxied out to take off for the strike. Morris was leading with Levine as his wingman. I was section leader with Lassiter to fly on my wing.

We took off with forty-eight fighters and rendez-voused with sixty-two SBD's and TBF's. There was the usual slow flying on the way to the target to conserve all possible fuel. The SBD's and TBF's couldn't fly very fast at best.

The Japs on the ground had more to fear from the dive bombers because they were so accurate, and the Zeros in the air had less to fear because of the smaller number of free gunners as compared to the Army bombers.

We began our weave as we neared New Ireland. We used the baffle weave, the logical outgrowth of our former attempts to have each section scissor with the other section of its division all the time. In the baffle weave each section could scissor with anybody it liked. The only planes that had to stay together were the two planes that composed a section.

It was just like a long, winding snake dance. The lead section at the front of the formation would follow a zigzag course above the bombers and all the other sections behind would follow the leader. The weave worked fine, because there was always a section with its guns pointed outward as the section ahead exposed its tails and started inward. Then the two planes in turn protected the tails of the Corsairs ahead of them.

The layers of planes above us began coming down too close. We had to dodge, slip and duck to avoid mid-air collisions. I always had to remember that I had a man flying a few feet below me.

I saw that Huck was lagging, so I throttled back to enable him to catch up. Then we stayed close together. When we passed over New Ireland I heard Johnny Morris call Levine and say he had to return to base because his wing tanks wouldn't purge.

We arrived near Rabaul. Ack-ack began to come up—a thick curtain of black and brown smokeballs. The dive bombers began their dive. AA exploded 500 feet below us. Not wishing to fly through the AA, I made a turn at 10,000 feet with some other fighters until I was to the right of the worst part of the AA.

Huck moved away from me and into battle formation as we began a steep dive, zigzagging as we went. I felt tense for a moment, then relaxed. The town of Rabaul with several vacant spots in the middle passed to the left as we flew over the outskirts and headed toward Simpson Harbor. Lights winked at us from the edge of the town and in the rim of the mountains. AA exploded to the left and to the right at our altitude. F4U's were off to the right and behind us.

I looked vigorously for Japs. We were in the stage

of the raid at which they liked to begin their attack. My head swiveled from side to side and back again.

Huck was lower than I was so I steepened my dive. Our speed was terrific. Lakunai airfield scooted past my port wing at nearly 300 knots. We began to level out at 3,000 feet. The field appeared to be grassy and dirty with a great many pockmarks on each side of the runway. Huge clouds of dust towered into the air above it.

The bombers were ahead and about 2,000 feet below us when I saw Huck falling behind me. I throttled back slightly and he caught up. F4U's and F6F's were behind and above us about 5,000 feet.

Huck had moved in closer. I smiled at him and could see a grin on his face. We were both happy to be aloft and unharmed.

I looked backward again as I searched the sky. A Zero performed an amazing pull-up. Perhaps he had been trying to catch Huck and me, because he was behind us. He zoomed straight into the sky for 1,500 feet, then did a vertical half-roll and started to level out, possibly to come down at us again.

At that moment an F4U from the higher cover swooped down. Smoke streamed from his wing, and tracers converged on the Zero. The Nip turned over and headed straight down, smoking. I watched for the splash, but in a matter of seconds it got too far to the rear for me to watch. Unidentified planes above and behind were chasing each other.

Huck and I were watching each other's tail closely as well as glancing all around. A Zero poised two thousand feet above and behind us, on the other side of Huck. I watched to see what he was going to do. He started down, heading for Huck. I waited until he had committed himself to his dive, then turned to the right and into him. It would be a deflection shot. I rapidly estimated his speed and took two-thirds of it for my mil lead, putting the pipper far ahead beyond the limits of my sight. Then I squeezed the trigger. My tracers headed for the Jap and some crossed in front of him. He abruptly changed his mind about attacking and pulled up into a right *chandelle*, which I could not follow without being sucked away from Huck.

When Huck saw me suddenly turn toward him he knew instantly what was happening and headed my way. As soon as we had crossed each other we both turned and scissored back to our original position.

Perhaps that little act of scissoring is the reason that I am alive today, instead of Huck. Perhaps if we hadn't scissored back, I might have done things differently than Huck and both of us would have survived. No man can tell.

That was the last clear memory I have of Huck—in his battle position off to my right. After that my memory consists entirely of momentary flashes and sensations.

It was after I had glanced to the left to check for incoming Japs and then to the right to check on Huck, it seems to me now, that I caught a quick glimpse of Huck's plane sweeping toward me. Then it disappeared. Afterthoughts even make it seem that I saw a flash of red as from the meatballs of a Jap plane and an instantaneous movement beneath my plane. I rolled my plane until the wings were nearly vertical to look below—first right, then left. Huck was not to be seen. I kicked right rudder and aileron and banked toward his last-seen position. I looked backward and down for a few moments and then leveled out and banked to the left to see what I could see, fully expecting to see Huck or perhaps Huck and a Jap plane. Nothing.

I weaved to and fro, desperately looking for Huck, swinging my tail from side to side to look behind. Nothing there. He had completely disappeared into thin air. That was not as unusual as it may sound, because the pale blue camouflage of the Corsairs made them invisible at a few hundred feet, particularly if the observer could not gaze at one spot very long.

At that moment I thought, perhaps Huck just got lost from me and we'll pick each other up in a few more seconds. About a minute later, I saw a lone F4U off to my left. "Ah—there you are Huck—why in the hell did you get way out there?" I said to myself. I moved over to the U and read its number. It was not Huck!

A lone F6F came along and we scissored a few times directly over the rear bombers. I didn't feel very worried about Huck after the initial surprise of his disappearance. I expected him to be along any minute since we had Corsairs guarding us above and behind, and if Huck had got into trouble he could have dived and taken cover with the bombers.

A Zero dived on the bombers from the starboard side. I swung over and gave him a few squirts with my trigger and he broke away to the right trying to coax me out after him. He was out of range, but I shot to scare him away from the bombers.

The F6F had gone wandering off by itself to the other side of the bombers. I stayed where I was, keeping a sharp lookout to the rear.

During one of my gentle weaves by which I was able to watch my tail, I saw a Zero diving on me. He began firing as I watched, smoke trailing from his wings. The Jap wasn't using tracers—another Nip trick, so that you wouldn't know anybody was shooting at you until you were hit. I stuck the nose of my Corsair down in a steep dive and watched my spottled rear-vision mirror as the Zero pulled up and disappeared to the rear.

A few minutes later another Zero came diving down on my tail. I could easily distinguish the brown-painted wings with their red circles when the wing tilted down at me. He was a poor shot and missed. I went into a steeper dive this time, because the second Nip had been approaching faster than the other. I didn't know whether he was still on my tail or not, but I was down to the water and had to pull out. Immediately I kicked the tail out of the way and saw the Zero turning back, disappointed.

We were flying down St. George's Channel. Apparently all aerial opposition had ceased. The only plane that might have been enemy was far above—completely out of sight. All I could see was the arcing vapor trail of a fighter that had just pulled out of its dive. It could have been a Jap or it could have been a Flying Foxhole (P-38).

There were several lone F4U's with the bomber formation. I went from plane to plane looking at their numbers, but there was no #798 among them. I hoped Huck was flying with the other formation of bombers or else was flying in one of the two plane sections which I hadn't observed closely.

Presently I joined up with a fellow in an F4U who had a bushy mustache and was flying with his hood open. I opened my own hood as I moved into the wing position. He smiled at me and held up one finger. I held up two fingers. He nodded and smiled again. The finger he displayed meant he had shot down one Jap. The two I displayed had meant V-for-Victory! Of course, he didn't know.

We passed over the field at 1,500 feet, then over a second time at 500 feet according to the rules. He patted his head and pointed to me, then broke away to the left. I saw that he was going to cut another plane out, so I flew straight ahead and fell in behind the other U.

As I made my straightaway approach to land after successfully evading a very tall tree, which poked its trunk up in the very path I should have liked to make my approach, the tower shot some red flares at the plane ahead and then at me.

I poured on the coal and took a wave-off and retracted my wheels to cut down the drag. When I gained some speed I raised my flaps 10 degrees at a time, so that I wouldn't mush into the ground. The Corsair loses about 200 feet when flaps are raised completely, due to the sudden loss in lift.

At the end of the runway I looked down and saw a crashed plane, evidently the same bearded pilot I had flown with a few minutes before.

I swung wide to give the rat race over the field a chance to clear up and for some of the other U's to land, then made my landing. All along the strip were groups of men on small hills and embankments watching the landing and crashing planes.

I followed the white taxi jeep to my revetment, revved up the engine for a final magneto check and parked my plane. "Has seven nine eight come back yet?" I asked the mechanic.

"Not that I know of," he replied.

I began to get really worried.

Back at the ready tent I told Schaefer all I knew and he telephoned it in to the command post.

"Where's Lassiter?"

"When did you last see Huck?" everybody asked.

We held out hope for him, until the hour came that we knew he could no longer be airborne.

All day and night it was on my mind: What in the hell happened to Huck? I began to think he had turned to shoot a Zero off my tail and somehow the Zero had turned into him and shot him instead. It was the sudden disappearance—the not-knowing what had happened—that made the sight of his vacant bed all the worse.

That evening after chow I looked up some pilots from VMF 217 who had been high cover and had been behind us, fighting off Zeros.

"I saw a Zero dive on a single F4U and shoot at him," one pilot told me. "The U nosed over and pulled away from the Zero—apparently unhurt. The Zero then pulled up in a left *chandelle* and I turned to the left and shot him down. He exploded."

"After my wingman and I had been sucked out wide after that Zeke, we were attacked by several Zeros and got our planes shot up badly. I was nicked by a bullet that grazed my right shoulder. My wingman had to make a wheels-up landing."

"That must have been me that dived away," I told him.

Lassiter was the only fighter shot down. Three crashes had occurred when our planes returned to the field, but nobody got hurt very bad.

At night it seemed lonely to see Lassiter's empty bed and to see his clothes, favorite pipe and tobacco, a little loose change, some old letters, the pillow still dented where his head had lain. I couldn't believe that big, burly Huck was dead. I felt that he'd be getting back sometime.

The following day, Major Gordon came by and told us one of the neighboring pilots had seen an F4U that was smoking and skimming low over the water, getting ready to make a water landing.

"If only I knew how he got hit without me knowing it, it would ease my mind a lot," I said. "We were only at 3,000 feet over Simpson Harbor. He was there one minute and then he just seemed to disappear. I might have been looking right at him though, and not seen him because of his camouflage."

"Hell," the skipper replied. "You can't fight a safe war. If you do, you aren't doing your duty. You've got to expect such things to happen, Zed. You needn't feel too bad about it. He's gone now and all we can do is hope that the Japs didn't get him. Maybe Dumbo might pick him up yet."

I then felt that he had landed okay and probably got into shore, somewhere. I only hoped he didn't meet up with any Japs, for he had told us, "They'll never take me a prisoner—not as long as my forty-five works. I'll fight until they kill me."

Huck never came back.

We had a couple of air raids that night. The AA took up a steady pounding of the seemingly empty sky. The racket grew so loud we couldn't hear the airplane.

When the bursting red spangles of the AA indicated the Nipponese plane was heading our way, we jumped into our foxhole. I hadn't been there over three seconds when there came a blinding flash above the treetops and white-hot pieces of confetti and streamers showered down near us. Instantaneously, a loud ground-shaking bomb blast reverberated and Wilson tumbled into the foxhole headfirst. In a few moments other men jumped into the foxhole. Levine had been lying in his sack when he saw the light from the phosphorous bomb. He fell to the floor on his stomach, then jumped up and ran for it when the chance came. The red glow of a fire came from the Army area a few hundred feet east of us.

The next morning, Hazlett and I went over to look at the bomb crater. It measured about twenty feet wide and had greatly enlarged the foxhole where an Army soldier had been. General Hodge, living a few feet away, had narrowly escaped being hit.

Leaflets had been dropped on Rabaul telling the people to get out because the city was going to be bombed. Five squadrons of bombers, Army B-24's, B-25's and Marine SBD's and TBF's, went up to give it a real pasting along with several of the airfields. I was very disappointed that it was my non-flying day. I keenly wanted to watch the destruction of the city. It was the only city in the South Pacific that our forces could attack. All the other places were mere clusters of huts. I envied the pilots in the European war theatre for the chance of dropping bombs and strafing such inviting targets, even if they had to meet more AA and defending fighters.

I was becoming more "eager" all the time. Every hour of flying that I lost due to bad weather or canceled hops brought a multitude of gripes from me. I had decided I would put in at least one hundred hours for the third tour of duty. The only way to get any Japs would be to get a chance at them and the best way to get chances would be to fly more often. Yet I didn't want to get too eager, because there was the common belief that when a pilot became that way his days were numbered.

Now that Huck and Craig were lost, I just wanted to kill Japs. I didn't care whether they were on the ground or in the air. I realized I could not become a hero. Time was now too short and the Japs too cagey, so I reaped satisfaction in doing all I could to damn them and theirs to their "immortal glory."

Although we bombed the airfields at Rabaul every day we continued to be met by from thirty to forty Zeros. Our aerial photographers would show every one of the five fields knocked out of action and we would send another strike up a couple of hours later, which would be met by more swarms of Zeros. It was much the same as a man trying to kill five gophers. After he has reduced the gophers down to one, he stands over one hole with his club ready and the gopher pops up in another. He runs over to that hole and the gopher pops up in another. Ad infinitum.

Jap shipping had been reduced to a trickle. Most of it was done by destroyers, barges and submarines operating at night.

Somebody back in Washington, D.C., had a bright idea to sow some mines in Simpson Harbor at Rabaul with the purpose of impeding the Jap shipping by their nuisance value. Consequently, orders were received at Bougainville. One torpedo bomber squadron was assigned the mission, but when the time came another was given the hop, because they had had previous experience in laying mines.

At the briefing they were told, "Make it good, because Washington has its eye on us tonight."

In the dark hours of February 14, 1944, the torpedo bombers of VMTB 233 and Major Roland F. Smith's VMTB 232 took off on the operation that was to result in tragedy for 233.

The Commanding Officer of VMTB 233, Major Conn, found the Japs unusually interested in what was happening that night. For several previous nights the bombers had followed the prescribed route and altitude to drop their bombs, and the Japs were able to predict easily enough where the Americans would fly.

The TBM's were to fly up in three groups of eight each. The first group lost one plane. As they headed back home the C.O. tried to radio the other TBF's to warn them to turn back but he couldn't make radio cantact. The second group lost two planes. Before the third group arrived at its assigned interval of nearly an hour, the B-24 which had been harassing Rabaul to distract the attention of the Japs was shot down.

The third group of planes found every searchlight and AA gun in the area pointed their way when they flew at 800 feet over the water at the slow speed of 160 knots to drop their parachute-mines, weighing 1,600 pounds apiece. Plane after plane disintegrated in mid-air and fell in flames. Only three of them got away. One pilot failed to be in the correct location on his first pass and had the nerve to turn around and go back to do it. He had the luck to escape.

And the next night the Army wanted them to go up again! One of the majors was ready to give up his wings and his commission rather than have his boys try it again. There was such a stink that the high command thought it wise to drop the affair.

My good friend and former roommate of cadet days, Cornelius, never came back from that mission. A total of six planes and eighteen men were senselessly lost that night.

The military ''chain of command'' comes in handy in such untidy affairs. The bright idea originates from on high and is transmitted through the generals and the colonels to the majors who give the orders to the men who do the dying. It is all very impersonal, so that if a mistake has been made, few are the people who know where to place the heavy finger of responsibility—and the finger is rarely pointed.

The following day we taxied to take off for the strike. Yeager's tailwheel went flat when we arrived at the end of the runway. A small tractor came to tow his plane away. I checked my gun sight and found it wouldn't go on. I motioned to Estes, one of the mechanics from my squadron, who was standing on the tractor. He came over and I yelled above the roar of the engine and gestured with my hands. He took the light bulb out of Yeager's plane and installed it in mine. The electrical sight still wouldn't work.

All the planes had taken off except mine. I didn't know what to do. I figured I could guess fairly close where the pipper of my sight would be if it worked, so I took off. When I was airborne, I heard Yeager radio that he would catch up if he could get an extra plane.

The fighters and bombers were still circling in their rendezvous when I joined. Soon after, we started for Rabaul, 225 nautical miles away. Twenty minutes later, Yeager joined me. I knew it was Yeager because he got close enough for me to see his face. I slipped back into wing position on him.

A few miles past Buka Island, the last land until we would arrive at New Britain, Steve's plane smoked slightly and dropped down. I knew he had run out of gas in one wing tank.

A few minutes later he turned to go back to base. We were halfway to Rabaul when my engine sputtered. I reached down and switched fuel tanks and flipped on my emergency fuel pump to maintain a stream of gasoline to the engine. My engine sputtered to a stop and I dropped behind the other planes. I pointed my nose down to maintain 130 knots flying speed and checked to make sure my fuel selector valve was engaged on the reserve tank. It was unusual for the Corsair's engine to stop from running out a wing tank after a new tank had been cut in so soon, but I was not unduly worried.

I kept dropping lower and still the engine failed to start. I came down from 16,000 feet to 12,000, then 10,000. I became worried and glanced down to see which way the whitecaps were breaking. I knew the whitecaps broke on the downwind side and streamed upwind. I began to think I would be making a water landing. It was important to land upwind so the contact with the water would be as slow as possible. I wondered if anybody in the formation had seen me go down. Pulling the mixture lever back to lean and shoving the lever gently forward I cleaned the cylinders of excess gasoline. The engine barked and coughed and took up its steady snore once again.

I really wasn't afraid of the water landing. I just didn't like the idea of getting wet, or perhaps landing on a Jap-held island.

There was a three-plane division near the rear of the fighter formation, which had not yet split up to begin scissoring. I joined up on the third man and recognized Wilson.

Upon smelling fumes in my cockpit I looked down. In a forward compartment on the floor, ahead of my rudder bar, I saw a pool of red liquid. I didn't know whether it was gasoline or hydraulic fluid.

When Wilson looked my way, I signaled good-by to him and peeled away. As I did so I heard him say, "Is that you, Bekins?"

Fluid was spraying out and my hydraulic pressure was slowly decreasing as I headed for home base. Off to my right and 3,000 feet below, long after I had left the formation, I saw a lone airplane heading in the opposite direction. I swung around into him and he turned into me, but he couldn't turn sharp enough. I was in a good position to boresight him, when I recognized the plane as an F4U. Wheeling away in a left *chandelle* I started for home again. When I looked back I saw the lone F4U following me. "What the hell is a lone U doing clear up here?" I asked myself.

I throttled back and reduced my RPM so the plane could catch up to me, but he turned around. I thought his actions peculiar so I turned around and chased him to get his number, but here were too many specks on my windshield and soon he was lost among them and outdistanced me when I weaved from side to side to keep him in sight. The last I saw, he was heading for Rabaul, all alone.

A few days before, an F4U was reported to have fired on two or three American planes and some of the pilots wondered if the Japs had captured an F4U and were using it against us. Several weeks previously a pilot had been disabled by AA and crashlanded safely on Lakunai airfield without burning his plane. The pilot had always maintained he woud rather land on the airstrip itself than bail out or land near Japanese ground forces. He thought the airfield personnel would treat him more decently. We wondered if he had thrown the switch which would automatically destroy his IFF equipment, a highly secret piece of radio equipment we all carried which sent out signals to show we were friends to allied radar search units.

I had to use the emergency hand pump to get enough hydraulic pressure to lower my wheels and I landed without flaps on the bomber strip, which was longer than the fighter strip. I was able to pump open the cowl flaps, intercooler and oil cooler flaps, in order to taxi without heating up the engine too much.

When I reported to Schaefer, I laughingly told him I had run up against "that Jap Corsair." Forever after, when I came down from hops, Schaef would ask, "Didja see anything of a Jap flying one of our planes today, Zed?"

Morris came back slightly wounded when a 7.7 mm went through his plastic canopy at the top and to the right, causing a multitude of small flesh wounds in his neck, hair and on the right side of the temple. He also had some AA holes in his plane. To add to his nicknames of "Stoneface" and "Hatchet" we called him "Purple Hatchet," because he would receive the Purple Heart.

A 20-mm shell had struck Levine's plane in the tail. A 12.7 mm (50 caliber) went through his right wing. With three 7.7's in the right wing, a 20 mm had knocked a rocker box off a cylinder head and another 12.7 mm had penetrated from the left and above and had been stopped by the armor plating behind Levine.

Levine's plane had smoked badly all the way from Rabaul to Cape St. George; then the smoking stopped until he neared home. Oil had streamed all over the left side of the fuselage and belly of the plane, and covered the windshield. He had done well to bring the plane back and land it safely. He had made the tightest turning approach in his life, because he could only see where he was going by looking out to the side in a turn.

"I'd have never got those arrows if I hadn't been too eager to get a Zero," Levine told us. "There were too many of them hanging around us and I lost sight of them for a moment. The next thing I knew, they had sneaked up on us."

It was on the 15th day of February, 1944 that our surface craft landed troops and supplies upon the Green Islands (Nissan Island) 115 miles east of Rabaul. The long-awaited invasion had taken place after a preliminary patrol had landed a few days before and reported only 50 Japanese on the island, who were there to man that important intermediary barge hideout between New Ireland, New Britain and the Bougainville area.

Some of our fighter planes had taken off before dawn and arrived on station over the landing at 0630. Fifteen minutes later a surprise struck the task force and the men on the shore in the form of fifteen unescorted Val dive bombers.

One division from VMF 212 shot down every plane in a group of six they found. Captain Philip C. De-Long knocked down three all by himself. AA shot down two.

One Jap bomber made a direct hit on one of our cruisers, with less disastrous effects than might be anticipated.

Only a few of the thirty-two planes that were patrolling over the landing got into action. Some were ordered to remain at their high levels to ward off other attacks that might come in, and those lower had a hard time locating the Japs because most of them had scattered and had to be hunted down individually.

The sending of unescorted dive bombers was practically suicide for the Japs. We fighter pilots even licked our chops when they sent dive bombers with fighter escort. The bombers all had tail gunners, which sometimes knocked American planes down, but generally they were easy kills.

That evening, Schaefer came around to tell us we had the predawn take-off at 0630. We didn't gripe about that, because we thought it might give us a good chance to hit some Vals that would likely stage another attack. It was dark when the dusk patrol came back from Green Island at 2000. The weather was bad and it was beginning to rain. Suddenly we heard a crash and the wail of the siren. I was about to walk down to the strip where it happened, but I decided it might interfere with my sleep.

Somebody came along and told us it was a pilot from VMF 217 who had cracked up. He seemed to have something wrong with his night vision, because he had cracked up twice before during night flying. The pilot had mistaken the space between the lighted fighter strip and the lighted bombed strip for the field on which he was supposed to land. After already taking two wave-offs, he had landed in the area filled with revetments, taxi-ways and trees. He hit a tree and revetment but somehow escaped unhurt. A week later he was killed in combat.

I woke up at 0245 and thought it was 0345 by the luminous dial of my watch. A sudden cannonading had awakened me. When I discovered it was an hour too soon, I couldn't get back to sleep. I worried about the predawn. I was confident of doing the right thing on the runway, but I was afraid I would receive one of the old type planes, in which it was necessary to bend down to reach the wheel retracting lever. In the daytime, I had barely cleared the tops of the trees at the end of the runway, and with the addition of darkness and not being able to see, an amount of uncertainty was created. The wheels nearly always had to be retracted to permit a plane to climb fast enough to evade the trees.

Again, the gain was worth the risk. Thoughts of getting a Val or Zero filled my mind. After a breakfast of hotcakes we went across the strip to our new ready room. The sky was very dark from low-hanging clouds. It had rained during the night until an hour before.

"I hope we don't get to take-off," one of the pilots said.

"Me too. I don't like the looks of that sky," answered another.

There was a horizon when one looked to the east. It was the line separating dark clouds, which retained a hint of their whiteness, and the dark gloom of the night jungle.

We taxied 4,200 feet along the winding, dipping road, without any lights. We could distinguish the white coral road but faintly and our wings narrowly missed the obstructions on either side.

When my turn came to take off, I lined the plane up with the runway and gave 'er the gun. The lights were too far apart, but not so far as to be unsafe. A total of eight lights extended the length of the runway on each side. I made a good take-off and retracted my wheels as soon as I left the ground. I had been assigned a new plane with the handily placed retraction lever and had plenty of clearance by the time I reached the trees. Turning to the left I cleared my slipstream from the take-off groove.

In a few seconds I was flying over Jap-held territory and out to sea. From my altitude the horizon had disappeared. The sky and the dark sea blended into a gray haze.

While flying wing on Morris, with my hood partly open because the outside was coated with an oily substance or water particles, vibration of the air, alternate compression and decompression, hurt my ears. I guarded against vertigo with quick glances at my artificial horizon.

We arrived on station fifteen minutes early and found the Islands visible in the golden glow of the coming sunrise. When dawn arrived and made visible all the switches and dials in my cockpit, I solved a major crisis. I had noticed that my oil temperature had risen to 120 degrees—much too high. At first I thought it would be necessary to return to base, but on checking my cylinder-head temperature and oil pressure and finding them okay, I didn't know what was wrong. If I opened my cooler flaps to decrease the oil temperature, the air resistance would put me behind the other planes.

I didn't want to go back to base, because it was precisely the moment we expected and hoped the enemy would start another attack. When I was able to see better with daylight I found that my master heating switch was on. I turned it off, the oil temperature dropped to 75 degrees in a few seconds, and I felt very much relieved.

The Japs must have learned their lesson, because after two hours without any sign of them we were told to return to base and pancake.

We went into a long dive that took us from 16,000 feet to 2,000 feet at a high rate of speed. Although I had turned on my defroster and master heating switch, my windshield continued to fog up. I couldn't wipe it off, because the fog formed between the bullet-proof glass and the plastic windscreen. I opened my hood a trifle and stuck my gloved hands into the cold air and scooped the air inside. This cleared the windshield off in a matter of minutes. In a dogfight the foggy windshield could easily result in disaster.

That afternoon after I had become airborne, flying a plane my squadron borrowed from VMF 217, we were near Buka Passage when I saw my left wing-folding indicator flap stick into the air. The flap was engineered to stay down when the folding wings of the Corsair remain safely spread and locked. When one of the flaps was up it indicated the wing was not locked in the spread position and might fold at any time. I remembered how one of the pilots at Espiritu Santo had been killed when his wing folded in mid-air and pinned him in the cockpit.

I could see the large steel locking pin still in place, but there was no telling when it would come loose. I hoped the indicator door was faulty and had sprung up, because of a weak spring. It was a matter of life and death.

After the patrol, Levine, Morris and I flew a line abreast formation and strafed the northwest tip of Buka in the midst of a rainstorm. I flipped some .50's into some buildings next to a pier and into some huts. We burst out into the clear. Levine was not with us.

"Reverse course for another run," I heard Morris say. We began to turn around. Then he said, "I must return to base. I have a leak in my hydraulic system." I stayed with Morris.

As we left the vicinity we heard Levine call excitedly, "I've found a barge, I've found a barge! I'm going to make two more strafing runs."

Morris and I won a race with a rain squall to the end of the runway. Levine came in a few minutes later. He was a very excited man. After he had made two runs on the camouflaged barge, the Japs for some reason had moved it away from shore into the bay. Perhaps they wanted the strafer to ignore their buildings. Levine thought there were 3 or 4 Japs in the crew. After expending 1,600 rounds of .50 calibers, he left it smoking slightly. There wasn't much in it that would burn.

Every morning the weather looked nice and clear, but every afternoon the volcano was obscured in massive clouds with bases as low as 3,000 feet, extending out to sea for miles and spreading to engulf the mountain ranges on Bougainville. Many rain squalls occurred and nearly every afternoon at 1600 one came over the field, lasting from two to eight hours.

Hazlett and I joked together at night. "When one of us whistles over the radio, the other will drop out of formation and we'll sneak off together and form our own roving high cover." We were both eager to get Japs. Hazlett had shot down three but he wanted five at least. I wanted any at all. Our plan was actually the same one that some of the aces had used earlier in the Rabaul campaign to run up their scores, but it was also dereliction of duty, involving abandonment of positions assigned in the bomber cover.

On one trip to Rabaul, members of my division had to turn back one by one until I was the only one remaining. I had joined upon another spare man, whom I found to be Hazlett. I hoped he would lead me astray and off to the side of the formation, such as we had planned, jokingly. Then I would have an excuse for being at a place where I wasn't supposed to be, because it would be my job to go wherever he led. We remained with the bombers on that trip however. Zeros flitted by and some came through our formation at a tremendous speed. I was tempted to follow one, but I didn't. One pilot tried to and was shot down for his pains.

A B-24 was hit by AA and exploded in mid-air. Six members of the crew parachuted. We flew on helplessly and watched them drift over the ocean to a plantation near Rapopo, one of the Japanese airfields. I wondered when we landed if the Japs had caught and killed them yet.

The next day, when the other part of our squadron landed from their turn on the Rabaul trip, one of our boys didn't come back. It was R. A. Schaeffer, the smooth-faced rosy-cheeked lad who had been a campus Romeo not so long before. His buddy and section leader, I. E. Moore, told us what he knew about it:

"I started after a Zero, but quit, when I saw four others perched up high starting to come down on me. I turned back to the formation then. The only thing I can think of is that Schaef left my wing and went after the Zero. I saw a Zero going down not very long after that."

One of our pilots told us, "When the Zeros started coming around, all the planes above us who were high cover deserted the bombers and went wandering off, acting as a roving high cover on their own. That left only the close and low cover of six sections to protect the bombers and practically all of them were from 222. That is why Schaeffer got shot down—we had no high cover."

The 145-plane formation of TBF's, SBD's, F6F's, P-40's and F4U's had met fifty Jap fighter planes and claimed to have shot down twenty-three. VF 17 came back from that flight on February 19th and claimed sixteen Zeros to surpass VMF 215's record of 135½.

We read in the Bougainville *Bulldozer* where two PB4Y's (B-24's) of VMD-254, piloted by Major J. R. Christensen and Captain J. Q. Yawn and their crewmen, had taken pictures of Truk. These Marines had performed one of the most daring photographic missions of the war. They took off from Sterling Island at night on February 3, 1944 and flew 1,000 miles to the northwest to mysterious spine-chilling Truk. The next morning they were over their target at 20,000 feet and saw below them most of the Japanese Combined Fleet consisting of the 63,000-ton battleship *Musashi*, one carrier, nine or ten cruisers, twenty destroyers, twelve submarines, and many cargo ships. They arrived overhead without being seen, but soon a battleship opened up with AA and two or three Zekes started up to intercept them. After 20 to 30 thrilling minutes over the target they tossed out a six-pound bomb so they could claim that the Marines were the first to bomb Truk and dived for home. Six hours later they landed at the Piva strip at Bougainville.

Admiral Koga, the Japanese Commander of the Combined Fleet, had considered the photo plane (the Japs only sighted one plane) a sign of bad news and weighted anchor on February 10, 1944, never to return to Truk. Some of the fleet went to Yokosuka and part to Singapore. Bad weather delayed the departure of some fifty ships—merchants and others.

Thirteen days after the photo mission, Mitscher's Task Force 58 struck and found that the Japanese fleet had escaped them. They received solace by sinking so many ships and destroying so many airplanes as to render Truk nearly defenseless.

After sunset, Gunner George Schaefer came around to our tent. "What'd ya hear about Schaef?" we asked him.

"Well, I talked to a New Zealander based over at Torokina, who had seen a smoking F4U make a water landing about one mile offshore from Cape Gazelle. He felt sure the pilot got out without any trouble. Incidentally, that's what I came to talk to you about. How would you boys like to make a predawn takeoff?"

"Now George, you know better than to ask us a question like that. How would you like to have an arm cut off?"

"Not even if it was to help poor old Schaef?" George asked.

"Well now, that's a different matter. If it would help Schaef, we're willing to do anything. What's the big scoop?"

"Well, here it is. We feel sure that he is floating just off-shore from New Britain in his little yellow raft—unless the Japs find him tonight. We want to get some fighters up there early in the morning, by dawn at the latest, to keep the Japs from getting out in the daylight to find him. Dumbo can land and pick him up and you boys can keep the Zeros and shore batteries out of action. Surely you'd be willing to miss the strike and your chances of getting a Zero, to help, wouldn't you? Besides, you're liable to have plenty of chances at Zeros if you take this little job."

"Roger!" we answered.

I woke up at 0230 and wasn't able to get back to sleep, expecting George to come around any moment to wake us up. He didn't arrive until 0530.

Operations had objected to our special search and

had canceled it, because they were going to send up a Dumbo and its fighter escort later in the morning anyway.

"That might be too late," we grumbled.

Nevertheless, Dumbo did pick up Schaeffer. When he got out of his sinking plane, he had tied his rubber life raft to him securely and had began swimming away from shore towing the raft. The Japs had shot at him from shore, but they didn't come after him. Evidently they were afraid of getting strafed.

He broke out his raft after a while and continued to paddle with his hands toward the open sea. Finally, he became so exhausted he just lay there, not caring whether he lived or died. He had been badly burned on his hands and face and was in such bad shape he couldn't have lasted many more hours when Dumbo rescued him. They took him to the hospital at the Treasury Islands, where he was visited the next day by the skipper, Schaefer, I. E. Moore and Doc Brittingham.

He had knocked down the Zero he went after and its buddies had shot him down.

We were scheduled to escort some Army B-25's to hit Lakunai airfield at Rabaul. Because of their speed (the fastest of the bombers we met) they were a pleasure to escort. We could make the flight in three hours instead of the usual four when we flew with SBD's.

Yeager was grounded because of a sore back, a recurrence of an injury of his collegiate days. Instead Ralph Langley, one of the two newest members of our squadron, flew wing on me.

Morris failed to get off the deck when his tailwheel

went flat, so we flew a three-plane division until Levine left us and joined up with another three-plane division. The weather was good and the Army B-25 bombers hit with a good pattern of bombs, unlike many of their drops which landed uselessly in the water.

That strike of March 20th was worthy of special notice, because *not one Zero was seen!* Had we at last completely neutralized the airpower at Rabaul, after weeks of daily poundings and after littering the bottom of Simpson Harbor with wrecked Jap ships and planes and the broken bodies of our American and New Zealand pilots?

"What happened to all the Zeros at Rabaul? Why didn't they come up and fight?" That was the question on everybody's lips.

That evening we learned some startling news from the two daily mimeographed news sheets, named the Torokina *Times* and the Bougainville *Bulldozer:* Truk had been hit by a large force of U. S. Warships including eighteen carriers. Admiral Mitscher's TF 58 claimed 200,000 tons of shipping sunk and 325 planes wrecked—planes which would have reinforced those at Rabaul. We presumed the Japs had either sent their fighters to Truk as reinforcements or else were out of gasoline, due to the sinking of a convoy of two tankers and other ships heading toward Rabaul a few days before.

Some pilots claimed the Japs had built underground hangars and were repairing all their planes to put them in the air for one surprise strike. Once before, they said, the Japs had staged no interception. Then they had hit hard with surprise. But the attack never materialized.

On our last trip to Sydney, Levine had purchased a diminutive wire-haired terrier not much larger than his fist. This piece of canine pulchritude he named Nicky. Watching Li'l Red Dog and Nicky play gave us our liveliest entertainment in the evenings. Dumb Li'l Red was smart enough to maul and bite his fragile playmate gently. Nicky on the other hand barred no holds and often gave Red the worst of the deal, sometimes getting Red's nose between his jaws and then squeezing.

Li'l Red Dog in particular and Nicky in general delighted to go down by the showers and take a bath in the pool of soapy water where the water drained from the showers. Nicky regarded himself a connoisseur of beautiful soap—which he ate. After eating about one-fourth of a bar he usually began to foam at the mouth and blow bubbles.

A thick vine hung down about seventy feet from a tree near the showers. Some of us emulated Tarzan and swung back and forth on the vine, which was nearly six inches thick. After we saw a movie called *Tarzan Triumphs* the vine was especially popular. Tarzan's jungle was a very civilized place compared to what we saw on Bougainville, not nearly as dense and without as many thick vines hanging from the trees.

The beach sloped very gently into the ocean and was composed of a grayish-black sand with extremely fine grains, the finest I had ever seen. Undoubtedly the smoke and ashes from the volcanoes on Bougainville had fallen or been washed into the sea to form the beach.

The water was warm. We tried to catch some of the

small breakers and ride them in. Tiring of this, we ducked each other. Then we grabbed handfuls of the black sand and flung it until each of us looked as black as the Bougainville natives. Thus we had our only recreation since our arrival on the combat tour. There was a volley ball court near the showers, but it was used mainly by those squadrons living closest to it.

It was after the Zeros had disappeared from Rabaul that I began to take inventory of myself, while shaving, since I might have to live with myself a few more weeks after all. I noticed something glisten in my hair as I gazed into the mirror with soap spread over my face. After several tries, I pulled out the glistening hair. My hair had turned to silver! I looked at my eyes in the mirror and noticed deep lines radiating outward from the corners and below. I knew that most of them were caused by squinting while flying. Then I realized that the furrows in my brow for the first time wouldn't smooth out.

It came to me then that I was getting old. Old before my time due to the strain of combat and the constant tension of being on the alert (consciously or subconsciously), on the ground and in the air. I aged mentally during those few moments that I looked at myself in the mirror. No longer was I the youth just out of college and aviation training with a certain disregard of danger. I had become an adult—more conscious of the possibility of death, but in a way that resulted in a cooler, more efficient performance of duty.

I felt robbed. Robbed of my youthfulness, of the years in which I should have been unfettered and unattached, and of the journeys I had planned in my boyish mind before the war sent me on a long one, a journey of no return for some of my buddies. And yet I marveled. I marveled at myself and at my friends for having been able to take so much with apparently slight effects. True, we tossed more in our sleep and were jumpier during the daytime. Hands that lit cigarettes trembled perceptibly, I had noticed. But in the main we had survived.

I marveled to think of the strange mental powers in the human mind that disciplines a man to the point where he will step into a mass of nearly seven tons of intricate metal and soar six miles above the earth to search for other men whom he has been told to kill. These are men he has never seen before, men who have never done him any personal harm. Yet, this sense of duty causes him to shoot and be shot, kill and be killed.

Then when it is all over, his individual death or accomplishments have not helped to win the war very much. Much less than one ant carrying away one grain of sand in the leveling of a giant anthill. But the value of the man and of the ant is undeniable. When there are enough men and enough ants, working hard enough and long enough, the mission is accomplished.

Despite the knowledge that any day might be our last, we never seriously mentioned getting killed. We talked about it jokingly, especially to the married men in the squadron. "Don't worry," some of us would say. "If you don't come back tonight, we'll go back and take care of your wife for you."

I sometimes would try my best to cheer the men up with songs, among them:

BLOODY RABAUL

Once down to Sydney from Vella I strolled,
From a place called bloody Rabaul.

I met an old sergeant, he said Pardon me please,
You've blood on your tunic and mud on your
   knees.

Da-De-Ah, Da-De-Ah,
You've blood on your tunic and mud on your
   knees.

Now listen here Doggie, you bloody damned
   fool,
I just got back from a raid on Rabaul.

Where shrapnel is flying and comforts are few,
And good men are dying for Bastards like you.

Da-De-Ah, Da-De-Ah,
Where good men are dying for Bastards like
you.

And, to the tune of "Take Me Out to the Ball
Game":

LET ME FLY TO RABAUL TOWN

Let me fly to Rabal town,
Let me go to Gazelle.
Over New Ireland and Simpson too,
The weather looks bad, but we're sure to get
   through.

Let me drop, drop, drop, on Rapopo,
If there's no fire, it's a shame.
For it's four, five, six bombs we've dropped,
And they're all in train.

Where all the songs originated, few men knew. The good ones, however, spread as rapidly as a brush fire once they were started.

The daily news sheet told us about the Gilbert and Marshall Islands being invaded. We were glad to hear about it, because it would shorten the war. I hated to think of the numerous islands to be conquered before we got to Japan, and hoped the high command would use the leapfrog method we had found so successful.

Our own war had become more active. In our back yard the Japs had pushed the Army back 2,000 yards and captured the small landing field hacked out of the jungle for the Piper Cubs that were used for artillery observation. Some of the Fiji Islanders, who had been engaged in scouting and patrol for the American Army, were sent to help repel the Japs. They loved to take Jap heads and were greatly feared.

I was happy to hear that the Army's 37th Division was one of those upon whom I had to place my trust, for I had heard they were one of the crack American outfits. They had seen action at Munda after being brought from Guadalcanal. The Marine ground forces had been sent back to the rear to rest up after they had taken the beachhead. In a very short time after the Army took over the place had blossomed out with motion picture theatres and USO shows, and now ice cream parlors were being built. With life beginning to get that comfortable, we Marines knew that we would be moving on to take another island, where the pattern would be repeated.

A sure sign that Bougainville was civilized was the funny sight of Army military police standing at the crossroads in the middle of the jungle directing traffic. It was an accomplishment to have a road there at all, let alone something to drive on it.

One of the M.P.'s told me there were 400 M.P.'s on the island with a two-star general to command them! When he heard my exclamation of amazement, he said: "Yes, I know there's a lot of us for a place this small. If they would put us in the front lines we could take this island."

A VMF 218 pilot had been shot down over New Britain and bailed out only three miles inland from Tobera airfield. He immediately began walking and reached the Warangoi River after three days. He got in his rubber life raft and floated down the river, traveling only at night. At noon of the sixth day, he arrived at the mouth of the river. As soon as it became dark he made a beeline for the open sea in his raft and after floating for two nights was rescued. He was very happy to get back and was still in good physical condition when rescued. He owed his survival to the excellent condition he was in before becoming lost.

That was the best rescue story I had heard. It was all so real for us, because we might get shot down and have to face the same situation the very next day. Later, we learned that his wounds nearly caused him to lose the sight of one of his eyes. He was killed after he returned to the States. The student he was instructing put their plane into a spin too close to the ground.

A Japanese convoy outward bound from Rabaul was sunk and seventy prisoners were taken. They were pilots and aviation mechanics, who said that all aviation personnel were being evacuated from Rabaul. Another convoy that was heading for Rabaul was also sunk.

With the notable absence of nearly all enemy

planes over Rabaul (no more than six had been seen at one time), fewer fighters were sent along to escort the American bombers. If the Japanese had only been tricking us instead of being genuinely caught with their planes down, they could have scored a disastrous attack upon our formations. We still wondered where the Zeros had gone, but the consensus of opinion was that they had gone to reinforce Truk.

Most of the time only three divisions of fighter planes were called upon to cover four three-plane Army formations, flying in a rectangular pattern. A week before and the same attack would have been sent out with two to three times as many fighters for the same number of bombers.

The Zeros had been absent from Rabaul for over two days when my squadron was assigned—ironically enough—to be roving high cover on a strike. This was the coveted position we had wanted for a long time. Our job was to escort SBD's and TBF's to hit Lakunai.

Levine was flying as wingman on me and Langley on Morris. When we were directly over Rabaul at 27,000 feet and the Japs were putting up their ack-ack, I heard Levine's voice desperately call me. "Foster, wait for me, wait for me—my engine's cutting out. Something's wrong with my engine!"

I had already noticed he was lagging and had made a turn to permit him to slip to the inside of the turn in order to stay up with me. I throttled back and kept turning as Levine caught up. Just before he called me I had seen a section of U's heading for us and I pulled over them, Levine ducking down a few feet to miss them. Since two planes comprising a section are usually flying close together they should maneuver together instead of in opposite directions. I wondered what was wrong with Levine. Morris led us toward Cape Gazelle as I radioed Levine. "How are you?"

"Okay for now," was the answer.

At 17,000 feet over Cape Gazelle, Morris did a right turn to head back over Rabaul. I knew that Levine would not like that idea with his missing engine. "Do you want to go home?" I radioed Levine.

"Affirmative, affirmative—I want to go home," he answered.

"Morris from Foster—we are returning to base, over," I said through my throat mike—a message Morris never received.

After we had landed safely on the deck at Piva strip, Levine told me his plane had started to lose power over Rabaul and he was busy looking over his dials and gauges trying to find out what was wrong with the engine, all the while trying to fly wing on me. He had looked up from his instrument panel just in time to see the other planes heading for us and to shove his stick forward just enough to miss them. He was still shaking from that narrow escape when his engine momentarily stopped. Then he called me. Levine said his high blower had gone out, and he couldn't get over 27 inches of manifold pressure. His fuel pressure kept dropping and his engine cut cold. It did this two or three times, then began to function when we dropped to lower altitude.

Despite the absence of Zeros, the Japanese AA and operational troubles continued to get more than their share of Americans. It was ironical that we should lose a fighter pilot over Rabaul without a shot being fired at him, but such proved to be the case.

On February 24th our squadron furnished the only escort for one twenty-plane B-24 bombing formation. Another squadron provided the same amount of cover for the following bombers. Levine did not take off at first, because his radio wouldn't work, but he borrowed another plane and caught up to us as we passed near Buka Island.

We were at 20,000 feet as we passed over the coast of New Britain and headed for Vunakanau airfield.

"Williams from Leach, I am having engine trouble. Follow me," Leach radioed to his division leader. Williams looked for Jesse.

The ceiling was 12,000 feet over Rabaul. The weather was too bad over our targets but an alternate target had been selected and that was the city of Rabaul. The formation leader, however, thought the ceiling was too low and would make them too easy targets for the Jap AA, so he called up his men and told them to dump their loads on the Jalu River on New Ireland while going back home.

I was plenty angry. We had gone to a lot of effort scissoring over the bombers, risking our lives in mid-air collisions and engine failures. We had used all the gasoline and human effort that was necessary for a real bombing mission and then they dumped their bombs upon a river! I did not blame them too much for not going in under the low ceiling, but I hated to see the bombs entirely wasted.

"Nice bombing, boys—you sure flattened that river," I called over the radio.

On the way home I saw a fighter plane do some slow rolls and a loop, so I put the nose of my plane on a cloud and rotated around it three consecutive times. In a Corsair one can do as many slow rolls as desired, without straightening out between them to gain speed.

Then I tried a loop, after getting clear of all planes. Down went my nose. Then back on the stick. The plane began to climb vertically. I eased the throttle forward for more power and tugged back on the stick. For some reason the Corsair is reluctant to be pulled over on its back; it seems to want to head straight up and claw at the air as best it can. Over I went on my back, then forward on the stick to round off the top of the loop and back on it gently as the plane gathered speed in its upside-down dive. Back stronger and it began to level out of the dive. I ran into some turbulent air that tossed the plane up and down, the sign of a good loop, for it was the slipstream of my own propeller.

Other fighters began to do acrobatics. Some of us had a tail chase. Then we began to make mock runs upon the bombers and watched the gunners following us with their machine guns. I knew they were getting as much fun out of it as we were, but someone called up over the radio and asked us to "Please discontinue making runs upon the bomber formation."

After we landed, we learned Leach hadn't got back. Between what all the pilots heard over the radio, each contributing bits of information that others had missed, we decided he had gone down for sure. His last reported position was between New Ireland and Duke of York Island. Leach had calmly sent out his position reports as he glided down to make a landing in dangerous waters, within sight of Rabaul.

Our mechanics rushed the servicing of our airplanes and as soon as four were ready to fly, one of the divisions took off to search for Leach. When four more were ready, another division took off. Finally, it came my division's turn.

We flew at 300 feet on the way up to Cape St. George. As we neared the Cape, one of the planes to my left spotted an object in the water and circled to get a better look. A half a minute later I circled to the right to look at something I had seen. It proved to be a piece of debris resembling a broken crate, with what appeared to be an orange floating beside it. I dived over it at fifty feet, but saw nothing of vital interest.

We continued on our way and flew up St. George's Channel. I saw Okie's division going up the east coast of New Ireland and heard Hazlett say, "There's two barges in the second cove."

As we neared the Duke of York Island, I heard Major Gordon call and say he'd found Jesse. He left Wilson and Hughes of his division to circle the location, while he climbed up to a higher altitude to give his radio more range, so that he could call Dane base at Torokina or Shepherd base at Green Island and tell them to rush a Dumbo up. Meanwhile, Wilson radioed the position to the rest of us on the secret VHF channel.

Yeager and I arrived at the spot and found three other planes circling, but for the life of me, I couldn't see Leach. Although Wilson would dive down and zoom his position, neither Yeager nor I could spot it.

"This is Yeager, my gas is running low. I will return to base by myself." Yeager's plane left our circle and headed for home.

After fifteen minutes or so of circling I finally spied the raft. I could see Leach lying on his back paddling with a backstroke away from Duke of York Island and toward the ocean. He had a current of about ten knots to paddle against.

I could readily understand why so many downed aviators had not been found. With the sun and Rabaul at my back I could see him plainly, but on the rest of my circuit in the late afternoon sun and with its reflection in the water he was invisible.

Major Gordon came down and rejoined us after getting Shepherd base to call Dane base to tell Dumbo to come at once. I got out my dye marker to drop on Leach. I had brought an extra package along for the purpose. I called over the radio and announced my intentions, but Wilson beat me to it.

Many circles later we heard Dumbo call over the radio saying they couldn't come up because they couldn't land back at base at night, even with the help of searchlights! At 1740 we were informed by Shepherd base of Dumbo's transmission and we heard Dumbo's escort being told to pancake.

Everyone had left, because they were running short of fuel, except Williams, Morris and I. We knew we had to go too, because our fuel supply was getting low and it was over 200 miles to home base. The other two planes started to leave. I flew toward Leach and blinked my running lights. T-O-M-O-R-R-O-W I flashed in code.

"Quit fooling around and come on, Zed," one of the others yelled over the radio.

They had started for home. I pointed my nose away from Leach and looked backward. Jesse was on his back on the raft still paddling against the current. I waggled my wings from side to side in farewell and applied throttle to catch the other planes.

That was the last time any of us ever saw Jesse.

As we passed the south tip of New Ireland, Williams and I swung over and gave a tripod installation a burst. It was just above that point where the radar station had been located which Bob Hanson had been strafing when hit by ack-ack. Several 500-pound bombs had knocked out the positions since, and evidently the Japs hadn't constructed more.

The next day a search was conducted for Leach by the division whose turn it was to fly. There were many clouds and rain squalls, the wind was strong and the water had become choppy. Nobody was able to find him.

Williams and I went down to squadron to try to take off with any extra planes that might return and be in a state of readiness. Major Gordon and a few others had already taken the first available planes. When there were enough for Williams and myself, we couldn't get clearance to take off because of the weather. Five minutes later a bad rain squall settled down over the field.

Leach must have felt heartened the day before when we found him, and considerably disheartened when he saw the last of us leave after circling for nearly two hours. I could imagine what he thought the next day if he was still out there floating around and all the planes overlooking him. "Fools," he would drawl, "they can't see me. Why don't they think to look this way?"

A major from one of the newly arrived squadrons led his wingman on a strafing hop over Buka airfield. They thought they saw a seaplane and came back for a second pass to get it. By that time the AA was ready for them and threw up a lot of stuff. The wingman pulled up thinking he had been hit. The major called and said he couldn't see, because of oil. No more was seen of the major, except for reports from ground observers along the coast of Bougainville, saying that they saw an F4U go into a dive and go straight into the water.

That evening, Schaefer came around, "How'd you like to go up in the morning with Sapp and Jones to look for Leach?" he asked me. "Witt will be going too, I think. You're the only one who has seen Leach who'll be along. Jones has got keen eyes and you seem to have extra good eyesight, too. It will have to be a predawn take-off if you want to go."

"Okay. I'll go," I answered.

George came in and roused me and after some breakfast we got down to the ready room for an 0530 take-off. It was still plenty dark. We were delayed by practice firing of the artillery but took off early enough to arrive at Cape St. George soon after sunup.

I was skirting the shore while the others were spaced evenly abreast over the water. After a few minutes I saw a cove with something white sticking up. I turned to the right and saw a sailboat in the cove and a canoe. The canoe was filled with four natives.

A couple of hundred yards up the shore, I received a surprise—a Jap barge was trying to get to shore at full speed. I couldn't turn sharply enough to bring my sights to bear, but I was able to go over it close enough to look inside. It seemed to be filled with bales covered by matting, and with several people in the bow and stern.

"Witt from Zed. I've found a live barge over here and am going to make some runs on it."

I circled to the left and came down with all guns firing, pulling out of the dive just in time to miss hitting it. A left *chandelle* regained much of my lost altitude and permitted me to turn sharply back for another try. I saw Witt approaching to help. The barge had stopped.

When I was in position for my second firing run, I heard Sapp call over the radio, "Come on—we'll get the barges later." I continued my run from a higher altitude this time, so my bullets poured into the inside of the barge. I went on ahead and caught Witt; then we caught up to Sapp and Jones, who were circling to wait for us.

We continued our search at 200 feet when Sapp started to circle an object in the water. I began to feel excited, hoping it was Leach. We all circled until we recognized the object as a tree.

We searched on. A minute later, I saw something and turned to get a better view. It looked like a raft. I thought sure that was what it was. I got another look when I circled closer to it and saw it wasn't a raft, but a canoe, or so I thought. I circled again, this time flying directly over it. Dipping my wing at the sea to get it out of the way I recognized a yellow tree stump with limbs rising in the air and waving in the gentle sea, looking just like people.

We searched methodically up and down the channel, going for several miles past Duke of York Island. On one sweep we discovered a small cargo boat anchored near a reef offshore from the Duke of York. I zoomed it as I happened to be closest. There were several bundles of cargo hidden under thatchwork. We ignored it for the time being and went on.

One more final sweep and we decided Leach wasn't on the water. We formed into a column and attacked a barge making for shore on the Duke of York. After we left it smoking, we went around again, each of us blazing away. It began to burn. There was a minor explosion. Soon it sank. Nobody escaped.

We hit the cargo boat, which looked about 75 feet long, and left it smoking badly.

We had been searching with our hoods open and our goggles perched high on our foreheads so that we could see better. The wind hurt the eyes and the noise and compression of the wind hurt the ears. All the while, we had to keep a sharp eye above us for Zeros, because only a few days before, when everyone had thought there were no longer Zeros at Rabaul, five Japs had jumped some Corsairs which were low over the water. The Corsairs knocked down one Zero, but they all returned back to base badly shot up in exchange. Only the sturdiness of their airplanes brought the pilots back.

Flying close to the shoreline of New Ireland on our way back to Bougainville, I saw a flash. I thought sure it was Leach in the jungle trying to signal me with his reflection mirror. I turned over to the spot. Instead of a mirror, I found a sailboat crammed with the most motley assortment of characters I had ever seen. They were dressed in colorful red, yellow and blue clothes. Most of them were natives, but some were lighter-skinned, either Japs, Chinese or possibly French. They sailed in the tree and mountain shadows along the water's edge, but seemed unafraid of being shot at. They just waved as I passed them by. I didn't want to kill a lot of natives just to get three or four Japs, although many of the other pilots did not share this point of view, figuring the natives deserved to die for associating with the Japanese.

We landed after an unsuccessful search—the last to be conducted for Leach.

"Some Dumbo pilot must be feeling like a heel by now," Jones said.

"The guy who gave Dumbo the order to return to base the other night ought to get a court-martial," Major Gordon declared vehemently.

During the latter part of February, one of those miraculous escapes occurred that makes a fatalistic person, who believes that he will not die until his "time comes," all the more certain of his belief. An F4U approached for a landing, but spun in and burned up. The pilot, who had been too low to parachute, escaped!

Our water supply was shut off until the wreckage was cleared from the small river.

Conversely, other accidents happened which should have resulted in only scratches and bruises, but pilots received broken necks instead. Two airplanes were shot down on different occasions as they approached the field for a landing. They collided with the huge shells fired by our 155-mm Long Toms.

The Army P-38's began to carry 500-pound bombs to drop on the city of Rabaul and other targets. Some of the Corsairs of VF 17 also carried some bombs. I hoped to pack some myself, but no arrangements appeared to be forthcoming to convert our Marine fighter planes.

Okie McLean received about the worst fright of his life—not in combat, but in a cloud. The clouds were very thick and came down to the water. He got in the cloud trying to get to Rabaul to escort some bombers. With unreliable instruments and the nearness of the clouds to the water, he thought for a few minutes that his time had come.

I was also frightened in the same manner. I was flying wing as the third man in a three-plane formation as our fourth man hadn't been able to take off. The division leader used too much throttle for me to keep up with him and I lost him as he turned away from me inside the clouds. I immediately stopped trying to keep up and went to my instruments. Finally I came out into a clear spot only 100 feet off the water and saw the other two planes not far away and heading for home.

That was not as bad as the fright I received one day on a test hop. Pilots had claimed that the engine of an F4U kept cutting out on take-off. I was available when it was repaired, so I took it up for a test. I said a brief prayer before taking off and the engine sounded fine. After taking it up to high altitudes and testing the supercharger, magnetos and other items, I chose the opportunity to fly completely around the circumference of Bougainville and Buka Island, a distance of 300 nautical miles, about 75 miles shorter than flying from Munda to Rabaul.

The engine had been overhauled and I had to take it easy, so I flew low and slow enough to inspect the shores for barges or Japanese. The thought of the accurate AA on Ballale Island gave me an uncomfortable feeling, but I was able to fly halfway between Ballale and Kahili.

It wasn't until I reached the northwest tip of Buka Island that I spotted an untouched but empty barge. It was in the middle of an open bay. I suspected a trap, because it was so easily seen, but made three firing runs on it anyway, without making much of an impression. I was just pulling out of my third dive when I heard the steady beat of my engine change. It went flat and became rough. I lost power.

Immediately I headed for the open sea, hoping to land on the other side of an island, where the only friendly natives on Buka were reported to be located. Even so, I had grave fears the Japs would see me go down and be along to reclaim me or my body.

I made it to the desired spot and still I had sufficient power to remain in the air. I set my course for home, staying a few miles off the shore. After I had limped back home and landed safely, I learned one of the magnetos had gone completely out and the other was not far from it after carrying the ignition load by itself from the tip of Buka.

Papers were captured from the Japanese on February 23rd which indicated that the American observation planes were not to be fired upon (probably not to give away gun positions). An Army lieutenant gave us a very good talk one evening in the messhall and told us leaflets had been dropped to the Japs in the jungle telling them they had fought honorably and there wasn't any use of them staying in the jungle to starve. By surrendering they would receive lots of good food. The leaflets also told them about the Japanese losses on the Central Pacific Islands and that Rabaul was being bombed every day so they could not get any more reinforcements or supplies.

The Japanese paper revealed that they had 27,000 men able to participate in a forthcoming attack, to begin the first week in March, probably about March 7th. They had prepared artillery positions and several 77 mm's and 150 mm's were available although none had been moved into position yet, as far as we knew.

The lieutenant commented, "We believe we can hold the outer perimeter against any attack the Japs might launch, but we want the Seabees and Marine Air Group 24 to strengthen the internal defenses, just in case. The documents we captured contained maps that were surprisingly accurate. They had this messhall plotted and they were planning to sight in with their first few rounds on the crossroads a few hundred feet away.

"All the planes will be flown to a field out of danger, probably down to the Treasuries and Vella Lavella. Those pilots who have to stay here are to remain in their foxholes as much as possible, if anything ever comes from the information we've learned.''

The lieutenant went on to tell us that General MacArthur had declared Bougainville ''secured'' some time before. We pilots asked each other, ''Who's got who secured?''

In view of the possible attack by the Japanese, we pilots began to take a greater interest in our ground defenses. Many of the men, including some Army higher-ups, thought it impossible for the Japs to drag artillery and bring shells some fifty miles through the jungle and swamps and over the mountains to stage an attack.

How wrong they were.

13.
ATTACK!

FLAME BELCHED MIGHTILY from the muzzle of the
155-mm "Long Tom" and the loudest earth-shaking
blast I ever heard sought to pierce my eardrums. I
was standing on tiptoe with my hands over my ears
and my mouth open, to equalize the pressure and
save myself from a punctured eardrum, when the
concussion of the shot made the sandbag wall waver
unsteadily and the camouflage netting overhead
shake as if it were the web of a gigantic spider.

The shot was terrifying. One of the officers with me
was very frank in admitting that he was afraid of the
big gun. "Let's get out of here before they fire that
thing again," he whispered in my ear. As we drove
away in our borrowed jeep he tried to apologize for
dragging the rest of us away. "I don't know why it is,
but I just can't stand being near one of those things
when it's fired. I can't take it. If I was ever assigned to
be on the crew I would do anything to get out of it."

We had left much of the camp area behind and were
out to look over our artillery positions, which had
become increasingly active. We found several batteries of Long Toms along the road, each in a
camouflaged position, surrounded by sandbags and
covered with netting. A wide area of grass had been
cut in the swampy ground to give unhindered visibil-

ity. Watchtowers had been constructed to keep an eye out for American planes that might fly near the path of the shells. All of the Long Toms we saw were manned by colored soldiers, with usually a white lieutenant in charge of each squad.

Our jeep passed over a bridge which crossed a stream of water resembling a light grade of motor oil flowing to the sea. We became engulfed in a sea of grass on each side of the road.

Upon reaching a clearing on the left we stopped at another gun emplacement. The gun was a 155-mm Howitzer which had a comparatively short barrel and was manned entirely by Marines.

I noticed the thick wall of sandbags built around the gun. There was an abandoned emplacement a few feet away and the sandbag revetment around it was scattered on the ground. "I suppose the blast knocks a few of those sandbags away once in a while judging by the looks of the old location," I commented to one of the Marines.

"Yeah, it's got quite a concussion effect. But it doesn't push them outward from the blast, it sucks them in!"

We flyers were all surprised for we thought the outgoing air pushed them away. Instead it was the air rushing back into the vacuum created by the blast that was forceful enough to pull ordinary barricades down and strip the bark from the trees.

"I would like to go to the outer defenses," I told the crew members. "Do I just follow the road?"

"You are at the outer defenses now."

"Do you mean to say there isn't anything between us and the Japs? I don't see any protection around here at all."

"That's right, there isn't a damned thing between

you and the Japs right this minute, except some swamp, which we are depending on to keep the Japs away from our position. We've got some wire strung along with tin cans tied to it and some flares that go off when the wire is touched."

It had become dark and the time came when the battery was scheduled to take its turn firing. The cannon was aimed by sighting through a rear-vision mirror arrangement and by turning the gun in the right direction by lining up a pole with a dim light back of the gun with the required number of degrees.

The explosion of the howitzer was not quite as bad as the Long Tom, but it was bad enough.

We drove back the way we had come and stopped by the Long Toms to watch them do some night firing. A short distance up the road a USO show was playing.

Back at the tents we found Hazlett shaving the hair off Jule's head. The twenty-five-year-old prematurely balding Koetsch had been told that shaving the scalp would make it grow new hair, so most of his third combat tour he went around monk-like with a bald pate fringed with reddish hair. In the sunstroke-laden sunshine he knotted a handkerchief at each corner and spread it over his unprotected head. With his rusty mustache and his meerschaum pipe, Jules Koetsch looked the picture of a comfortable German.

I was sleeping soundly on the morning of March the eighth for I anticipated having the day off and hoped to pay another visit to our front line defenses.

A loud noise stirred my consciousness. The noise came again. I became more awake. A few seconds later I heard a loud explosion. "Damn that new artillery position. Why'n-the-hell did they have to put it so close," I said to myself and turned over on my other side to go back to sleep.

"Those are Jap shells!" Panky's voice rang out loud and clear in spite of the early hour.

"CRACK!" Another explosion and I became fully awake.

"Wake up! The Japs are shelling us!" someone screamed outside.

Swinging my feet out of the bunk and into the waiting "air raid" shoes, I grabbed my steel helmet and ran out the door yelling, "Wake up, wake up. Hit the foxhole," hitting it myself and being joined in matter of moments by several others.

Thirty seconds later and CR-ACK! An extremely loud blast came from close by.

CR-ACK! Another close hit.

CR-UMP, CR-UMP! They were hitting farther away.

I looked at my watch and it was a minute or two after 0600. We crouched close together under the protection of the timber roof Levine and I had built. Nobody helped us work on the foxhole, but when the time came to use it we found ourselves on the exposed ends where a slanting piece of shrapnel could dive beneath the logs.

Shells were exploding near and far all over the vicinity. After an hour they slowed in frequency and stopped, probably while the Japs took time out for breakfast.

We climbed out of the foxhole. Our tent was riddled with shrapnel that had pierced the canvas roof and holed the floor. If Levine had waited any longer in hitting the foxhole, he would have received a piece of shrapnel in the chest. One would have got me in the stomach.

There were four jagged holes in the seat of my pants. Luckily, I hadn't been wearing them at the time, because they were hanging on a nail over my bed. All the mattresses had been pierced and Levine's flying suit had several holes in it.

In the foxhole, twenty feet from where we were, Hazlett had taken refuge with some pilots from another squadron. Two of the men with him had been hit in the shoulder and arms. The third had been so slightly wounded he didn't even know it until he saw the blood running. Sand from the rim of the foxhole was blasted into Hazlett's back.

Forty feet from our tent a tree had stopped and exploded a passing shell, which had chopped off a limb and then sprayed the ground and the tents with shrapnel.

The tent nearest the tree was badly wrecked and had to be completely evacuated. For a few minutes there was competition as each pilot dug shrapnel out of the ground for souvenirs. Some of it was razor sharp on the jagged edges.

The planes all took off for a safer place. "Goldarn our luck," Morris moaned, "we *would* have the day off when they started this shelling so we have to stay and take it."

Then we all pitched in and remodeled our foxhole, covering it over entirely with heavy logs and building a sloping L-shaped entrance so no shrapnel could get us that way. We left a hole at each end to help relieve the concussion effect of shells.

While we were chopping fallen trees for the logs, the Japs began to shell us again. I threw myself flat on the ground until the scream of the shell passed overhead. Then I followed Koetsch and Hazlett as we sprinted for our foxhole 100 yards away. The wail of another shell approached and we fell as close to the earth as possible. The shell burst close. After one more mad dash we hit the foxhole.

We noticed that the shelling came heavily at hourly intervals with a minor barrage every half hour. In between there were a few stray shells whistling overhead. We kept a close check on the time and moved to the foxholes when it came time for the regular barrages. Sometimes the Japs fooled us by changing their schedules, however.

George Schaefer came back from a hectic time at the runway. One of the first shells fired had struck the ground about twelve feet in front of Kitty Hobb's airplane as he taxied out to take off. Kitty leaped and fell out of the cockpit and ran with his parachute banging against his knees to the protective side of a dirt embankment. There he found two mechanics and they all huddled together, afraid the next shell would get them.

When the shelling eased up and the remaining planes left, Okie McLean received a hotseat and a case of jangled nerves when the old plane he was flying caught fire while he was taking off. Somehow he managed to stamp it out. The battery located beneath his seat had shorted out.

The first shell fired by the Japs had killed a Marine walking to the neighboring messhall for breakfast. Scuttlebutt came, which was never substantiated, saying that an officer about to get on a plane to leave for rear areas and then home had his right leg cut off by a shell. There were many tales of narrow escapes: a shell passing one foot over a man's head, another fellow leaving a foxhole thirty seconds before it received a direct hit, another fellow's bed being sprayed by shrapnel a couple of seconds after he had been blown from it onto the floor. Between 100 to 200 shells had hit our positions. They wrecked three F4U's on Piva South (Yoke) strip. At Piva Uncle strip one B-24 was ruined. Nineteen other planes were damaged but repairable. One man was dead and twelve wounded.

Li'l Red Dog hadn't taken cover at first and was found bleeding from a shrapnel wound in the tip of the nose.

Strange as it may seem, while Hawaii, Midway and many areas back in the States maintained blackouts or dimouts, we on the most advanced bases were permitted to burn as many lights as we needed unless there was an actual enemy raid in progress. With the advent of the Japanese shelling within a day of the forecast, we knew that any light at night would be enough to draw 77-mm or larger shells upon our heads, so for the first time we voluntarily blacked-out our camp area.

That night we were to be thankful that we had improved our foxhole, because it was to become a night of terror and exhaustion—a night we would all remember as long as we lived.

We huddled closer together in our foxhole. It was comforting to feel the warmth of the next body and to know that you were not alone to face the coming night. Outside, the last lingering fingers of sunlight were retreating away to the west and clawing the cloak of darkness over our beachhead and the 40,000 Japanese trying to drive us into the sea.

It had been one of those Solomon Island sunsets where the clouds are touched with the most vivid reds and yellows with a smear of the two spread overhead, as if the artist had flung his paint pots in a rage at the canvas of blue, then like a naughty schoolboy, had deliberately rubbed out the picture he had been painting. The long plume of smoke trailing from the volcano overlooking us had pointed down the prevailing wind like a golden arrow toward Rabaul—still a formidable enemy stronghold.

We had not been able to enjoy the scene for long before the first artillery barrage of the evening began coming our way.

"Hit the foxhole, men!" rang out that old familiar cry.

Now there were seven of us seated on the bench we had installed that very afternoon. We were squeezed together. It was dark as an elephant's belly inside our shelter. We had covered it with timbers and then heaped the dirt in a large pile on top of it all.

Remembering the officers who had claimed it was impossible to bring big guns half the length of Bougainville to shell us, I remarked to the fellows seated beside me, "I'll bet there's a lot of red faces around the island today, boys."

"Yeah, but not nearly as crimson as some of the patches of ground have become since this morning," one of them replied.

The Japs had perfect positions to shell our "Little Anzio." The perimeter and everything within our position was overlooked by jungle-covered, Jap-infested hills that increased in height and erupted literally in the conical shape of Mount Bagana well over a mile above the sea.

CR-UMP! CR-UMP! CR-UMP! Shells landed in our area, but not close enough to worry about. CR-ACK! A small avalanche of dirt cascaded down the wall of the foxhole and down my back.

Blam! Blam! I relaxed. The shells were moving

away from us and toward the beach.

When darkness arrived outside and brought with it thoughts of sleep, I wondered how we would endure the night. Already I was tired of sitting down.

Levine stood up as tall as he could without scraping the logs overhead and began to grope his way to the entrance.

"Where ya' goin'?"

"To hell with this old stuff. I'm going to get out of here. I'm going to take a mattress over to the next foxhole and stay there."

The tall, dark-haired pilot picked up Nicky, the diminutive wire-haired terrier, and departed. He had only been gone for five minutes. We heard him wrestling with the bulky mattress in the tent nearby. Then we heard the soul-chilling explosion of a very close hit.

"Did it get ya'—Levine?"

"Hell no, I'm okay. It was a little too close for comfort though." We heard his voice answer with a hesitation that sounded as if he first had to reassure himself.

The shell we thought might have hit Levine proved to be the opening gun of a fierce barrage. The Japs seemed to have boresighted the place where most of us fighter pilots lived and were intent upon wiping us out. Every shell appeared to be coming right for us. Then just when the next forward hit of the walking shells would get us for sure, the range lifted and the Japs shelled some other sector.

"Looks like we'll live a while longer," Fred Hughes quipped.

Blam! Blam! CR-ACK! The barrage began to creep toward us again. We heard the awesome whistling noises of shells passing us by. The shells going over sounded like a noiseless train rushing through a tunnel with the *whish* of split air resounding as it passed. We learned very quickly from their threatening tone whether they would hit near or far.

"They say you'll never hear the one that gets you," Bekins exclaimed in a voice meant to be encouraging. "As long as we don't hear them, we'll be all right."

"That's only hearsay, Bekins. Maybe nobody has ever lived through a hit to tell whether he heard it coming or not. Personally, I would rather not hear any of 'em coming at all." I finished talking to listen. The shells began to strike nearer again. The explosions were louder and there was less warning of their coming. We began to get really worried and wondered if we might be now experiencing the last few minutes of our lives.

At last the shelling lifted and our spirits brightened, for we were still alive. My wrist watch read 2230.

"*Hey you!* Down in that foxhole, get your gas masks. The Japs have begun to use gas!" I poked my head out of an entrance and saw a sentry moving away to warn the other foxholers.

"*Gas!*" The ejaculation came from the fellows with me. We looked at each other in consternation, although it was too dark to see anybody.

I called to the sentry, "Wait a minute, what do you mean the Japs are using gas? Are you sure?"

"I dunno. They wanted a doctor to come down by the strip just a little while ago. They said the Japs have begun to use gas!"

We all sat down again. "I hope they are using gas. That'll shorten this war," Hughes said. "Of course, it'll catch a lot of men on this island without their masks."

Then I began to smell something peculiar.

"Does anybody here smell anything strange, besides me?" Willie Hazlett asked.

"Yes, I do. I know I've smelled it somewhere before, though."

"Maybe it's gas!"

"Mebbe so."

"It smells like one of those insect bombs to me," one of the fellows said. Immediately we realized that was what it must be. Evidently a piece of shrapnel had holed one of the cans filled with compressed air and liquid insect poison, which was now spraying out uncontrolled.

"Hope it kills some of the mosquitoes in here."

"Are you sure it doesn't smell like garlic, geraniums, bitter almonds or any of those other poison gas smells?" Morris wanted to know with anxiety traced in his voice.

I pulled out my gas mask and tried it on to make sure it fit snugly. Bekins also thought that was a good idea, but found his mask container filled with odds and ends: a knife, sewing kit, spare flashlight batteries, bottle opener and other assorted bric-a-brac. "I'd be in a helluva fix if this was a real gas alarm. Who knows, maybe it is, maybe we'll all keel over dead in about five more minutes."

A few days before, scuttlebutt came that the Japs had used poison gas on some of our troops defending the perimeter, but nothing more was heard about it, so we assumed it to be false.

Now that we were actually facing an all-out assault on our positions by the Japs, along with their intense artillery bombardment, I realized just how hopeless our position could become. If the Japs used gas and caught our Army troops on the perimeter with their masks down, they would be able to break through without resistance, then divide our internal defenses and drive us all to the water's edge. It would be a South Pacific Dunkerque, without enough ships available to rescue more than a small minority of the men. It was not an appealing picture.

Midnight came and found us very drowsy, but unable to get any sleep. The bench became as unyielding as granite the longer we sat on it. Our nerves, already jolted by four and a half months of active combat flying, had begun to wear long before. Now I secretly wondered if we would come out of the night in one of those shaking, shell-shocked conditions. We held our breath every time one hit close.

The steel helmet on my head pressed downward with ever-increasing weight. When I sat upright and my head balanced on my shoulders, it wasn't hard to support, but when my sleepy head nodded forward, the weight of the helmet accelerated the downward motion and drove my chin against my chest with an audible clack of my teeth.

Finally, I leaned forward until my head touched the dirt wall facing me; this supported part of the burden. Somehow, I managed to relax for a few seconds at a time. Every time I began to doze my body fell lower and my head was pushed backward, the foxhole wall giving me the straightarm.

There wasn't any hope of getting a particle of rest in that postion, so I took my poncho and lay down on my belly to spread it underneath the bench. Then I crawled between the legs that dangled and lay down.

It felt good to lie down in spite of the clods and rocks taking turns at carving my back bone. I found that a rock made an excellent pillow, providing one wore his steel helmet.

When I began to fall into a halfhearted slumber with the explosions of the battle sounding in my ears, I daydreamed: I was back sleeping between clean white sheets on the bed of our screened-in back porch, listening to the sigh of the poplar trees as the fresh canyon breeze rushed through their branches and rubbed the leaves against one another. I could hear the low, dull bumping and grinding of boulders bouncing along the bottom of the creek bed and the roar of the rushing waters of the swollen and muddy mountain creek—changed into a turbulent river by a summer rainstorm.

A movement by my feet aroused me completely. I felt an animal cross over one of my spread-out legs, making a complete turn and lie down between them with its head resting on my stomach. I reached down and received the warm, moist caress of a friendly tongue on my hand.

It was Li'l Red Dog. I chuckled to myself over silly, awkward Red—Koetsch's dog. He was getting quite a travel record behind him, flying from Australia to New Caledonia, the New Hebrides and all over the Solomons, experiencing air raids, shellings and Spam—more than most dogs could boast.

After fighting and living together we were undergoing an ordeal over which we had not the slightest control. We couldn't shove the stick forward and bend the throttle to the firewall to get the hell out. We just had to stay there—like the poor guys in the infantry have always had to do—and take it, hoping that our number wasn't up, yet.

The tempo of the shelling increased to a constant stream of projectiles. Jap shells were coming at us and ours were passing overhead, going the other way. The boom of our own artillery and the *baloom, brrumph* and CR-ACK of bursting shells sounded as though Rip Van Winkle and his merry cronies were having an invitational bowling tournament with the Bougainville champions. I counted an explosion every three seconds, but many were from our own guns. However, a Jap shell passed over or burst short of us every five seconds.

Every man in the foxhole was silent. Then one fellow's leg began to shake uncontrollably. He tried to hold it still with his hands. The rest of us were taut with anxiety, for the Japs were placing their shot right in our area.

"I don't mind telling you boys—this is the scaredest I've ever been in all my life," Bekins told us in a quavering vibrato.

I grinned a worried, wry grin and my voice floated up from below. "You're not the only one!" I had smiled not because I was happy, but it struck me as humorous to see how really tense and worried all of my big, strong Marine pals were—not that I was any less worried.

We heard shrapnel flying through the canvas roofs and the wooden floors of the tents and ricocheting among the branches of a nearby banyan tree. There was so much shrapnel flying around outside, all a person would have to do to earn a Purple Heart would be to stick one finger out of the top of the foxhole.

"As bad off as we are in here, compared to being outside right now, this foxhole is my idea of heaven," one of the boys told us as if he was reconciling himself to the situation.

A sudden yell of pain made all of us jump momentarily. *"Ough! Oh, Oh, Oh, oooh! I've been hit!"* Hughes was jumping around near the entrance of the foxhole with a slight hop and a constant moan of pain. "I'm running for the doctor!"

Just after he dashed up the incline leading away from our hole to go over to a neighboring foxhole where Doc Brittingham was located, another shell exploded very close. We wondered if it got him.

"Where's the piece of shrapnel that hit Hughes?" I asked, closing my eyes as a pile of dirt cascaded past my face.

"He didn't say he got hit—he said he got bit!" Morris told me in an exasperated voice.

"*Bit?*" Li'l Red Dog jumped in alarm and bumped his head against the bench as I hurriedly brushed the overhanging legs apart to get clear of the bench. "What bit him?"

We looked all over the bench, dirt walls, roof and the deck with the beam of our one flashlight, but couldn't see anything that moved.

The barrage lifted and Hughes came back after half an hour, feeling much better. He had found Doc Brittingham with Ace Newlands and George Schaefer in the other foxhole. Doc was seated in the corner, swathed in his raincoat and hat and wearing his gas mask.

"I felt something crawl over my hand that felt soft and almost furry. Without thinking, I moved my hand. Then it bit me. I've never had anything sting me like that before, it was ten times worse than a hornet. I thought it might be something poisonous so I ran right over to the Doc, before I could fall over dead. When I think of it now, it could have been one of those long centipedes we've seen in the jungles and over at the messhall—You know, the ones about eight inches long and as thick as a broomstick."

Hughes also told us that some of the Japs were

infiltrating behind our lines. I regretted leaving my .45 automatic up in the tent, but touched the long hunting knife I always wore strapped to my belt and felt better.

The concentrated shelling stopped about 0200 and was replaced by just a few stray explosions at unexpected places. As if we hadn't already been through enough to make the evening memorable enough, another odor penetrated our foxhole.

"It smells like gasoline."

"Who would go around spilling gasoline at this hour of the night?"

"Mebbe a jeep's gas tank got hit."

The fumes became so concentrated in our hole, they began to affect me. "This stuff is so powerful in here I'm getting a headache. I've never had any bad effects from gasoline before. It might be some kind of poison gas the Japs are using that is made to smell like gasoline, so we won't use our masks—That's about the way those Japs would pull a gas attack."

Evidently the other fellows thought that might be the truth for they followed my example and put on their gas masks—that is all but two did. They had forgotten theirs.

To protect themselves as best they could, handkerchiefs were dampened from the canteen and the two breathed through moist cloth. Everything was silent except for the distant shelling and the wheeze of our breathing. When minutes passed and nothing happened to our two-legged maskless guinea pigs, the rest of us bravely took our masks off.

When dawn finally arrived and brought with it a lull in the shelling, we scrambled from our foxhole. We were as happy to get out as we had been to get in the night before.

A shell had clipped a sapling in back of our tent about fifteen feet away. Another had struck a tree not far from Levine's unprotected foxhole. We found Levine still alive and untouched, although shrapnel had sprayed all about him. Some of the tents were a shambles, riddled with holes. A truck across the street wore a gasoline tank with a gaping hole in it.

Rejoicing in our survival, we hungrily made our way past several shell craters to the messhall where we came face to face with our breakfast. It was Spam—the illegitimate ham!

We were indeed gluttons for punishment.

14.
FLIGHT TO "SAFETY"

MUNCHING BREAD AND jam we stood around our foxhole exchanging experiences with some of the neighboring denizens of the "underground." We thought we were going to have a respite from the shelling: scuttlebutt said our Army and Marine artillery had knocked out fifty-four Japanese positions and there weren't any more left. Another rumor claimed the Japs had exhausted their supply of shells. Ten men had been wounded during the night, two seriously.

There was no way of knowing about the newest scuttlebutt, but we learned that the old one about the Japanese use of poison gas had been totally false. The new "dope" also was proven to be false when a shell scuttled overhead and blew up a tent near the pilot's area. We all jumped into the foxhole in time to evade the shrapnel from the next one—a close hit.

Levine picked a piece of hot shrapnel out of the wall of our foxhole, directly opposite the entrance. "Looks like we've got a little visitor, boys," he commented.

With shells bursting all around us again, any of us could have exposed one square inch of flesh, I felt, and become eligible for the Purple Heart.

When things quieted down, Levine and I laid mattresses on the floor of our protected foxhole so we could spend the night in comfort.

It began to rain, with the sun continuing to shine throughout. Morris, Levine and I stripped down to our shorts so our clothes wouldn't get wet and spread ponchos over every sizable leak in our foxhole and shoveled dirt on top. Then we rushed a trench to completion around the whole to carry off the rain-water. Despite all the preparations a steady trickle of water poured into the foxhole, so we just dug a hole to capture it.

We thought the last of our airplanes had been flown out that morning and that we would remain where we were indefinitely. Most of the pilots had disappeared from the area. With the foxhole all fixed up and the thought in the back of my mind that I might get to see more of what it was like for our ground forces, I secretly began to look forward to the future, however uncertain it might be. It was therefore with a feeling of reluctance that I heard a jeep drive up and George Schaefer yelling, "I need three pilots!"

Morris, Levine and I scrambled out of our foxhole. I grabbed my shaving gear and put it in one pocket. I put a small book on *How to Speak Russian in Six Weeks Without a Master,* that I had purchased in Sydney and had been studying ever since, in another pocket and a vest-pocketsized book, *Principles of the Gospel,* in the same pocket as my shaving kit. My helmet and my gas mask completed my baggage.

Under cover of a light, sprinkly rain we volunteers sped down the road and drove across the open land-ing strip as fast as we could go. Jap artillery observers on the hills were able to see practically every move-ment in the area; besides, a few snipers had infiltrated our lines.

At the ready room we put on our flight gear and our parachutes. My gloves had been taken by somebody else—They were one article of clothing that I never flew without.

We were to fly the last of the fighter planes out from under the Japanese noses and shells. They were three planes which had been so beat up and out of condition that, up until then, they had been unable to fly away. One had an engine which had cut out on take-off. The other two were from another squadron and we didn't even know what might be wrong with them. At any rate, with nearly $100,000 of taxpayer's money tied-up in each plane in cash alone, and with their greatly increased value in the actual combat zone— they had to be saved if humanly possible.

We had intended to utilize the poor visibility of the rainstorm to hide our movements from the Japanese so as not to draw their fire. Now, as we rode on the jeep for the revetment area, the rain stopped. Off to our left a few hundred feet we could see the densely foliaged hills, where the Japanese were located. I wondered how many eyes were watching us at that moment. We heard the explosions of Japanese mortars and cannonfire bursting across the strip from us.

With faithful George driving like mad and the rest of us hanging on for dear life we drove up the taxiway and let Morris jump off at his plane. Then on to the Service Squadron area, a place totally unfamiliar to me, where Levine and I jumped off.

Our planes were parked in a revetment without any protecting embankment except at the rear. They were on the exposed side of the embankment and faced the Jap positions—and in full view of the enemy. A TBF parked next to us was sending up a tall column of black smoke from its flaming guts, where a

Jap shell had struck a few minutes before.

"Better hurry, the Japs are starting to shell again and there's a 500-pound bomb in the middle of that TBF that might go off any time," a mechanic shouted to me as he gave me a boost onto the wing of the F4U.

I dumped my gas mask and helmet on top of my oxygen bottle. Then I wrestled with the shoulder straps and nearly pulled a tendon loose in my left arm trying to get them over and the safety belt fastened. There was one mechanic for each plane, and mine just stood on the ground not giving any help with my harnessing and wishing to hell we would hurry up before we drew the enemy artillery shells our way.

My engine kicked over and caught without any trouble. Levine's coughed and died a couple of times; then it too joined the chorus. I knew the Japs could surely hear the engines now and would know what was up. The oil pressure rose within thirty seconds, and I thumbed the chocks away and held the brakes while the mech took them from the wheels. He waved his arm and off I went.

With my throttle forward to give me all the speed I dared on the winding, dipping taxi-way, I broke all speed records for the unfamiliar course and after taxiing half the length of the strip entered the take-off area. George was parked in his jeep watching to see if we would make it all right and ready to pick up the pieces if we didn't. I thought it was pretty brave of him to stick around like that when he knew we must have become the center of Jap attention.

Holding my brakes I ran the engine up for a hurried magneto check, then dashed out onto the runway, swinging to the right, and started my take-off, lining up with the runway and locking my tailwheel as I went.

Shoving the throttle up to 43 inches of manifold pressure for a fast take-off, but not enough to strain the engine too much, I got off the ground safely and quickly turned to the left so that I wouldn't pass over some Japs waiting to take pot shots at me.

Not bothering to retract my wheels or close the hatch, I headed seaward and within five minutes was coming in for a landing on the Torokina airstrip, by the beach.

My plane was one of the old "bird-cage" models. I had become used to the newer "bubble-canopy" type with their increased vision and safer landing characteristics. I made a bumpy landing on the metal Marston mat at Torokina and a cross wind gave me a scare when it started to blow me off the runway. My left brake was almost a complete failure, but—by gunning the engine and using the rudder and with luck, I kept from running off.

Levine came in for a landing as soon as I had taxied off the strip, followed by Morris.

"I sure got a scare coming in for the landing," Levine told us. "I pulled back on the stick and it wouldn't come back, no matter how hard I tried. I managed to land okay and then I discovered that my helmet and gas mask had gotten in between the stick and the seat and blocked it from coming back."

Leaving instructions with some mechanics to fix the left brake on my plane, we all walked over to the tower and reported our names and plane numbers to the New Zealand operations officer. A truck took us inland a fraction of a mile to a bivouac area. Here we were assigned a tent and issued a three-day supply of K rations.

The first thing we did after finding the location of the nearest foxhole was to plunk ourselves down on the cots. We hadn't slept for approximately thirty hours. During the night, I had felt sure I couldn't possibly fly the next day even if I had to, I was so tired, sleepy and miserable. When the time came to fly though, with the added incentive furnished by the Japs, I had forgotten about my exhaustion. For three hours we were dead to the world.

It was the craving in our bellies as much as the ring of the mess gong that awoke us in time to eat some hot bully beef hash, with bread and jam—topped off with canned peaches for dessert.

I had only half of my peach eaten, when a siren rang for us to hit the foxholes. The Japs began shelling the area.

And so it went, all that day and into a night marked by repeated dives for the foxhole, when shells struck the vicinity and tilted the nearest latrine at a crazy angle. We awoke to see that some of our squadron mates had returned to Bougainville. They had flown the planes away early on the first morning of the shelling and had been living at Ondonga, near Munda, ever since. They had to fly up to Green Island to patrol all day from the recently completed airstrip, then fly back to Ondonga at night.

Hughes, York and I borrowed a jeep and dashed up the road to our vacated tents to pack a few valuables. Before returning to the Torokina strip, however, we drove around to the prisoner-of-war cage. The Marine POW cage was rumored to consist of a single strand of barbed wire enclosing an empty space about four feet square, in keeping with Marine policy of taking no prisoners.

We found the Army POW enclosure to consist of a plentiful supply of wire fencing, with two separate stockades inside, one for the officers and one for the enlisted men. Two tents provided shelter. The Japanese prisoners were busily digging foxholes to protect themselves from their own shelling.

With the officer in charge we approached the barbed wire, while an M.P. went inside to summon one of the Nips. "This one is the friendliest of the lot," we were told. "Most of them act pretty sullen all the time, but this one is always smiling and acts as if he is trying to please. He understands English better than the others do."

The other POW's didn't pay any attention to us after a first quick glance. Many of them had tried to commit suicide to avoid being captured. It was a disgrace to be captured. The Japanese government took the attitude that prisoners of the Americans were officially dead.

When I saw the Jap soldier approaching, I felt very strange. Here for the first time I met my enemy face to face, with no hostile acts permitted. I looked at him appraisingly. All that I had heard about the "bandy-legged Jap" appeared to be true. I rose half a head taller than the Japanese, who was dressed only in a pair of shorts and shoes.

The "son of heaven" came to a halt and saluted, his face wreathed in a toothy grin. "Hello," I told him coldly. He grinned even more broadly and executed a quick little bow from the waist in acknowledgment, muttering a word unintelligible to me.

I looked at the sweating stockily built torso. "You-working-hard?" I paused between each word and acted the part of a man throwing shovelfuls of dirt over his shoulder.

"Yesss, yesss. We"—he gesticulated—"work

busy." Then he imitated the motion of a shell coming from the Jap positions and exploding, accompanying the action with appropriate whistles and grunts.

While the Army officer talked to him in Japanese, I noticed the eyes of the Jap focus upon my .45 automatic slung under my left armpit with its handle toward him. Hughes also saw it and drew me backwards two paces. He expected the Jap to reach through the wire and grab my pistol any moment. I rather hoped he would, just for the excitement. I had taken care to remove all the cartridges from it.

Late that afternoon Morris, Levine and I flew down to Ondonga. Morris flew a different plane than the one he had rescued from the Japs, but Levine and I flew the same old clunkers, and once again my brake failed when we landed in a stiff crosswind that was bringing splattering drops of rain with it. As always it was a problem to keep the plane from ground-looping, but my efforts were successful.

Ondonga became memorable, because it was the only place we had encountered in the South Pacific which provided hot water—and it steeped us in lovely steam and enabled stubby whiskers to make a fast exit from our faces.

Most of the Blackcat crews lived at Ondonga at that time. Every night one or more of the black-painted PBY's would take off, no matter how bad the weather. With their radar and bombs they harassed and sank enemy shipping. The worst part about night flying, the pilots thought, was the chance of running into unseen turbulent clouds capable of tearing the wings off their planes.

Every day our pilots flew up to Green Island, 300 miles away. After patrolling and standing by on the alert, they would return at night—until the day came that Green Island could at last accommodate all of VMF 222 and part of VMF 223.

The day before, Major Don Sapp, who always made the most of his opportunities with his excellent marksmanship, had knocked down two more Zekes to run his total up to ten. It happened to be the first day in several that I hadn't gone to Rabaul. Jones had sighted some Zeros over Rabaul and tallyhoed their position. Sapp beat Jones to them. While the Japs circled Tobera airfield in the landing traffic circle, Sapp rode up behind and shot one down; it crashed on the runway amid a black cloud of smoke. He then moved on up the line and hit another, which crashed beside the runway. He shot another that started going down and holed one more, but the AA was so heavy by that time he didn't attempt to see what happened to the last two planes. He claimed it was so thick he could have walked on it.

It had only been a few days before that Sapp led Langley in a strafing attack on a Japanese cargo vessel over 100 feet long, leaving it in flames. He had become the outstanding pilot in the squadron, largely due to his sharpshooting ability and luck at encountering opportune situations. After instructing and practicing gunnery at Miami, Florida, "Slap Happy Sappy the Mental Midget," as he called himself, had made his skill pay off in company with his fighting spirit.

I drove up to my former place of abode to assemble my gear for the move to Green Island. The commander of the Seabees had thought so highly of the foxhole we had left that he had taken it for his very own.

During the two days and one night I had been shelled, 60 per cent of the total Japanese shells fired had landed in the pilots' area. Approximately eighty-seven shells had attempted to saturate a space smaller than a city block. In the small triangular tent area used for the seven tents of my squadron, with only a few yards of ground remaining unused, at least four shells had exploded in the trees or on the ground.

The situation was dark on Bougainville. In fact, some of the Army generals had completed detailed plans for the evacuation of all the forces from our beachhead. The Japs had broken through some of our outer defenses. Although they had sacrificed several hundred men in attacking, they had exacted their toll of American lives.

For the first time in World War II, the Negro troops received a real tryout in battle. Their first night in the front line foxholes the cunning Japanese rattled tin cans, yelled, whispered, shot and exercised many of their tricks calculated to throw horror into the enemy and get him to reveal his position. Through the night, our colored boys in camouflage remained at their posts and like seasoned troops dutifully kept the Japs in the dark regarding their location.

Some of the outfits on the island, who had been concerned with aviation, had been instructed in forming an inner defense system. Many had suffered quite heavy casualties from the shelling. Some mechanics from VMF 215 had knocked out three Jap foxholes, losing one of their own men.

Nine nights after the shelling had begun a dark figure stood near the messhall, within fifty yards of my former residence. For three nights the shadow was observed and challenged by sentries, but it always melted away. Then they captured it and discovered a Japanese soldier. Nobody knew why he never had tried to steal food. He was very hungry.

One of the Negro messmen was found two weeks after the first day of the shelling. He was cowering in the darkest corner of his foxhole, with cans of rations stacked in the corners. Those who found him claimed that he hadn't been out of the hole since the start of the Jap attack.

The Japanese had installed a heavy AA gun near our landing strip and had shot the wing from the Flying Grasshopper American observation airplane. Neither of the two occupants escaped the death plunge.

From the observer of our take-off in the last three F4U's to leave Piva Y strip, I learned that the last plane had no sooner become airborne when an artillery shell exploded close behind it. That pilot must have been Johnny Morris, using up some more of his "nine lives."

We took off for Green Island in our F4U's carrying everything we would need until the rest of our baggage could be sent up. From the air, Green Island looked like an emerald circlet containing a center stone of blue sapphire.

On the ground we had a rude awakening. Not enough mattresses and blankets were available, so each of us had a choice of one or the other, but not both. A long tent contained canvas cots for our use. The messhall and the tents were immersed in a gooey mass of mud and the whole was overshadowed by the trees of the jungle and serviced by a solitary road. Near the landing strip the constant coral dust and human sweat created a hard exterior for all of the Marines and New Zealanders. There were no shower baths. Water was precious. We were able to solve this problem by swimming in the lagoon, staying close to shore because we did not know just what the local shark population might favor in the way of dessert.

I wondered what Admiral Halsey had thought of the island during his thirty-minute visit a couple of days before.

If the Japanese had been alert they might have shot down our favorite admiral. I was in one of the Corsairs providing protection to the PBY which carried Halsey to the island. As we approached our destination one of the Corsairs on patrol over the island made a playful run at the flying boat. "Stop it! I am carrying Admiral Halsey aboard!" someone on the PBY screamed over the radio.

"What a poor damn fool that was, who told us the admiral was on board his plane," one of us commented when we landed. "If the Japs picked that up on their radio they would probably send all the remaining Zeros down from Rabaul to shoot him down."

Frankly, at the time I rather hoped the Japs had heard the transmission. I couldn't think of better bait than Admiral "Bull" Halsey to stir the rats out of their hole at Rabaul, and I was hungry for Jap planes.

Admiral Halsey must have considered everything ready for occupancy because it was not long until Green Island became an integral cog in our plans for staging attacks on Rabaul and Kavieng.

The second day of my arrival on Green Island I was walking along the flight strip when I stepped aside to let a jeep pass. Immediately I shouted at the driver and I met William Wood again. Now a captain, he was in charge of Marine Air Group 14's transportation. He only had time for five minutes of conversation. Our friendship had begun at the Bahama Room

in a Miami hotel on New Year's eve, 1942. I had been a
second lieutenant in the Marine Corps less than two
months when I walked into the lounge and began
talking to a friendly, heavy set first lieutenant—
Wood. I hung breathlessly on his every word about
the Corps for he appeared to be "salty."

He introduced me to people or pointed them out
and I immediately forget their names, for in those
days most were unknown to the public. Upon subsequent recollection I realized the gathering had been
somewhat illustrious to say the least.

Major "Zach" Scott of the U.S. Army Air Corps
came in with his cousin, Toby Wing, a former motion
picture star who was with the transoceanic flyer,
Dick Merrill.

"Whitney" (R. W. Whitehead), the Commanding
Officer of the Rangoon Squadron of the American
Volunteer Group, was there clinking glasses with
other ex-Flying Tigers; Curtis Smith, who was the
AVG adjutant under Chennault, and Greg Boyington,
formerly executive officer of the Adam and Eve
Squadron.

They were all in civilian clothes except for Scott
and enjoying the courtesy of millionaire Bill Pawley,
who was president of the firm that had assembled the
flyers and sent them to China.

One of the ex-AVG boys who later added three
more planes to his score of 6 wasn't present at the
party. Like Boyington he later went to the Solomons.
He was Eddie Overend, C.O. of Marine Fighting
Squadron VMF 321, which had been relieved at
Bougainville early in February.

The next time I saw First Lieutenant Wood was at
North Island, California. I had been preparing to

check out on flying from an aircraft carrier and he was about to ship overseas. That was the last of January, 1943.

At Vella Lavella he passed by in a speeding jeep with another officer—one shout and a wave of the hand and he was gone. I had no inkling he was anywhere near my location.

Each time we met he always invited me to visit him. Every time I had attempted to do so, he had just been moved. This time, we pilots were moved to new quarters several miles distant and I didn't get to see him again.

For the first time Marine B-25's (PBJ's) appeared in the South Pacific, making strikes on Rabaul and other targets. Later, they performed many night harassing missions and when the AA became too intense they would drop a flash bomb that blinded all the Japanese gunners for the next ten minutes.

We griped about the lack of enemy planes and wondered why we weren't sent to New Guinea to help the Army flyers clean out the Japanese aviation there. Some of us thought the Army wanted to keep that melon for themselves so that their new high-ranking ace, Dick Bong, could ring up a new record. Until then, practically all the American flyers with a score of twenty planes or more during World War II had been Marines. We supposed that both the Army and Navy were getting a little bit tired of having the Marines in the limelight and wanted to keep us out of the juicy fighting.

All we had to look forward to was the strafing of Japanese barges which were plentiful near Wide Bay and Simpson Harbor. Then we received orders from General MacArthur prohibiting us from attacking the enemy on New Britain south of a line drawn on the maps, which deprived us of the happy hunting ground at Wide Bay. That area was to be considered part of the Southwest Pacific Area and we were to confine ourselves to the South Pacific Area.

After days of dawn take-offs, all-day patrolling, dusk landings and strikes on Rabaul, we wondered where the next forward step would be taken toward Tokyo. Scuttlebutt came that a Marine division was preparing to make a landing at the large base of Kavieng on the far end of New Ireland Island. Other rumors said we would hurdle over the hedge of New Britain and New Ireland and establish an airbase in the Admiralty Islands on the other side.

When we were ordered to attack Kavieng with a large formation of SBD's and TBF's we felt sure it was the start of the preliminary softening-up process before the Marines landed. It was to be the first time those land-based bombers had struck at the Japanese base, although a Navy carrier strike and allied heavy bombers had paid visits to Kavieng.

All the planes took off from Green Island with a full load of fuel. We flew at a high altitude close to the long, narrow coast of New Ireland, a rapier pointed toward the Palau Islands, 1,520 miles distant. Truk was off to our starboard 725 miles away. Never had I seen the South Pacific Area so maplike. I could see Rabaul and could almost look the length of New Britain to New Guinea over 200 miles to the west. We flew past such places as Cape Matanamberam, Namatanai (one of the Jap bases) and others more easily pronounced, Kaf Kaf and But But.

Five hours after our take-off we fighter pilots returned to Green Island, with very sore hind ends, an interesting geography lesson and little else to reward us. Army P-39's guarded the home base in our absence.

James A. Wally returned from a strike on

Namatanai airfield. He had been tail-end Charlie in a dive, when he saw a streak in the water near the mouth of a river. He thought it was a boat so he went over to strafe it. Much to his surprise and the enemy's, he discovered a Jap float plane taking off!

After diving at it and firing a few rounds he came back for another run. The float plane was then airborne and as he approached again it lifted its nose to fire back at him. A wing dropped and hit the water and the plane cartwheeled wing over wing in the middle of a heavy splash. Wally never knew for sure whether he had shot it down with bullets or whether it just spun in. It really didn't matter—at least it was another dead Jap.

After Wally's success, Jonesy and I received permission to form a patrol. Levine and Mack wanted to go along too, so we four took off on what was officially a barge hunt at the Feni Islands, forty miles closer to New Britain. We felt sure that a "wind" would blow us over by Namatanai airfield to watch for enemy planes, however.

We gave three barges which Bekins had hit a few hours before another going over. Then we headed for New Ireland. We never fulfilled our desire, because we found a plane circling a pilot in a one-man life raft with the yellow-orange of dye marker trailing behind.

We left Levine with the other pilot and went on to guide the Dumbo forty miles to the pilot by radio. When we returned to the raft, it had been lost by the planes circling over it. Then followed fifteen minutes of searching in a line abreast formation until Jones saw the raft.

When the Dumbo arrived we witnessed a beautiful demonstration of air-sea rescue. Dumbo flew near the pilot and dropped four smoke bombs in a neat row. It then landed into the wind and taxied through the center of the smoke columns. The pilot and his raft were hauled aboard and Dumbo took off straight ahead.

With a low supply of gasoline we returned to base.

Around most of Green Island a shelf of coral extended for about fifty feet and then dropped off perpendicularly into the deep blue ocean. When we got a chance we climbed down a 75 foot coral cliff to the shelf. By clinging to the roots of pandanus trees that were somehow successfully clinging to the upper face of the cliff, we navigated the remaining distance via a rickety bamboo native ladder, which had the top three rungs missing.

The cat-eyes (hard operculums used to close the entrance of gastropod shells) were plentiful, but a white color instead of the beautiful greens, blues and browns we liked so well.

Numerous caves had been formed along the base of the cliff by undermining wave action. Stalagmites and stalactites abounded in the caves and along the bottom of the cliff. Native woven baskets and mats, made from the bark of the coconut tree, were to be found around the blackened remains of old fires. The cracked and empty shells of mollusks which some native or Jap had eaten were scattered about the sand.

As the last few days of our combat tour drew close, each of us became a little more careful so we wouldn't slip up and get killed when relief was so near. Some of the fellows remarked they were going to spend that last week of flying with their cockpit hatches open and one hand on their ripcord, all ready to jump at the slightest sign of trouble.

Ironically, Major Gordon's division received nearly their greatest amount of action at the end of the combat tour.

An Army pilot was in a life raft at Lauwi Point near Rabaul. When the Dumbo came along to rescue him, escorted by Al Gordon and his boys, he was being shelled by the Japanese from the shore. The Dumbo met with heavy shellfire, which came within thirty feet when it attempted to pick up the pilot. Meanwhile, Gordon led his division on repeated strafing runs on the enemy gun positions, attempting to divert their fire. The Japs turned loose their AA on the Marine Corsairs and Bekins' plane was hit. He was able to notify the others he was going down, so they didn't lose his position. Bekins then made a water landing not far from Duke of York Island, but far enough from shore so that he wasn't shelled.

Meanwhile, Lieutenant York's Corsair had a bad hunk ripped from the elevator and stabilizer by the Jap barrage, and he headed for Green Island, accompanied by Hughes.

A second Dumbo came along with its own Corsair escort. Major Gordon, in final efforts to keep the Japs from firing at the big flying boat, made two heroic runs in the face of the Japs and made them duck. The escorting fighters didn't attempt to help him out at all. After over five hours of flying, Al made it back to base and landed with ten gallons of gas remaining in his tanks.

The Dumbo rescued both the Army pilot and Bekins and returned them safely to Green Island. The Army man told us that two natives had paddled out in a canoe and urged him to get in, saying they were friendly and would take him to a safe place. He got in their canoe and tied his raft on behind. When they headed for shore he jumped overboard and swam back to his raft. Although he had a pistol, he didn't try to shoot the traitors, as most of us would have.

New squadrons arrived to relieve us, VMF 212 and VMF 321. It was only appropriate that Merrill Swenson from my home town was in 212. Small as it was, the old home city always coincidentally managed to keep a pilot representative right up in the foremost bases at all times. Lowell Whittaker, another home town boy, was back on Bougainville.

They brought word that our fears had been justified back at Efate. Over six pilots had been killed in night flying training accidents due to weather or unknown causes. Many of them were dive bomber pilots. I was relieved to learn that Jack. J Foster was still in one piece. Although he and I had practically the same name, we were not related. We had become acquainted as cadets when I opened a letter and was greeted by "Dearest Jack." At first, I thought it was a mash note, and then I learned of another Jack Foster.

J. J. had done some good work dive-bombing Rabaul during the tough days. When he brought home three different airplanes so shot up they were unfit to fly, his C.O. decided to send him back to the rest area ahead of schedule, because it looked like his number was about up.

I had hoped for months that we would have some 20-mm cannon installed in the Corsairs for use on the last trip, but they never came until after we left. The squadrons that remained began to carry bombs on their F4U's under the leadership of the Chance-Vought representative, who did some of the flying—Charles A. Lindbergh, the first pilot to fly the Atlantic Ocean alone.

No longer was there any great incentive for a fighter pilot in the area, since few enemy planes had been seen. Outside of the dark days of Guadalcanal, we had been present to see the Japanese dreams of empire wither on a vine—which we had helped to sever.

It is an adage of the sea that one meets his former shipmates all over the world.

We had stopped overnight at Guadalcanal on our way back to the New Hebrides, when I met one of mine—Joe Pfahnel, a Navy pilot of Austrian descent who had been with me in that first embryo class of twenty-five aspiring aviation cadets at Oakland, California.

Joe was flying from one of the baby escort carriers and didn't like it. All he did was fly patrols, and he hadn't seen any action to speak of as compensation. "It's the most tiresome job in the world," he told me. "If we were on one of the larger carriers we would at least get to participate in some of the strikes they've been staging. On top of that, one torpedo and these baby carriers are done for. Take the *Luscombe Bay,* for instance; it was right alongside our carrier when it got hit and it went down in fifteen minutes!"

As usual upon such meetings I learned of more casualties among my original twenty-five. Only the day before, dark, handsome Jack Zehrung had taken a wave-off as he started to land on the carrier. His torpedo bomber cleared the side of the ship and then fell off on a wing and dived into the sea. The 500-pound depth charge he was carrying had a faulty fuse and exploded.

"If only we had the old-type fuse," Joe told me, "Jack would have been here today. We've had a lot of trouble with the new ones. The substitute material in them cracks when it receives rough handling and the acid drains through and arms the charge. You never know whether you can depend on them being unarmed or not.''

Down at Efate, we had one last glorious party, sponsored by George Schaefer in farewell to the men he had served with for so many months—the men who would return to their homes while he remained behind to put in another six months of overseas duty. I had never noticed before, but when I saw George for what I realized would be the last time in months and perhaps the last time, forever—I saw that the man had the gray, drawn expression of a person who had already been away from home too long. I knew that if it was I being left behind, it would only be a short time before I began to crack up.

George and the pilots we were leaving who had not yet put in their three combat tours would provide the nucleus for a new 222. The pool at Efate would be raided for the rest of the complement.

Minus four pilots missing in action from our original group that had arrived in the New Hebrides so long before, we returned to Espiritu Santo to await our turn on one of the twin-engined Martin Mariners that would take us to Honolulu and then the States.

There was not a man among us who had not proved himself as a flyer. All the poor pilots who fight a violent war, all the good pilots whose luck had run out, and those in between whose luck had also run out—were left behind, permanently.

But our thoughts were only fleetingly of them, for we had gathered up our hospitalized pilot, R. A. Schaeffer, with his burns still painful from being shot down, and we were all going home. We could now sing the ''C Ration Stew Song'' and mean nearly every word of it:

I'm tired of their Spam and Vienna's
I'm sick of dehydrated chow,
I want a blonde and some liquor,
And a steak the size of a cow.
I don't like spinach and bacon,
And that horrible jungle brew.
My teeth can't stand their damned hard tack
And my Gawd! That C Ration Stew.

I'm down with the elephantiasis,
The jungle-rot and spik-itch.
If my kid starts out on his left foot,
I''ll shoot the little son-of-a——.
I'm sick of the sound of motors,
I'm done with F4U's.
They can jam all their lousy spaghetti
And Gawd-damn C Ration Stew.

We ate it from Ewa to Midway,
To Santos and right up the "Slot,"
Munda to Vella Lavella,
And Empress Augusta was hot.
We didn't mind their bombing and shelling,
We sniped at the sniper too.
There's only one thing we're afraid of,
That Gawd-damn C Ration Stew.

I'm going back to God's country,
I'm going to make me a change.
I'm tired of the beautiful tropics,
And sick of the mud and the rain.
I'm sick of those sneaking mosquitoes,
Sick of the scuttlebutt too.
To hell with the whole South Pacific,
And that Gawd-damn C Ration Stew!

EPILOGUE

WHAT SHOULD HAVE been a quiet trip back to the United States turned out to be exciting. We flew back to Hawaii in a twin-engined flying boat (PBM). After a couple of days, space became available in another PBM for the trip to the mainland. The squadron was divided up into three groups for the return. My group left Hawaii nearly six hours behind and was almost halfway to our destination when the plane began to have engine trouble and to lose oil pressure. It was midnight on a very dark night. None of us relished the thought of a forced landing on the ocean and we kept our fingers crossed. The pilot banked and headed back for Hawaii. Although we kept losing altitude we managed to reach the island safely after dawn.

The next night we traveled without incident and shortly after sunup we flew near the Golden Gate, past San Francisco, and landed in the harbor. When we reported to headquarters, several of us found that we had been promoted to the rank of captain two weeks before. The first night in the United States I slept until five o'clock in the morning, when the automatic alarm clock within me caused me to wake up. Then I went back to sleep and slumbered peacefully until noon. It was the first time I had been able to relax. Until then, I did not realize that even in the most comfortable beds overseas (which were in Sydney) I hadn't been able to "unlax" completely. There had always been the threat of future combat hanging over my head.

We were transported from San Francisco in a comfortable train compartment on The Lark to San Diego and reported in to the base at Miramar, sixteen miles distant. There we found most of the fellows of the flight echelon of VMF 215. They had just returned from their thirty-day leaves. Some had new brides and most of them had automobiles. I inquired of some of the married men what they thought of marriage and received answers ranging from "It's the only thing" to "It's just like the Marine Corps, you won't take anybody's word for it—you have to learn by experience."

When I talked to people about some of the overseas experiences and losing some of our squadron mates, my teeth began chattering and my diaphragm and stomach became as tense as if it were a chilly morning—although the sun was warm and shining. I knew then that my nerves were acting very strangely—nothing like that had ever happened to me before.

Maurine, the girl I had gone to college with, came down to Los Angeles and we were married on May 1, 1944. I was twenty-four years old and she was twenty-three. As we came out of the wedding chapel in Los Angeles we found a platoon of Marines lined up on both sides of the walk acting as a guard of honor. They were all rewarded by a kiss from the bride.

With the tight housing conditions of wartime I had great difficulty in getting any room reservations in the cities and at Palm Springs resorts even for a honeymoon. I had succeeded in reserving a room at a large hotel in Los Angeles. After the wedding reception in Inglewood I attempted to unlock the door to my hotel room that night preparatory to carrying my bride across the threshold. A woman's voice inside said, "Who is it? Who is it? What do you want?" The hotel had rented the same room twice and given both of us a key.

We went to Palm Springs and then to San Francisco for our honeymoon. At Oakland, California, we occupied a small "honeymoon cottage" through the courtesy of the wife of my pal of cadet days, Samuel E. Ellsworth Goldberg "Goldie". He had gone overseas with a Navy fighter squadron on an aircraft carrier just two weeks before I arrived back in the U.S.A.

When I had joined the Navy a few days after the Pearl Harbor attack I left a mother who was exceptionally young in her appearance and actions for sixty-two years of age. Upon my return from overseas two and a half years later, I returned to a mother old and wrinkled, looking like a frail grandmother. She was standing shakily when I entered the room, the tears streaming down her cheeks. "My son, my son," she sobbed weakly. "Thank God, you've come back."

When my father greeted me, he shook my hand gruffly. He didn't say very much, as usual, but he surely did grin.

I learned that the folks at home had been worrying more about me than I had. With my two older brothers Frederick and Monroe, now in the Marine Corps and Navy and about to be sent overseas, they, like so many other parents, would spend more sleepless nights.

When my thirty days' leave expired, I was assigned to El Toro Marine Air Base near Santa Ana, California. Several of us were sent there to fly Corsairs and to instruct the second lieutenants about to be sent overseas in the latest fighter tactics and Japanese tricks.

On my first flight as an instructor, my students and I were flying over the ocean on a gunnery hop not far from Catalina Island when one of the students radioed that he would have to return to base. I sent a plane back with him to see that he made it safely. A few minutes later we heard him radio that he was bailing out. Upon inquiry, the escort pilot informed me a naval vessel was below and was picking him up. He returned to base with a severely strained back. A routine board of investigation met to determine the cause of the crash and where blame was to be placed, if any. I escaped censure by the board because of my precaution in sending the escort pilot back with the ailing plane.

Subsequent training crashes seemed to exact nearly as high a toll of airplanes as we had lost in combat.

Koetsch and Hazlett were both anxious to go back over and shortly before Christmas of 1944 they were sent overseas—through no special efforts of their own. Koetsch—the woman hater of the squadron, had ruined his reputation by becoming engaged.

After a few weeks of flying, my left shoulder began to bother me. Soon it became so sore I couldn't even lift my arm to signal for turns when driving my automobile. It took me several minutes every day to accomplish the simple task of raising my left arm high above my head to close and open the cockpit cover of the F4U. This was a dangerous condition in case I ever had to make a fast exit from the cockpit. Consequently, I reported in to sick bay.

After needles had been jabbed in me and blood taken away, and after the doctor watched the contortions he had me do, I found myself grounded for three weeks. I learned I had chronic bursitis of the shoulder, chronic tropical fungus (on my ankles), was anemic, underweight and nervous. After three weeks my fungus infection was pretty well cleared up by means of X-ray treatments and my shoulder had improved. My shoulder injury may have occurred when someone jumped on me in a foxhole during an air raid, or else when I was making hurried preparations during the shelling at Bougainville to take the F4U away from the burning plane with the 500-pound bomb.

I was then put on a straight and level flying status, which meant I wasn't supposed to fly a plane except in gentle maneuvers.

That doctor was later shipped to a different base. The man who took his place grounded me indefinitely.

It was about this time that my wife began to feel nauseated in the mornings and the evenings. After consulting with the doctor, I came home one afternoon and announced to her, "Darling—you're going to have a baby." Subsequent developments proved that I was right.

During the time they had me grounded, the Marines kept me busy at other jobs. One of these was to train the pilots in firing air-to-ground rockets, one of the new innovations of warfare. Every day a group of enlisted men and I drove out to the rocket range at Trabuco Canyon and directed the pilots by radio, giving them advice on methods to improve their accuracy, and reporting their scores to them.

On April 9, 1945, just three days before President Roosevelt died, my wife gave birth to a boy with some of the longest hair ever seen on a newborn baby at St. Joseph's Hospital in Orange, California. In spite of myself I couldn't help but bring forth the biggest grin of 1945 at the news.

After giving me a few weeks to recover from the birth of the baby, a board of reclassification was called to decide my fate. They were to determine whether to send me back to regular flying duties, make me a ground officer, or give me a medical discharge. The board consisted of several majors, lieutenant commanders and lieutenant colonels.

I presented my side of the story and told of the vast improvement I had made, how healthy I was, and I concluded with Patrick Henry's words, slightly revised: "Give me liberty or give me flight."

The board then called in some of the former members of VMF 222 who had seen me under combat conditions, and other pilots who had been flight instructors with me.

Several weeks later I was greatly pleased to receive notification that the board had seen fit to return me to unrestricted flying. A great weight seemed to be lifted from my mind and I found it easier to smile.

There were plenty of things happening to the other fellows too. While the Philippines were being invaded, all the ground echelon of VMF 222 came back from overseas, six months after the flight echelon. Their long service (19 months) had an affect on them when they came back. Several became renegades and were willing to do anything to get out of the service. One technical sergeant was assigned to El Toro for duty and within thirty days he went over the hill. They caught him and brought him back after he'd had eighteen days of liberty. He went over the hill four times, eighteen days each, within the next twelve months and was reduced in rating to a corporal.

Three of the enlisted men who had served in VMF 222 were caught stealing gasoline at the base at Cherry Point, North Carolina, and were sentenced to three years' imprisonment at Mare Island.

Another was awaiting court-martial for going over the hill, when his discharge papers arrived. Instead of holding him for the court-martial, his Commanding Officer gave him a break and released him for discharge.

I learned that "Pop" Krantz, one of the plane mechanics, had a shell explode very close to him on Bougainville. Later, the gasoline tank of the plane he was working on blew up—which proved too much for his nerves. Frank Demos of Detroit, another enlisted man, had also received a case of shell shock on Bougainville.

The entire squadron along with all the other present had been commended for their work at the Piva Yoke airfields under the Jap shelling.

One evening on the streets of Hollywood, by sheer coincidence, I met MacDonald Summers, the Marine sergeant who had claimed to see chipmunks dressed in tuxedoes running around his bunk. He had been much more severely wounded than most of us had been informed. I had heard some of the men claim he was just pretending to be seeing things so he could get discharged. The truth of the matter was he had several inches of his scalp and skull blown away by a bomb at Munda. Particles of shrapnel and bone had pierced his brain. He had escaped death by a quarter of an inch. Without the protecting bone, a loud noise or explosion could kill him. At first he objected to an operation, thinking he would be all right; but later submitted to the delicate operation and a tantalum plate was placed in his skull. His stories about chipmunks were merely daily attempts to brighten the spirits of the other hospital patients.

At Guadalcanal we had seen what war was really like when men were brought into the hospital with their arms and legs blown off or a piece of artillery embedded in their chests. Unlike the stories, usually published—when the bombers came, the hospital attendants did not pile mattresses over the injured men to protect them from falling debris and take them to safety. Instead, they most often ran for their own lives. The helpless unprotected men in the hospital learned what real fear was as they listened to the droning overhead—and many of them found their God for the first time.

The last I heard of Summers he had been discharged for eight months and was learning to be a director of a concert orchestra and a concert singer. Evidently the former Montana cowboy and bit player in the movies had real talent, because he had a backer who had spent over $12,000 on him and was paying $40 per day for lessons. His voice had a range of four octaves and had been favorably compared with Ezio Pinza, considered by many to be the world's greatest baritone. He still had nightmares several times per week.

By December 1945, most of the VMF 222 enlisted personnel and myself had received discharges from the Marine Corps. About half of the former pilots were back overseas, many in night fighter squadrons flying the Grumman F6F or the P61 (''Black

Widow"). Some were in carrier squadrons. Major Sapp was commanding his own squadron and had narrowly missed out on the turkey shoot at Okinawa when so many relatively inexperienced Jap pilots, who were concentrating on the shipping, were blasted out of the sky.

Harold Spears, the 15-plane ace, had been killed in 1944 at El Toro during the landing turn while flying an SBD for the first time. The plane was too sluggish to respond to the controls and a wing hit the ground first. Major Warner was in the rear cockpit and was badly hurt. Spears' pal, Donald Aldrich, a 20-plane ace, followed him in death in 1947. During what started as a routine landing near Chicago his plane, an F4U, skidded over on its back in loose gravel and caught fire—trapping the pilot in his cockpit.

My pal, "Goldie," became missing in action off Formosa in September 1944 when his wingman became frightened, lost his head, and ran away while three Zeros were attacking.

And all the time until the declaration of peace, Rabaul and the surrounding Japanese positions were receiving their daily dosage of bombs and bullets and were in turn knocking down several American, Australian, and New Zealand airplanes. It was an unnecessary risk of lives and money, for our carrier planes and B-29's had been bombarding the home islands. The same held true at Guam and Peleliu—our flyers continued to be sent out to strafe and bomb when all we needed to do was sit back and wait for the Japs on the islands to die from starvation and disease, or just leave them isolated to live as they might until the war ended.

Meanwhile, our former squadron with its replacement pilots had gone from Green Island to Emireau (near and on the other side of Rabaul), where its enlisted personnel left for the States. Then it went to the Philippines, arriving too late to get in on the good shooting. Six pilots were lost on their last six weeks' tour, just bombing and strafing the Japanese in the Philippines.

My friend Levine had been shot down while strafing near Kavieng on New Ireland, but made a safe water landing and was rescued. All of those pilots I knew in VMF 222 when the rest of us left for the States returned safely.

According to his brother Myrl, who had been contacted by a former prisoner of the Japanese and our military casualty branch, Hugh Cornelius, the TBF pilot acquaintance of mine who was shot down over Simpson Harbor at Rabaul while engaged in the disastrous mine-laying venture of February 1944, survived the crash when he was shot down and was taken prisoner. He died in April 1944, according to Japanese records. Injuries as a result of the crash, lack of medical care and malnutrition were the causes as far as can be determined. His body was recovered and buried in 1948 at San Diego.

A prisoner at Rabaul who survived the war told a harrowing tale. After a severe bombing raid on March 2, 1944, when a large part of the city was burned up, a total of forty prisoners were taken out on the next two successive nights, blindfolded, handcuffed, and tied together. None were ever seen again. The Japanese said both groups had been killed by bombs, but rifle shots were heard on both nights. Were our missing pilots of VMF 222 with them?

The only man to come back from being shot down, of those mentioned in this book, was the indomitable Gregory Boyington, who was rescued during the last days of August 1945 from the Omori prison camp.

He and his wingman George Ashmun were last seen diving into some clouds after some Jap planes. On the other side of the clouds they fought several Zeros. Ashmun got one and Gregory got his second for the hop. But Zeros were pouring lead in Ashmun in spite of Pappy, who was weaving back and forth squirting .50 calibers, doing his best to defend George and oblivious of the bullets that were peppering his own Corsair. Ashmun never even tried to come out of that dive, but went straight in.

When Pappy pulled out low over the water his main gas tank exploded, directly in front of him. "I felt like my head had been stuck in a blast furnace door," he told reporters when he was rescued months later.

He turned his plane over on its back and pushed himself right through the plastic canopy, pulling his ripcord instantly. He was only one to two hundred feet off the water when he jumped and his chute streamed unopened as he hit the water on his side. The terrific impact stunned him.

When he came to, he found four Zeros strafing him. He took a couple of six-foot soundings at first, but was so tired that he just floated in the water after that and ducked his head, like an ostrich in the sand. His torn scalp dangled in front of his eyes, one ear was almost torn off, his throat had been deeply gashed and he had wounds in his ankle, thigh and both arms.

His Mae West had 200 holes in it, so he treaded water for two hours and then felt safe enough to open his life raft. He lay there waiting for Dumbo to come along. All the while the song "In a Rowboat Off Rabaul" sung to the tune of "The Battle Hymn of the

Republic" kept ringing in his ears:

> If your engine conks out now,
> You'll come down from forty thou'
> And you'll end up in a rowboat at Rabaul.
>
> In a rowboat off Rabaul,
> We are throwing in the towel,
> 'Cause they'll never send the Dumbo over here.
>
> We'll be prisoners of war,
> And we'll stay till forty-four
> Getting drunk on Saki and New Britain beer.

Boyington thought he saw some planes that might have been Corsairs searching for him, but the weather had closed in to hide him.

A submarine surfaced near him, purely by coincidence, with a large red "meatball" painted on the tarpaulin wrapped around the conning tower. The Japs took Greg aboard and gave him Saki, tea, biscuits and a package of Jap cigarettes and matches.

When the sub docked at Rabaul his hands were tied together and he was dragged blindfolded and naked up the street to be questioned all night.

He gave his true name to the Japs, but told them he was a ground operations officer who had just gone along on the flight that day to see what it was like. He never told them he had once been a Flying Tiger, for that would have meant sure death. He also concealed the fact from the Japs at Rabaul that he had ever shot down any Jap planes.

There must have been a slip-up of Japanese Intelligence somewhere, because they seemed unaware of Boyington's record.

For ten days Greg was questioned without medical treatment for his wounds. He wondered how his questioners could stand the stench.

There were twenty other airmen held prisoners at Rabaul. Pappy was made a special prisoner with no POW privileges.

On February 14th he was among six prisoners loaded aboard a Jap "Betty". There were two pilots up front and three guards in the cabin. Only one guard had a gun that Pappy could see, although he didn't know about the pilots. He thought about trying to overpower the guards and flying the bomber down to Bougainville and making a water landing near the American airstrip so as to avoid being shot down. The rest of the Allied prisoners were in no condition to try the plan except for Major Boyle, a pilot from VMF 212. He later regretted not making the attempt.

They landed at Truk. Someone gave Greg a powerful shove away from the plane. His blindfold slipped and he saw an F6F come over and blow the bomber up in flames.

They got in a slit trench for protection, because it was the time of the famous Navy carrier strike at Truk. An ugly Jap pilot with a scowl on his face came over and looked down at them. They all stood up at attention.

"I'm a Japanese pilot," the Jap said slowly and deliberately. "I'm a Japanese pilot—I'm a Japanese pilot." He pulled his pistol from its holster meaningfully. "If you bomb us—you die!"

The prisoners felt sure their end had come, for American planes were bombing and strafing the place unmercifully. With a final black look the Japanese pilot departed.

''He was a cheerful sonuva-gun wasn't he?'' Boyington exclaimed.

They were then taken to a concrete air raid shelter which was soon shattered by a thousand-pound bomb dropped a hundred feet away, without injuring any of the Americans very badly.

They were kept sixteen days in four by six cells with only one cup of water per day. They were then flown to Saipan and to Iwo Jima and then to Yokohama.

The prisoners' previous beating with rifle butts and boards were not nearly as bad as those they received at the secret prison camp at Ofuna where they were held thirteen months. They were slugged on the legs, back and rumps with a baseball bat. After a beating like that, Boyington could look over his shoulder and see his swollen rump.

He was slugged about 300 times on the jaw and still he survived, although some of the other prisoners were unable to take it.

He was transferred to Omouri prison camp on April 5, 1945, where politeness was the order of the day. The inmates had to bow every morning to the emperor. They had to bow from the waist whenever they wanted to go to the toilet and ask permission in Japanese. After returning they had to find the guard, bow to him again and thank him.

The majority of the prisoners were suffering from dysentery and some were not able to conform to the rules. They were beaten for their disobedience.

The spy and grapevine system was wonderful. Koreans and sometimes Japanese guards let them know secretly how the war was going.

One little guard called Pappy behind a door. The guard had been gone for a month. ''U.S. got good navy—ship sunk," the Jap told him with a diving gesture of his hands. "I swim." He gesticulated with the breast stroke.

When he heard reports about the atomic bomb, Boyington thought it was a fairy tale!

The prisoners were fed a conglomeration of rice and maize, which tasted like chalk. This was complemented by soy bean soup, with very little bean and lots of water. They were sometimes given a treat of fish heads or seaweed.

Boyington had lost 65 pounds since his capture and was down to 110. Resourceful as ever, he wangled a job as a slave boy (*Kobin*) in the kitchen of the Japanese mess, while at Ofuna. With a year-old hunger gnawing at his stomach he ate everything he got a chance at and balooned to 190 pounds. At Omouri he began to lose weight again.

On August 14th a guard told him the war was over. Five days later they were told they were no longer special prisoners and could talk; then the prisoners took over the camp, and the Japs deluged them with cod-liver oil and iron pills.

Cans of food were dropped from American planes. The rescue party, led by Commodore Roger Simpson and Commander Harold Stassen, came along in three Higgins boats and found the prisoners gorged and swollen from eating too much. Pappy had a jaundiced complexion and weighed in at 160 pounds.

Taken to Hawaii, the thirty-two-year-old multi-ace had the silver oak leaves of a lieutenant colonel pinned on his shoulders by General Moore. A few days later he landed at Oakland, California to be greeted by twenty of his "Black Sheep," newspaper photographers, reporters and newsreel cameramen.

That first night of the reunion, the Black Sheep

were herded to a private dining room of a ritzy San Francisco Hotel, where they were to graze, not on Zeros this time for those days were past, but on choice and expensive food. For several days, while awaiting Pappy's arrival, the Sheep had been bedded down at the hotel with all the bills footed by Chance-Vought, the manufacturer of the Corsair, which they had used with such deadly effect.

The Black Sheep thought they knew their old man thoroughly. Yet none of them really knew him. A few had received glimpses past the tough exterior, when he talked about his beloved mother and three children. None of them got to know the deep, inner man.

They didn't know that rough, gruff, but always polite Boyington had not only helped them all he could, but had called on a greater power to bring them back, safe and alive.

"I never taxi out to take off on any mission that I don't pray; not for myself but for their return and safety," Pappy had once told Chaplain M. Paetznick, his friend. "It may not be an elegant prayer, but it always stated what needed to be said."

After praying regularly while in the Jap prison camps, when tough Pappy landed in the States he managed to evade the commotion for a few moments and took Chaplain Paetznick aside:

"Padre," he said, "I'm an easy touch for your business now." Then he turned on his heel and once again rejoined his flock.

And so—at last—the great struggle ended and we returned to pick up our civilian lives again. During the postwar years I had no contact with any of my former squadron mates of VMF 222 except for visiting Bekins in Dallas, Texas, where I gave him a ride in my new Bellanca airplane, and for three telephone conversations with George Shaefer. I was dismayed, in July 1960, to learn he was afflicted with multiple sclerosis. During the war in Korea, I read in a national magazine where Marine Captain W. Hazlett and his wingman were "circling over a ground attack" in Korea. From this I jumped to the conclusion that "Willie" Hazlett was the one mentioned in the article.

Some of the men I had associated with or heard about overseas had become world-famous. Joe Foss, the Marine ace, had become governor of South Dakota.

Joe McCarthy, the former base legal officer at El Toro Marine Air Base who had given me some help in my legal difficulties and who was noted at that time only for his former occupation as judge, became a United States Senator from Wisconsin, and his actions in persecuting possible Communists had instilled a new word in the dictionary—"McCarthyism." By May of 1957 he had died of hepatitis. Some people have said that he began to die that day in the halls of Congress when they passed a resolution of censure, for he seemed to fade away physically and politically until the end came.

The skipper of the boat (PT 109) which had been cut in two by a Japanese destroyer in the Solomons—the Ambassador's son, John Fitzgerald Kennedy—was nominated in July 1960 for the Presidency of the United States by the Democratic Party. He had already become a Senator from Massachusetts, and had written a Pulitzer Prize-winning book. His thirty missions in the combat zone and heroic efforts on behalf of his crew when they were shipwrecked are a good indication of what this young man is made of. His bid for the Presidency was successful. Few of us achieve even one of the accomplishments he has.

The expansion of a nation or the spread through force of a new ideology are simply not worth the cost in lives and misery. If another great conflict comes along, then millions of young and old men and women will again be put into positions which they will have to swear to attack or to defend; again they will be indoctrinated with a hatred of their fellow men, who may or may not happen to have a different color of skin, or may happen to live on the other side of a political boundary, or perhaps may only happen to believe in different things than their attackers. Again stranger will kill stranger. A relatively small metal cylinder containing atoms in a certain arrangement may again be permitted to explode with the force of thousands of tons of dynamite.

Will mankind ever learn from history? It seems likely that it will not.

And yet one hopes. One who has faced a "hell in the heavens," or on land, or at sea, hopes fervently that at last mankind will learn to seek its destiny without turning against itself. And perhaps it is this hope—unjustified as it may be—which keeps those of us going who have seen war face-to-face.